T0229861

Intelligent Internet of Things for Smart Healthcare Systems

The book focuses on developments in artificial intelligence (AI) and internet of things (IoT) integration for smart healthcare, with an emphasis on current methodologies and frameworks for the design, growth, implementation, and creative use of such convergence technologies to provide insight into smart healthcare service demands. Concepts like signal recognition, computation, internet of health stuff, and so forth and their applications are covered. Development in connectivity and intelligent networks allowing for social adoption of ambient intelligence is also included.

Features:

- Introduces Intelligent IoT as applicable to the key areas of smart healthcare
- Discusses computational intelligence and IoT-based optimizations of smart healthcare systems
- Explores effective management of healthcare systems using dedicated IoT-based infrastructures
- Includes dedicated chapters on securing patient's confidential data
- Reviews diagnosis of critical diseases from medical imaging using advanced deep learning-based approaches

This book is aimed at researchers, professionals, and graduate students in intelligent systems, big data, cloud computing, information security, and healthcare systems.

Advances in Smart Healthcare Technologies

Editors:

Chinmay Chakraborty and Joel J. P. C. Rodrigues

This book series focuses on recent advances and different research areas in smart healthcare technologies including the Internet of Medical Things (IoMedT), e-Health, personalized medicine, sensing, big data, telemedicine, etc. under the healthcare informatics umbrella. The overall focus is on bringing together the latest industrial and academic progress, research, and development efforts within the rapidly maturing health informatics ecosystem. It aims to offer valuable perceptions to researchers and engineers on how to design and develop novel healthcare systems and how to improve patient information delivery care remotely. The potential for making faster advances in many scientific disciplines and improving the profitability and success of different enterprises is to be investigated.

Blockchain Technology in Healthcare Applications
Social, Economic, and Technological Implications
Bharat Bhushan, Nitin Rakesh, Yousef Farhaoui, Parma Nand Astya, and Bhuvan Unhelkar

Digital Health Transformation with Blockchain and Artificial Intelligence
Chinmay Chakraborty

Smart and Secure Internet of Healthcare Things
Nitin Gupta, Jagdeep Singh, Chinmay Chakraborty, Mamoun Alazab, and Dinh-Thuan Do

Practical Artificial Intelligence for Internet of Medical Things
Emerging Trends, Issues, and Challenges
Edited by Ben Othman Soufiene, Chinmay Chakraborty, and Faris A. Almalki

Intelligent Internet of Things for Smart Healthcare Systems
Edited by Durgesh Srivastava, Neha Sharma, Deepak Sinwar, Jabar H. Yousif, and Hari Prabhat Gupta

For more information about this series, please visit: www.routledge.com/Advances-in-Smart-Healthcare-Technologies/book-series/CRCASHT

Intelligent Internet of Things for Smart Healthcare Systems

Edited by
Durgesh Srivastava, Neha Sharma,
Deepak Sinwar, Jabar H. Yousif, and
Hari Prabhat Gupta

CRC Press
Taylor & Francis Group
Boca Raton London New York

CRC Press is an imprint of the
Taylor & Francis Group, an **informa** business

Designed cover image: © Shutterstock

First edition published 2023
by CRC Press
6000 Broken Sound Parkway NW, Suite 300, Boca Raton, FL 33487-2742

and by CRC Press
4 Park Square, Milton Park, Abingdon, Oxon, OX14 4RN

CRC Press is an imprint of Taylor & Francis Group, LLC

© 2023 selection and editorial matter, Durgesh Srivastava, Neha Sharma, Deepak Sinwar, Jabar H. Yousif, and Hari Prabhat Gupta; individual chapters, the contributors

ISBN: 9781032352862 (hbk)
ISBN: 9781032352879 (pbk)
ISBN: 9781003326182 (ebk)

DOI: 10.1201/9781003326182

Typeset in Times
by codeMantra

Contents

Editors

Durgesh Srivastava is an Associate Professor at the Chitkara University Institute of Engineering & Technology, Chitkara University, Rajpura, Punjab, India. He received his Ph.D. degree in Computer Science & Engineering from IKG Punjab Technical University, Jalandhar, Punjab, India in 2020. He received a B.Tech. degree in Information and Technology (IT) from MIET, Meerut, UP in 2006 and an M.E. in Software Engineering from the Birla Institute of Technology (BIT), Mesra, Ranchi, Jharkhand, India in 2008. He is an enthusiastic and motivating technocrat with 14 years of research and academic experience. His research interests include machine learning, soft computing, pattern recognition, software engineering, modeling, and design. He has published more than 30 papers in reputed international/national journals and conferences/seminars. As far as editorial experience is concerned, he is serving as an editor for CRC Press (Taylor & Francis). He has published several patents and copyrights in the field of computer software. He has organized and attended various workshops during his teaching career. He is a life member of a different professional society.

Neha Sharma is working as an Assistant Professor at the Computer Science and Engineering Department in Chitkara University, Rajpura. She has received her M.Tech. (CSE) and Ph.D. (Computer Science) degrees in the area of computer science with a vast teaching experience of 11 years in a reputed organization. She has more than 15 international publications in reputed peer-reviewed journals including IEEE xplore, SCOPUS, and SCI-indexed journals. Her main area of research is image processing, machine learning, deep learning, and cyber security. She has also published several national and international patents under the Intellectual Property Rights of the Government of India and abroad. She is actively associated with NAAC preparations at the university interface. She is associated with many high-impact society memberships like IEEE (senior member), ACM, and ISTE (lifetime member).

Deepak Sinwar is an Associate Professor at the Department of Computer and Communication Engineering, Manipal University Jaipur, Jaipur, Rajasthan, India. He received his Ph.D. and M.Tech. degrees in Computer Science and Engineering, respectively, and B.Tech. (with honors) in Information Technology. He has published more than 30 research papers in various international journals and more than 15 research papers at international conferences. As far as editorial experience is concerned, he is serving as an editor for reputed publishers including CRC Press (Taylor & Francis), Scrivener (Wiley), and IGI Global. He has published several patents and copyrights in the field of computer software. He is the organizing chair of international conferences on Innovations in Computational Intelligence and Computer Vision (ICICV-2022, ICICV-2021, and ICICV-2020) supported by Springer. Recently he has been awarded "Top Researcher of the Year 2021" by Manipal University Jaipur, India. He has organized and attended various workshops during his teaching career. His research interests include Computational Intelligence, Data Mining, Machine Learning, Reliability Theory, Computer Networks, and Pattern Recognition. He is an enthusiastic and motivating technocrat with 12 years of research and academic experience. He is a life member of the Indian Society for Technical Education, a senior member of IEEE, and a member of the ACM professional society.

Dr. Jabar H. Yousif, Associate Prof. at Faculty of Computing and Information Technology, Sohar University, Oman. Ph.D. in Information Science & Technology, UKM University, Malaysia. M.Sc. & B.Sc. in Computer Science, Basrah University, Iraq. Postdoctoral fellowship in Virtual Reality, UKM University, Malaysia. More than 25 years of teaching experience. He has published more than 100 papers & books in Artificial Intelligent, Cloud Computing, Soft Computing, Renewable Energy Modelling, Natural Language Processing, Arabic text Processing & Virtual Reality. Editorial board & reviewer for many scientific journals and conferences.

Hari Prabhat Gupta is an Assistant Professor in the Department of Computer Science and Engineering, Indian Institute of Technology (BHU) Varanasi, India. Previously, he was a Technical Lead in Samsung R&D Bangalore, India. He received his Ph.D. and M.Tech. degrees in Computer Science and Engineering from the Indian Institute of Technology Guwahati, and his B.E. degree in Computer Science and Engineering from Govt. Engineering College Ajmer, India. He is a senior member of IEEE. He has published more than 100 papers and finished multiple projects in the domain of IoT, Wireless Sensor Networks (WSN), and Human-Computer Interaction (HCI).

Contributors

Abdelhakeem M. B. Abdelrahman
Sudan University of Science and
Technology
Khartoum, Sudan

Eimad Abusham
Sohar University
Sohar, Oman

Saeid Hosseini
Sohar University
Sohar, Oman

Amro Al-Said Ahmad
Philadelphia University
Amman, Jordan

Abbas H. Hassin Alasadi
University of Basrah
Basrah, Iraq

Maryam Gharib Aljabri
Sohar University
Sohar, Oman

Sanad Al-Maskari
Sohar University
Sohar, Oman

Mahin Anup
Manipal University Jaipur
India

Shishir Singh Chauhan
Birla Institute of Technology
Ranchi, India

Nameer N. El-Emam
Philadelphia University
Amman, Jordan

Atika Fatma
Integral University
Lucknow, UP, India

Gauri Shanker Gupta
Birla Institute of Technology
Ranchi, India

Shikha Gupta
Chandigarh University
Mohali, India

Faten Salim Hanoon
University of Basrah
Basrah, Iraq

Praveen Kantha
BRCM CET
Bhiwani, India

Ahmad. K. Kayed
Sohar University
Sohar, Oman

Akhalesh Kumar
Maharishi University of
Information Technology
Lucknow, India

Sunil Kumar Maakar
Galgotias University
Greater Noida, India

Sudhanshu Mishra
Madan Mohan Malviya
University of Technology
Gorakhpur, India

Amit Mithal
Jaipur Engineering College &
Research Centre
Jaipur, India

Dipra Mitra
Amity University
Jharkhand, India

Rohit Mittal
Manipal University Jaipur
Jaipur, India

Akarsh K. Nair
Indian Institute of Information
Technology
Kottayam, India

Smriti Ojha
Madan Mohan Malviya University of
Technology
Gorakhpur, India

Mrinal Pathak
Birla Institute of Technology
Ranchi, India

Vibhakar Pathak
Arya College of Engineering & I.T.
Jaipur, India

Jayakrushna Sahoo
Indian Institute of Information
Technology
Kottayam, India

Sudeshna Sani
Koneru Lakshmaiah University
Guntur, India

Devika Sapra
Manipal University Jaipur
Jaipur, India

Hare Ram Singh
GNIOT
Greater Noida, India

Akruti Sinha
Manipal University Jaipur
Jaipur, India

Rakesh Kumar Sinha
Birla Institute of Technology
Ranchi, India

Deepak Sinwar
Manipal University Jaipur
Jaipur, India

Durgesh Srivastava
Chitkara University
Rajpura, India

Gaurav Srivastava
Manipal University Jaipur
Jaipur, India

Santosh Kumar Srivastava
Galgotias University
Greater Noida, India

Shivam Tiwari
G L Bajaj Institute of
Technology & Management
Greater Noida, India

**Shantha Visalakshi
Upendran**
Ethiraj College for Women
Chennai, India

Maram Bani Younes
Philadelphia University
Amman, Jordan

Jabar H. Yousif
Sohar University
Sohar, Oman

Preface

"Smart healthcare" is attracting a lot of interest from academics, government, business, and the healthcare sector, due to the growth of smart sensorial media, things, and cloud technology. The usage of healthcare monitoring systems in hospitals and other health facilities has increased dramatically, and portable healthcare monitoring systems based on new technologies are now a major concern for many countries around the world. Artificial intelligence (AI) has received a lot of interest as a result of the machine learning algorithms being used to deliver high-quality health care. However, the convergence of IoT and AI can provide new opportunities for both technologies. AI-driven IoT can play a significant role in smart healthcare by offering a better insight into healthcare data to support affordable personalized care. It can also support efficient processing and storage facilities for large IoT data streams (big data) that go beyond the capacities of individual "people", as well as provide real-time automatic decision-making. Although researchers have made progress in their individual studies of AI and IoT for health care, relatively little attention has been paid to designing cost-effective and affordable smart health devices.

Many facets of our healthcare business could be revolutionized by AI-driven IoT for smart healthcare; however, many technological obstacles must be solved before this opportunity can be realized. The book focuses on recent developments in AI and IoT integration for smart healthcare, with an emphasis on state-of-the-art methods, methodologies, and frameworks for the design, growth, implementation, and creative use of such convergence technologies to provide insight into smart healthcare service demands. The concepts like signal recognition, visualization, computation, instrumentation, AI, internet of health stuff, data mining, disease detection, telemedicine, and their applications will be covered. This book will help researchers who are working on the new developments in connectivity and intelligent networks that will allow for the social adoption of ambient intelligence.

The book focuses on providing deeper insights into computational intelligence and IoT-based techniques and procedures available for smart healthcare systems. This book will unveil several applications of metaheuristic approaches (i.e., swarm intelligence, genetic algorithm) in collaboration with IoT for the efficient management of smart healthcare systems. Some special features of this book include a comprehensive guide for utilizing computational models for reliability engineering, state-of-the-art swarm intelligence methods for solving complex problems and developing computer-aided models, high-quality and innovative research contributions, and a guide for applying computational optimization to healthcare systems. A chapter-wise summary is provided in the following,

Chapter 1 discusses the future of health care that is expected to be controlled by IoT devices either directly or through combinational applications. Authors categorized applications of smart healthcare into three main classes, viz. patient level, medico level, and hospital level. In addition, the chapter also includes the architecture of an IoT-based smart healthcare system, technological classifications of IoT, the role of IoT in smart healthcare, challenges, and observations, and future scopes.

Chapter 2 presents several applications of Intelligent IoT (I-IoT) for the smart healthcare system. The author investigates a variety of i-IoT system elements and presents the architecture of an i-IoT system, its aspects, and how these components communicate with one another. The existing healthcare systems where IoT-based solutions have been investigated are also included in this study. The i-IoT has assisted healthcare practitioners in monitoring and diagnosing a variety of health concerns, measuring a variety of health factors, and providing diagnostic facilities in remote places by utilizing these principles. Due to this, the healthcare sector has changed from being primarily focused on hospitals to one that is more patient-centric.

Chapter 3 deals with an examination of the Human Healthcare Internet of Things (H2IoT) state, including existing services, architecture, topology, tools, services, and healthcare applications. With a detailed background in IoT technology for smart healthcare systems, the authors present the architecture of healthcare architecture using a three-layer architecture and a five-layer architecture. In addition, they present several application areas, viz. glucose level sensing, blood pressure monitoring, body temperature monitoring, oxygen saturation monitoring, electrocardiogram (ECG) monitoring, wheelchair management system, rehabilitation system, etc.

Chapter 4 deals with the intensive investigation of a futuristic IoT-based smart healthcare system (SHCS) which concentrates on security features that need to be wrapped up with the trusted data and the data management strategies and techniques with respect to cloud computing and big data analytics. This chapter provides a complete review of different technologies dealing with IoT-enabled SHCS like big data analytics, cloud data management, and data governance. The prime objective of this chapter is to deliver the state-of-the-art understanding and update about information security and data management required for IoT-enabled SHCS.

Chapter 5 investigates the role of information security and data management in IoT-enabled SHCSs. It explores how sensitive health information is protected against cybercrime attacks and the associated risks in healthcare systems. At the same time, it also discusses how sensitive information is shared and transmitted among different entities in healthcare firms and units without losing the patient's privacy. Firstly, the main components of healthcare systems and how it is different from IoT-enabled SHCSs are investigated. Then, authors discussed about the main threats and vulnerabilities in the system. After that, some recent and sophisticated security solutions have been introduced to tackle these issues. Finally, the data management of several scenarios in the smart healthcare system is taken into consideration.

Chapter 6 presents a comparative and comprehensive analysis to study different architectures for building a smart healthcare system using big data analytics and AI. Authors explained in this chapter about big data and AI for smart healthcare systems. In addition, the background of AI and big data is presented with several important AI and big data analytics for smart healthcare systems. The chapter also discusses common methods and their implications followed by the most used frameworks in the field of smart healthcare systems that integrate both AI and big data analytics. Emerging trends in big data and AI with reference to the SHCS are also presented along with various challenges and issues in developing smart healthcare systems.

Chapter 7 first discusses computing services that facilitate and assist in real-time health monitoring and tracking, and then discusses the cloud computing services and technologies that provide individuals and consultants with accurate data. It also focuses on the challenges faced by healthcare systems accompanied by cloud computing.

Chapter 8 discusses the adoption of IoT-based healthcare systems worldwide. Starting with a brief introduction on the expansion of healthcare systems, the authors discuss the paradigm of an ideal healthcare system. In addition, they present a model for IoT-based healthcare systems in the future. They also present various sensors and wearable devices that can assist smart healthcare systems. It also discusses how a smart health monitoring system that can interface with network devices and applications is essential for supporting patients and physicians in monitoring, tracking, and gathering sensitive medical data.

Chapter 9 proposes the semantic similarity measurement between two medical terms in a single ontology or multiple ontologies in the international classification of diseases (ICD-10 V1.0) as a primary source. A comparison study is done to evaluate the obtained results and the results of human experts based on the correlation coefficient to verify the validity of the proposed method. The results show the possibility of efficiently implementing the proposed approach to measure the similarity in the biomedical domain.

Chapter 10 deals with the transforming approaches of IoT to the pharmaceutical sector. The chapter summarizes various IoT-related platforms which have created a new door to innovations in the field of the healthcare system and disease management. In addition, the authors present various AI-based approaches for the pharmaceutical sector including medical imaging, and IoT platform for disorder evaluation, diagnosis, prevention, and therapy.

Chapter 11 presents a systematic review of blockchain technology implications in the healthcare system. It is based on PRISMA guidelines for examining metadata analyses of selected studies to identify, extract, and analyze relevant publications across specific databases. Based on the review, several studies have proposed blockchain technology in the healthcare system, showing exciting results and solving critical challenges.

Chapter 12 presents a deep learning approach for the classification of Alzheimer's disease. The Alzheimer's brain MRI dataset was obtained from the open-access section of the Kaggle website. The dataset contains 6,400 images with a size of 176×208 pixels. It is divided into four classes (NonDemented, MildDemented, ModerateDemented, and VeryMildDemented), each with a non-uniform distribution of images. The efficacy of the proposed model is evaluated through accuracy, precision, recall, and F1 score. This chapter is aimed to find out whether the early diagnosis of Alzheimer's disease can be reliably performed by using magnetic resonance imaging of the brain together with a deep learning algorithm known as a convolutional neural network.

Chapter 13 shows a case study related to the health of plants using a deep learning strategy. CNN model has been used to present a deep learning strategy for classifying different types of succulent Tomato plants. In this, three classes of succulent plants have been analyzed. It is inadequate for model optimization or poses a challenge to additional succulent species that are unknown. As a result, our long-term goal is to increase better optimization and the number of succulent plant types, and to develop an Android app that will assist users in identifying succulent plants.

Chapter 14 deals with feature engineering for depression. Depression, a serious mental disorder that has become ubiquitous these days, contributes to increase in the number of suicides committed every year and poor functioning at both personal and professional levels. As handwriting can give insights into the functions of the human brain, this paper focuses on utilizing the science of analyzing handwriting to diagnose depression in individuals so that the necessary treatment and counseling can be provided to help the person recover. Key features are identified to detect the worldwide common disease, and then they are fed into automated handwriting-analyzing systems which can save tremendous amounts of time and energy in comparison to manual handwriting analysis.

The e-nose and chemical sensing technologies are introduced in Chapter 15. A quick comparison between biological and e-nose sensors is given in this chapter. It also provides a summary of the sensor's response, e-nose pattern identification, applications, problems, and relevant difficulties. Along with addressing e-nose applications, the authors also clarify the rationale behind using the technology. In terms of research challenges and issues, e-nose technologies are represented as a concluding point.

We hope that the works published in this book will be able to serve the concerned communities of Intelligent IoT for smart healthcare systems.

1 Internet of Things in Smart and Intelligent Healthcare Systems

Akarsh K. Nair and Jayakrushna Sahoo
Indian Institute of Information Technology

CONTENTS

1.1 INTRODUCTION

With the rapid evolution of information and communication technology (ICT), the world has witnessed a revolutionary change being undertaken by all technological domains. Among many other domains such as education, production, telecommunication, and so on, healthcare is one of the most benefited domains from the technological revolution. In the primary stages where artificial intelligence (AI) had caused a boom, healthcare applications had adapted themselves to match the changing needs of the technology. The

DOI: 10.1201/9781003326182-1

issue with AI was the incompleteness of the applications it had delivered in healthcare.[1] Even though multiple technologies such as decision support systems, patient–doctor interactive machines, expert systems, and so on make use of pure AI techniques, they did lack certain elements. All these were limited to software-based applications, and still, physical-level applications were missing. Such an issue had been overcome with the introduction of Internet of things (IoT)-based applications into healthcare. This has opened up a wide set of applications where IoT combined with AI has given revolutionary results. Such applications have proven their mettle at such a level that they have replaced their human counterparts in most cases.[2] In recent times, multiple newer terminologies have been introduced into healthcare with the application of such technologies. Some of the very common applications are digital healthcare, E-health, remote healthcare, and so on.

Health is a broad term that refers to a person's physical and social well-being. It is often defined as a state of complete physical and mental wellness. A healthy life is a basic human right. Unfortunately, many people in developing countries lack access to proper health services. This contributes to the global health problem. For ages, healthcare has been completely undertaken by human work capital. Technological advancements have been used in the healthcare industry more as a support rather than as a replacement for human capital. The confluence of several ICT technologies such as smart systems, cloud computing, social networks, and so on is opening up the possibilities of organizing these techniques into service relationships via the development of new healthcare service systems. These systems usually add value to the processes by incorporating different aspects into them such as individuals, languages, procedures, rule sets, and so on. Cloud computing-based smart healthcare systems, concomitant with electronic health records (EHRs), and novel sensor or mobile networks open up unparalleled possibilities for developing autonomous, smart, and sustainable healthcare systems.[3] Due to its sensitive nature, the induction of a completely autonomous process into healthcare is a highly debated topic. Intelligent healthcare (IH) is a comparatively newer terminology that is fast growing with the growth of ICT technology. Even though the term is widely used, it is still void of a formal definition. It can be said that the base of IH is developed from the regional healthcare information system models. Most of the currently discussed technologies such as telemedicine, digital hospitals, and E-health are the paving blocks for IH. Backed by IoT, the IH system capacitates healthcare services to be delivered to the needy irrespective of time or location.[4]

The IoT is one of the most vital and transformational technologies ever to be devised. It refers to a system that enables various devices to form a link with each other and perform various tasks. The concept of the IoT is that it connects objects to the internet and collects data about them and performs actions related to that objects. It makes use of information technology principles to store, retrieve, and transmit data without requiring manual intervention or human-to-human contact. The IoT is a megatrend that will transform the way businesses operate. Its various benefits include the ability to connect and communicate with various smart devices and systems. Therefore, starting an automation project is feasible in most domains. The IoT is a broad-based network that enables people to connect to each other. Its potential to transform various industries such as healthcare is evidenced by the number of applications that are being developed in this field.[5] Various medical devices and sensors can be considered as components of the IoT. Healthcare services provided through the IoT are expected to improve the quality of life and lower the cost of care. IoT has the potential to enable healthcare providers to collect and analyze real-time data from various sources. This could allow them to provide better and more accurate medical services to their patients. These include even vital measures such as blood pressure and pulse rate. With the help of the IoT, doctors can now collect and analyze these data through various smart devices connected to an online network. The IoT is going to transform healthcare by drastically lowering costs and improving the quality of care.[6]

Prior to IoT, interchange between patients and doctors was restricted to physical visits and digital communications. The scope of remote treatments was very limited, and continuous evaluation of personal health conditions by hospitals or doctors was not facilitated. IoT-enabled devices have opened up the era of remote health-monitoring systems and unleashed the possibility of retaining patient health without distance becoming a hindrance. It has also endowed medicos to perform excellent medical care and necessary procedures. The degree of patient contentment has also shown an exponential rise as continuous communications with doctors have been made more convenient and effective than ever. Additionally, continuous and remote monitoring of the health status of the diseased has made it possible to reduce the need for a lengthy stay at healthcare facilities and also reduces the chances of readmissions. Alongside all this, a keen reduction in the economical side has also been facilitated via such procedures. The quality of services provided at the same economical expense has increased as well as enhanced treatment results.[7] In the current scenario, it is hard to identify a system that is void of IoT devices in the healthcare sector. From digital healthcare assistants to smart personal healthcare systems and from basic expert systems to high-end surgical and therapeutic robots, IoT devices have proved their mettle in each and every sector possible. Now rather than classifying certain technology as smart and some as "not-smart," the context of healthcare has reached a level where the gap between both is very much narrow, and it will be hard to find "not-smart" devices in the coming years. It can be clearly inferred that IoT devices directly and their combinational applications have taken over the healthcare industry to such a level that it has become hard to not find IoT in healthcare industrial applications. In this chapter, we discuss IoT implementation, various applications, challenges, and the future scope of IoT in smart healthcare systems.

IoT is authentically changing the healthcare industry by readdressing the way devices and people connect to deliver healthcare solutions. Smart healthcare is widely used at the patient, physician, and hospital levels, and is not limited to few applications.

Patient-level IoT: Wearable devices such as fitness bands and other similar devices which make use of wireless connections aiming to measure things such as blood pressure, heart rate, glucometers, and so on belong to a category of smart IoT devices directly being used by patients. Such devices have the capability to act as reminder systems to remind certain things such as calorie counts and exercise routines and even act as alarm systems whenever a bodily measure acts anomalously such as blood pressure, oxygen level and so on. IoT has drastically changed the way people perceive lives, particularly in older people by facilitating constant monitoring of health conditions. This in turn has a high impact on the people surrounding them immediately.[8] Upon any shift or disruptions in the mundane activities of a person, altering systems send messages to selected personnel or health providers.

1. **Medico-level IoT:** With the help of wearable devices and home monitoring equipment, physicians can keep track of their patient's health more effectively. They can also keep an eye on the treatment plans and provide immediate medical attention when needed. Similarly, IoT enables healthcare professionals to monitor and connect with patients at an early stage of their illness and provide them with the best treatment options.
2. **Hospital-level IoT:** Aside from monitoring patients, there exist several other areas where IoT applications can be used to improve the healthcare delivery system. For instance, in hospitals, the use of wearable devices to monitor the locations of various medical equipment or medical staff in a real-time manner is highly resourceful. Similarly, IoT devices can also be employed for supply chain-related tasks such as keeping notes of various medical equipment and supplies. Another major concern in hospitals is the rapid spread of infectious diseases. With the help of IoT devices that can monitor hygiene, hospitals can prevent the spread of such infections.[8] IoT can also be employed for tasks related to asset management such as pharmacy inventory control, monitoring surrounding, and even temperature or humidity management in medical devices.

The application of IoT is not just limited to direct smart healthcare applications, but many indirect applications are also performed. One such major application is related to health insurance procedures. In the healthcare insurance sector, countless opportunities exist for IoT-based intelligent devices. In recent applications, several insurance companies have started making use of data generated by health-monitoring devices prior to insurance approval and other claim operations. By making use of such data, fraud claims can be minimized up to a level and eligible claims can be identified with ease. IoT devices can make such claim operations more transparent due to the existence of hard and reliable data.[9] Such data make the procedures more open and genuine, and also ensure that no underlying intentions exist on both sides. Insurance is one among many applications of IoT in smart health allied sectors. The following section will discuss the basic implementation of IoT in smart healthcare prior to performing a detailed application-based study.

1.2 IMPLEMENTATION OF IoT IN SMART HEALTHCARE

The accretion of healthcare-oriented IoT devices has opened up a huge number of opportunities for technological advancements and gradual autonomy. The peculiarity of IoT devices is the capability of generating huge amounts of data. Such huge amounts of data in the context of healthcare hold the key to transforming healthcare. The IoT model applied in healthcare-based applications aims at integrating the merits of IoT along with several other technologies depending upon the situation of the application. Certain protocols are set to be followed during the transmittance of data from countless sensors and healthcare devices at the patient's end to a particular device or network at the computing end. Basically, the arrangement of such devices and networks is referred to as healthcare IoT topology where all devices are orderly connected in a healthcare network scenario. Basically, a healthcare IoT system is comprised of three constituent elements. They are publishers, brokers, and subscribers.[10] A network of interconnected sensors and other healthcare devices is referred to as a publisher, and the peculiarity of such a network is that the individual components have the capability to work as a stand-alone device as well as a network when it comes to mapping the vitals of the diseased. Such information may include anything from blood pressure, pulse rate, oxygen level, and several other measures.[11] The information generated by the publisher will be sent in a contiguous manner to the next entity in the setting, i.e., the broker. Usually, the role of the broker is limited to data processing and storing in several devices, be it the cloud or any other similar device. The final component of the system is the subscriber whose role is to perform constant observations of the diseased via data obtained. Such data will be made accessible through different mediums such as smartphones, computers, and so on. Figure 1.1 provides an idea of the basic three components of an IoT-based healthcare system similar to the one mentioned above.

The publishers also have the capability of data processing and feedback generation after performing needed observation in case of changes observed or any other sort of anomalies detected in the conditions of the diseased. Such healthcare IoT systems accommodate individual components into a mixed framework where each component has an individual role to play in the healthcare network. The major issue of such healthcare IoT systems is the absence of a global topology as it is completely dependent upon the need of the time and situation. Due to this reason, it is to be noted that the system has undergone considerable structural changes in the past as well.[12] The primary phase when designing a new IoT-based healthcare system is to make a note of all the needs and activities that the system is expected to perform. As with all other systems, here also the success of the system is completely dependent upon its ability to satisfy its users, i.e., healthcare professionals and patients. Also due to the complexity and sensitivity of healthcare tasks, the system topology also needs to follow some predefined rules and measures during medical diagnosis operations.

When discussing the implementation of IoT in healthcare systems, another critical component should be discussed as well, i.e., the various technologies used. It is because of the fact that the selection of the right technology for the particular application is a major deciding factor when it comes to the performing ability of the system. Thus, when it comes to the integration of healthcare applications with IoT, advanced technologies are employed. Such technologies can be classified into three categories, i.e., recognition technologies, transmission technologies, and location technology. Figure 1.2 gives a graphical representation of the technological classification in IoT-based smart healthcare system implementation.

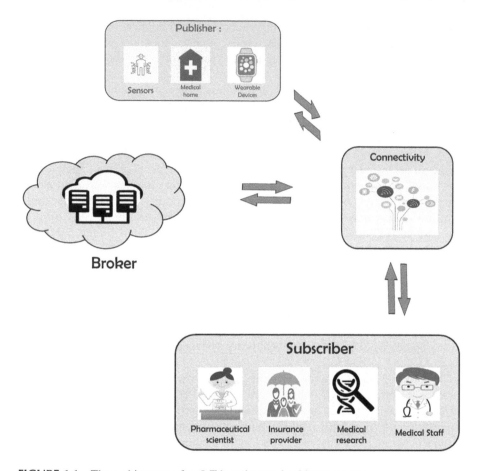

FIGURE 1.1 The architecture of an IoT-based smart healthcare system.

1.2.1 RECOGNITION TECHNOLOGY

A prime factor affecting the design of an IoT-based healthcare system is the reachability of the data generated from the sensors or similar devices at the patient's end. Such a process can only be performed with efficient recognition procedures for individual data generation points present throughout the network irrespective of their geographical locations. The recognition process begins with the system assigning individual and unique identifiers (UIDs) to every single node present in the network to ensure data individuality and easy recognition.[13] Generally, it can be said that every entity (living or non-living) that is part of a smart healthcare system is assigned a UID. As of now, several methodologies are followed for the above-mentioned procedures. Even though the separate addressing and recognition of all entities also help in the proper working of the system, the chances of changes made to the UID also exist in such systems due to situations such as system upgradation. Thus, the system should have a feature to perform self-update with the server devices in cases where UID changes are made to safeguard the fullness of

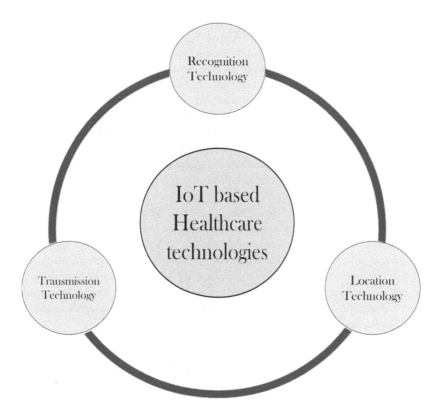

FIGURE 1.2 Technological classification of IoT.

the smart healthcare system. Also, this can be the rationale behind the fact that such modifications not only result in inefficient tracking procedures but also may cause unsatisfactory diagnostics.

1.2.2 TRANSMISSION TECHNOLOGY

Transmission technology plays the part of ensuring a stable connection between multiple entities that are part of the IoT-based healthcare network. In a broader sense, these technologies are of two types, i.e., short range and medium range.[14] As the name implies, short-range technologies comprise the protocols which are capable of establishing connections between devices in a very narrow geographical range, in most cases body area networks (BANs). As with medium-range technologies, they aim for data transmissions among long-range devices ("long" in IoT context) such as data transfer between servers or base stations and other smaller networks such as BAN. The word "long" in the context of IoT networks usually refers to a span of over 100 m and "short" usually implies a few centimeters to a couple of meters at maximum. Some of the very common transmission technologies include radiofrequency identification (RFID), Wi-Fi, Bluetooth, and so on.

1.2.3 LOCATION TECHNOLOGY

In the context of healthcare IoT networks, location technologies serve the purpose of identifying and tracking the location of a component object. They are also referred to as real-time location systems. Not only that, but they also aid in tracking the treatment procedures based on the administration of resources. The most-renowned and worldwide-used location identification technology is the global positioning system or GPS technology, which functions by making use of satellite data for tracking and identification purpose. The detection range of an object using GPS is valid till a line of sight persists between the object and a combination of four geo-location-identifying satellites.[14] In IoT-based healthcare applications, such technologies are used for tracking the positions of various hospital-related objects or entities such as ambulances, medical staff, patients, medical equipment, and so on. The major demerit of the GPS technology is its limitations to outdoor applications only. Basic structures inside buildings such as walls, pillars, and so on block the GPS signals or make them feeble. Such cases call for another similar technology known as a local positioning system or LPS. LPS systems are capable of object tracking using radio signals generated by moving objects and captured by dedicated receivers. The LPS can also be employed on systems making use of different short-distance communication technologies such as RFID, Wi-Fi, and so on.

1.3 ROLE OF IoT IN SMART HEALTHCARE

The rapid developments in the IoT technology have facilitated the medical sector in incorporating devices capable of performing real-time data analysis functions which were not even imaginable a few years back. Such functionalities have made healthcare tasks to be accessible to a higher number of users over the same period of time and still to produce exceptional results in the service sector at a considerably low cost. Technologies such as big data analysis and cloud computing have also facilitated efficient and reliable modes of data transmission among the patients and medical personnel. The exponential growth of IoT has also contributed to the progression of IoT-based healthcare applications such as medical diagnosis, personal care systems, health management applications, and so on.[16] The application of IoT in the healthcare industry can be broadly classified into two main categories depending upon their line of work, i.e., service sector and applications. Tasks that are related to the developmental stage of an IoT system are referred to as the service sector in the smart healthcare context. Similarly, application means the real-life application of IoT systems such as diagnosis, monitoring tasks, and so on. We will go through a small study of both divisions in the coming section.

1.3.1 SERVICES PERFORMED BY IoT IN SMART HEALTHCARE

Services and concepts have entirely modified the healthcare sector by giving efficient solutions to long-lasting technological problems. The need for more services is ever existing, and the count is getting added on a daily basis with the rise in technological advancements. In the current scenario, such services are just becoming a regular

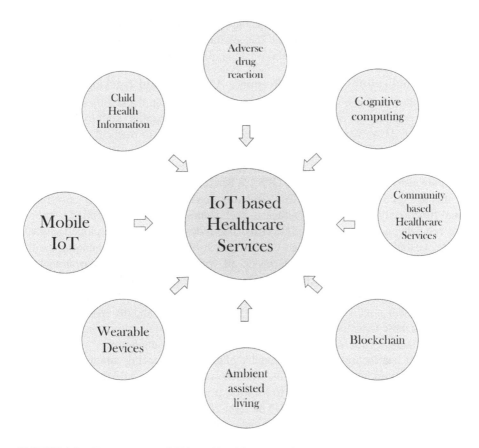

FIGURE 1.3   Some common IoT-based healthcare services.

part of IoT-based healthcare systems. The interpretation given to the term "services" is not a distinctive or individual one as they are common for multiple applications. The individuality of a system is completely based on the application running on it.[17] Even though we will not be studying the topic in detail, some of the very common IoT-based healthcare services are depicted in Figure 1.3.

1.3.2   APPLICATIONS OF IoT IN SMART HEALTHCARE

As mentioned earlier, healthcare IoT services are mainly employed for developing various IoT-based applications. Academicians and analysts from the domain have suggested several other concepts aimed at the service sector. It can be said that services or concepts are more oriented toward the likes of the developers, whereas applications give prime consideration to their users. The technological advancements in IoT have meant that greater volumes of cheaper and user-friendly devices have been made available to the general public such as wearable devices, healthcare systems, and similar other gadgets. Such systems serve their purpose by collecting information from patients related to health status and disease conditions, and even help in generating alerts when needed. In the coming section, we will perform a study on the different IoT-based healthcare applications available as of now.[18] Based on the levels and needs, smart healthcare applications can be divided into the following.

1.3.2.1 Applications Related to Resource Allocation and Tracking

Resource allocation and tracking technology based on IoT in the healthcare industry helps in keeping a note of physical entities related to the hospital, both living as well as non-living. From basic medical equipment or machines to medical personnel or patients, such applications can be used to understand the current situation. Usually, such applications making use of IoT for tracking functionalities in medical environments are also referred to as "indoor GPS". When it comes to tracking and monitoring, the majorly used IoT device is RFID. Tracking tasks is one of the major unconventional functionalities of IoT in healthcare. Such solutions are mostly applied to problems requiring actions on a real-time basis. The industry has now developed several IoT devices and applications based on the context of tracking and managing medical equipment, medics, and patients inside all varieties of medical environments.[19] Mostly such applications function by making use of embedded devices (capable of performing location identification) attached to whatsoever asset whose details are to be known. Each asset will be marked with a unique identifier and the system functions by tracking these tags. Such devices can be applied to hospital units, rooms, and even shelf-level storage cum tracking for authentic functionality autonomy.

These IoT healthcare systems are capable of governing, storing, and working upon the data generated by the RFID cards. In other ways, it can be said that the purpose of such systems is not just limited to location tracking but make inferences related to supply chain management as well. The level of stock, usage over a particular time period, frequency, and all sorts of such measures can be inferred when proper data analysis can be done on the generated data. The major purpose of IoT-based tracking systems in the healthcare sector is to facilitate the generation of well-formulated decisions and perform on-time treatments.[20] Tracking via medical IoT applications entitles real-time warning and surveillance systems. All such measures ensure a better quality of treatment and higher patient-level satisfaction.

1.3.2.2 Applications Based on Remote Patient Monitoring Systems

Remote patient monitoring systems are one of the most useful and relevant IoT-based healthcare applications used throughout the world. Such systems are usually considered extensions of regular medical systems with the exception that the patients can be monitored remotely. Taking into consideration the multiple capabilities of IoT devices, such monitoring systems were devised. They make use of a "cocktail" of devices and applications depending upon the need of the situation. The usual system is comprised of three health sensors, i.e., the heart rate sensor, temperature measuring sensor, and galvanic skin response sensor. With the aid of these three parameters, medical professionals can make several other inferences. Remote patient monitoring systems have facilitated medical experts to monitor, analyze, and keep a track of their patients in a constant manner.

The major motto of such systems is to provide ready access to healthcare professionals for physically unstable and critical patients on a regular basis. From a doctor's perspective, it enables them to do round-the-clock assessments and provide consistent treatment assistance irrespective of locations. The systems also aim at offering mobile treatment support to enable a quicker response in case of medical emergencies.[21] As of now, such remote monitoring systems are being developed using low-powered dedicated sensors with each one having a dedicated purpose. In the future, it is also expected to add small cameras and similar devices for real-time multimedia data streaming.

1.3.2.3   Robotics-Based Smart Health Applications

During the corona outbreak in Wuhan, to cope with the high staff shortage and to scale the number of critical ICU units and resources, multiple field hospitals employed IoT robots for medical assistance. Even though such robots were not used for treatment-related functions, they were employed for tasks such as disinfection, medicine delivery, temperature monitoring, and so on within the hospital environment. The claims from the authorities state that such a measure had surely helped to efficiently manage the already-overloaded medical staff as well as bring down the contraction of diseases among medical personnel.[22] The corona era has surely opened up the view of the practical feasibility of robotics and healthcare automation made possible.

Robotics and automation of healthcare tasks are two very significant IoT-based applications in smart healthcare. With the help of dedicated machinery, intelligent robots are capable of doing certain jobs on their own with minimal human intervention. Such systems are constructed with the aid of statistical pattern recognition techniques, deep learning techniques, parametric and non-parametric algorithms, and so on. Robotics in smart healthcare scenarios helps in forming an IoT-based network of interconnected robots.[23] Such connections help in performing data transfer via IoT principles without the need for human-to-human or human-to-computer interaction cycles.

The main purpose of the application of robotics in smart healthcare is as efficient data-collection points as well as automated data processing centers. Also, the growing scope of robotics has facilitated its applications being visible in complex surgical procedures for more precision-based tasks. Robotic tasks in smart healthcare are not just limited to microlevel IoT applications but are also made available on a larger scale in mechanical and electrical applications.[24] The penultimate aim of such methodologies is to make healthcare more performance-oriented and patient-centric, ensuring easier rehabilitation and care for patients.

1.3.2.4   Smart Hospital-Based Applications

Smart hospitals are establishments that make use of IoT to monitor and control several types of vitals of patients such as pulse rate, blood pressure, and so on in a remote manner. Smart hospitals mainly function using IoT applications capable of monitoring patients and generating alarms in case of emergencies. Even though the principle remains constant, the method of implementation will change depending on the need of the institution. Such applications make use of combinations of IoT with cloud computing, and different AI techniques such as machine learning, deep learning, and so on.[25] It can be inferred that a smart hospital is such an environment where

IT services are used to create healthcare automation and specialized supplementary procedures.

The role of IoT devices in smart healthcare is not just limited to sensory devices, but they also act as communication aids for recording purposes as well as mediums for displaying data. Also, various pre-collected medical parameters and post-operational data can be made use of by IoT applications in smart hospitals. Therefore, we can say that the usage of IoT applications in smart hospitals has really catalyzed the healthcare industry and also plays a major role in varying levels of healthcare applications.[26] The prime motto of such intuitions is in designing, developing, and constructing new clinical procedures using IoT applications. They also aim to optimize the usage of the already-available infrastructure as well as to form a digitalized network with high-end internet of medical things (IoMT) technologies.

1.3.2.5 Hospital Information Management System

Another major application of IoT in a hospital-based environment is the hospital information and management system. Such a system uses IoT principles along with other technologies and provides a detailed source of information regarding the patient's medical history. IoT applications are used to connect several physical and analog devices via the internet with actuators and sensors as data-collecting agents. Such data will be stored in the hospital information management systems and analyzed by medical personnel at a later time. Even though the basic elements of such systems are related to the patient's health history, they are not limited to those applications only.[27] They also aid in allied systems such as financial and commerce management, communication systems, medical documentation, administrative systems, and even medical support systems.

In the case of systems aiming at other managerial tasks, their expertise lies in remote control of databases. The use of IoT applications ensures the ready availability of data irrespective of geographical location for authorized users. Such systems covert hospitals to more of a patient-centric view and ensure efficient medical environments in technological perspective as well. Using the IoT, hospital information and management systems can improve healthcare coordination and patient safety. It can also handle different aspects of a healthcare facility's operations very efficiently.

Even though several other applications exist, we have only discussed a handful of instances. Figure 1.4 provides a basic idea of the several IoT-based healthcare applications that are already being used commercially.

1.4 CHALLENGES AND OBSERVATIONS MADE

In recent years, the healthcare industry has been subjected to high-intensity technological developments in an attempt to revolutionize health-related problem-solving tasks. This has given rise to better healthcare services being made available at a click's distance. With the introduction of smart sensors, cloud devices, and several communication techniques, IoT has completely transformed the healthcare sector.[28] Similar to any other technology, IoT also faces particular challenges and issues that need to be rectified on the way forward. We will discuss some of the issues while staying within the scope of our work.

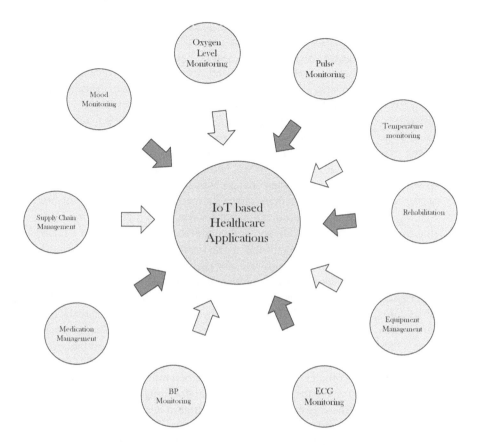

FIGURE 1.4 Various IoT-based healthcare applications at a glance.

1. **Data security and privacy:** A major issue related to IoT environments was their resource-constraint nature when it comes to particular tasks. The incorporation of cloud computing has not only alleviated memory-related issues up to a certain level but also opened up a new set of issues related cyber-attacks. The sensitive nature of healthcare data implies that such an issue needed to be taken care of in immediate way. Several methodologies have been tried and tested as preventive measures for the same. Some of the major ones were related to user authentication, security boosting, password encryption, increased security protocols, and so on.[29] The highly connected nature of IoT implies that any bug in the system can totally compromise the system resulting in high levels of privacy breaches and data loss. The only solution, in the long run, is to create better and more secure environments with high-end cryptographic techniques and secure algorithms.

2. **Expandability:** As with any other "networking environment," expandability is a huge concern in healthcare IoT implementations as well. This feature enables the capability of systems to work in varying environments without incurring latency issues and ensures efficient resource usage as well. Hence,

expandability is a highly desired feature when producing systems aiming for future use cases as well. As with the case of IoT in healthcare, heterogeneity is a real concern when it comes to the network structure.[30] The number and type of sensors as well as other allied devices keep on varying. This, in turn, puts an inverse effect on the system's capability for expanding, and thus, the issue needs to be tackled efficiently with proper research.

3. **Update cost:** Lately, sudden technological developments are happening all around the healthcare industry which in turn requires constant updating of the existing devices and technologies to stay compatible with the rest. As in other cases, IoT systems in the healthcare sector are also designed in such a way that several other devices will be connected to it making it a proper network, in the particular case its medical equipment or sensors. Such networks need extensive maintenance as well as high updating costs that can end up in increased financial investments than what could be taken out.[31] Such an issue is not just limited to the institutional level but also applicable to the end users. Thus, proposal for the introduction of cost-effective low-maintenance sensors is high and the very need of future.

4. **Energy consumption:** In the healthcare industry due to the need for stable procedures, most of the IoT systems are run on stored power, mostly batteries. Hence, once a system is implemented, the task of replacing a battery is hard. Thus, the alternative solution is to go for high-power batteries, which again ends up in increased costs.[32] Hence, the need of the future is to develop power-efficient systems or systems that are capable of producing their needed power via some medium preferably through renewable sources of energy. Also, these systems can be influential in dealing with the energy crisis going on around the globe.

5. **Regularity issues:** The context of healthcare IoT has witnessed a huge boom over the years, and thus, the number of devices and their producers is high. This simply means that there exists a huge heterogeneity in the type and working of these devices. Similarly, their mode of design and operation, as well as their working protocols, will also vary. Thus, the need for a standard protocol for the manufacture and working of these devices is high. Only then, we can ensure a consistent standard when it comes to communication protocols, data processing, and so on.

6. **Continual surveillance:** Certain healthcare scenarios need constant monitoring of the diseased throughout a particular period of time during treatment procedures such as for cardiac ICU patients, chronic disease cases, and so on.[31] This calls for real-time video-streaming functionalities that need to be incorporated into IoT settings more efficiently.

7. **Coping with changing diseases:** Mobile applications are a huge part of smart healthcare IoT applications, and as of now, multiple mobile apps and platforms are available in the market aiming to take care of certain diseases. The major issue with such platforms is that they have a limited stratum of application meaning that they aim for a single or very few diseases. Such devices or applications should have the ability to upgrade according to the need of the user, implying that with the changing scenarios of newer

diseases appearing in society, it should also have the provisions to incorporate them into the system.

8. **Environmental concerns:** The rapid advancements in healthcare-based IoT devices have also increased the need for the usage of more biomedical sensors and devices with high semiconductor components. Such devices have a high need for certain metals and chemicals during their production as well. Such an issue will surely put high pressure on environmental resources. Thus, the need for a regulatory authority having the sole power to govern all the procedures related to the production of such materials is evident.[33] Also, in the long run, more stress should be put into developing such devices with either biodegradable or reusable materials.

1.5 FUTURE SCOPE

The past decade had seen the takeover of healthcare by IoT- and AI-based technologies. This had given rise to a condition where the industry, as well as academia, has started shifting their concentration to the IoT market space. The latest CES event saw a huge rise in the sheer number of companies working on IoT-based healthcare products such as personal care robots, smart home monitoring systems, smart sensor devices, and so on. Extensive studies estimate that by 2025, the wearable IoT technology market is expected to triple in volume as compared to 2019. Wearable technology is one of the most effective additions of IoT in healthcare and has all the potential to take the technology forward in the coming decades. This single technology can change the way healthcare functions in uncountable ways by just changing the sensors and monitoring activities they perform, thus adding to its growing scope.

1.5.1 What Is the Real Scope of the IoMT in the Future?

Beyond the hype around healthcare IoT, the COVID-19 pandemic has sparked discussions about the future of the IoT-connected healthcare industry and the safety it can offer for medical professionals and patients. The complexity of the issues has forced many hospitals and treatment centers to opt for telehealth services rather than ensuring the physical presence of the diseased and in turn, increasing risks of contractions. Also in the long-lasting attempt to develop cost-efficient diagnosis and treatment methodology, wearable technologies have taken the industry pretty far toward the aim.[34] Wearable devices could help hospitals cut costs by allowing some patients to be treated at home.

Another technology that will play a huge role in the future of IoT in healthcare is the introduction of fifth-generation (5G) networks. These networks provide faster connectivity and better security. The building block of IoT devices is a highly efficient connectivity channel, and 5G network can facilitate that with ease. Faster cellular data transfer speeds allow IoT devices to connect and exchange data much faster. Some of the new applications that are being made available to the public include home healthcare monitoring devices that can help patients keep track of their medication adherence and monitor their oxygen levels, and even temperature.[35] The new pandemic experience and the advancements in the field of IoT will surely encourage more people to get on board with the technology.

1.5.2   WHAT DOES THE FUTURE HOLD FOR SMART HEALTHCARE?

With the addition of multiple technologies such as the cloud and AI, IoT devices are making smart healthcare even smarter and the scope is alleviating from just patient data transfer applications to higher use cases. For instance, smart glucose monitoring systems and smart insulin pens are just a couple of technologies that are already making use of IoT combined with cloud services and performing high-end data analytics operations. They are capable of not just capturing continuous glucose level data, but they also perform data uploading to the cloud or some other remote server devices where analytics can be performed. Based on the analysis result, the insulin pump has the intelligence to determine the amount of dosage.[36] Similarly, another application is related to smart cameras for monitoring elderly or diseased people. Such cameras identify any changes happening in the mundane tasks of the people and take necessary actions.

As of now, AI is gradually converting the conventional tag of IoT devices as "data-collection points" to "smart devices" capable of performing meaningful procedures. The other applications of IoMT that are expected to create a trend in the near future include the deployment of small-scale robots and virtual agents, facilitating interaction with the diseased. With a combination of data generated via IoT devices and sensors and other compatible vocal assistants, the patients can have personal healthcare assistants developed according to individual needs.[37] Similarly, wearable technologies along with data mining techniques have been employed related to COVID-19 tasks in recent times. From tracking to bodily measures, they have to track the patient's activities and even trace unidentifiable contacts.

The end line is that the future of IoT in smart health is very bright if it is able to adapt. As in the past with AI, applications based on pure technology are limited and incomplete. They fail to adapt in the long run and get outdated very quickly. The era of pure AI was over with the emergence of IoT. Even though now the trend is for AI-enabled IoT in every field, we cannot say that it is permanent. The future holds different needs, and technologies perish when failing to adapt.

The combinational applications of IoT with the cloud are facing huge issues in the current scenarios due to the latency associated with cloud services. The industry is on a search for alternatives for the cloud which can provide real-time or at least near-real-time processing capabilities. It is expected that in the very near future, we will see a total replacement of the cloud by edge and fog computing technologies. Edge computing simply means to take the processing closer to the source of the data, and it is an ideal combination for IoT applications. In the field of healthcare where every second of time lost in processing can result in huge losses, edge computing is the ideal contender due to its real-time processing capabilities and cheap infrastructural needs.[38] Fog is also a similar technology with similar expectations. When it comes to the security side as well, IoT needs certain support.[15] The industry is gradually trying to incorporate blockchain with IoT in an attempt to find a solution for the issues, and by far, the results show that they have succeeded up to a certain level. Blockchain enables the creation of a strong network among devices and intra-organizational bodies to perform secure procedures. It can also play a major role in healthcare supply chain management.

It is pretty clear from previous experiences that the survival of a technology is always a matter of its capability to adapt to the needs. If IoT can do that, the coming era will witness a total revolution similar to Industrial Revolution 4.0. Else, it will be part of a long list of other technologies which have perished due to their inability to adapt and thus survive.

1.6   CONCLUSION

To sum up, the scope of smart healthcare in the current era is huge. For isolated users, such systems can provide enhanced health management services individually. On-time and appropriate medical aids can be made available at times of emergencies, and the methods of operation of such services can be highly individualized. From the medical institutional point of view, smart healthcare systems provide a much more cost-effective solution along with ensuring lessened pressure and improving the experience of the user as a whole. Similarly, from a research perspective, smart healthcare opens up the scope for facilitating quicker and cost-effective research methodologies as well as improved efficiency. The inclusion of IoT into the mix has facilitated a new era of smart medical systems. IoT is a very efficient tool that has facilitated quality healthcare to be made available at a click's distance, unlike previous times when it was limited to hospitals and research institutions. As a result of IoT incorporation, several new technologies have been introduced into smart healthcare systems such as wearable technologies, remote healthcare systems, personalized healthcare systems, smart pills, and so on. All these have resulted in a total increase in user experience as well as efficient treatments being ensured for all users. This has eradicated the previously existing gap related to the physical distance between the patients and the doctors as it has enabled healthcare professionals to give the same attention to several people at the same time irrespective of their geographical position or status. The future of healthcare is expected to be controlled by IoT devices either directly or through combinational applications. The current trend of pure IoT is slowly getting saturated, and the industry is moving toward more combinations of IoT along with AI, blockchain, edge computing, and so on. Either way, the trend clearly says one thing. In the context of healthcare systems, IoT is here to stay for a long period of time if it has the capability to upgrade and adapt according to the requirements.

REFERENCES

[1] Aghdam, Z. N., Rahmani, A. M. and Hosseinzadeh, M. [2020], 'The role of the internet of things in healthcare: future trends and challenges', *Computer Methods and Programs in Biomedicine*, 199, 105903.

[2] Ahad, A., Tahir, M., Aman Sheikh, M., Ahmed, K. I., Mughees, A. and Numani, A. [2020], 'Technologies trend towards 5g network for smart health-care using Iot: A review', *Sensors* 20(14), 4047.

[3] Awaisi, K. S., Hussain, S., Ahmed, M., Khan, A. A. and Ahmed, G. [2020], 'Leveraging Iot and fog computing in healthcare systems', *IEEE Internet of Things Magazine* 3(2), 52–56.

[4] Banerjee, A., Chakraborty, C., Kumar, A. and Biswas, D. [2020], Emerging trends in Iot and big data analytics for biomedical and healthcare technologies, in *Handbook of Data Science Approaches for Biomedical Engineering*, Elsevier, pp. 121–152, edited by Valentia Emilia Balas, Vijender Kumar Solanki, Raghvendra Kumar, and Manju Khari, ISBN 978-0-12-818318, Amsterdam, Netherlands.

[5] Cáceres, C., Rosário, J. M. and Amaya, D. [2018], Proposal of a smart hospital based on internet of things (Iot) concept, in *Sipaim–Miccai Biomedical Workshop*, Springer, pp. 93–104, edited by Natasha Lepore, Jorge Brieva, Eduardo Romero, Daniel Racoceanu, Leo Joskowicz, Granada, Spain.

[6] Celesti, A., Lay-Ekuakille, A., Wan, J., Fazio, M., Celesti, F., Romano, A., Bramanti, P. and Villari, M. [2020], 'Information management in Iot cloudbased tele-rehabilitation as a service for smart cities: Comparison of nosql approaches', *Measurement* 151, 107218.

[7] Chawla, M. N. [2020], 'Ai, Iot and wearable technology for smart healthcare – a review', *International Journal of Green Energy* 7(1), 9–13.

[8] Dang, L. M., Piran, M., Han, D., Min, K., Moon, H. et al. [2019], 'A survey on internet of things and cloud computing for healthcare', *Electronics* 8(7), 768.

[9] Gatouillat, A., Badr, Y., Massot, B. and Sejdić, E. [2018], 'Internet of medical things: A review of recent contributions dealing with cyber-physical systems in medicine', *IEEE Internet of Things Journal* 5(5), 3810–3822.

[10] Greco, L., Percannella, G., Ritrovato, P., Tortorella, F. and Vento, M. [2020], 'Trends in Iot based solutions for healthcare: Moving ai to the edge', *Pattern Recognition Letters* 135, 346–353.

[11] Hathaliya, J. J. and Tanwar, S. [2020], 'An exhaustive survey on security and privacy issues in healthcare 4.0', *Computer Communications* 153, 311–335.

[12] Hinterberger, L., Weber, B., Fischer, S., Neubauer, K. and Hackenberg, R. [2020], 'Iot device identification and recognition (Iotag)', *Cloud Computing* 2020, 17.

[13] Huang, J., Wu, X., Huang, W., Wu, X. and Wang, S. [2021], 'Internet of things in health management systems: A review', *International Journal of Communication Systems* 34(4), e4683.

[14] Islam, M. M., Rahaman, A. and Islam, M. R. [2020a], 'Development of smart healthcare monitoring system in Iot environment', *SN Computer Science* 1, 1–11.

[15] Zou, N., Liang, S. and He, D. [2020], '*Issues and Challenges of User and Data Interaction in Healthcare-Related Iot: A Systematic Review*'. Library Hi Tech, Bingley, UK.

[16] Kadhim, K. T., Alsahlany, A. M., Wadi, S. M. and Kadhum, H. T. [2020], 'An overview of patient's health status monitoring system based on internet of things (Iot)', *Wireless Personal Communications* 114(3), 2235–2262.

[17] Khanna, A. and Kaur, S. [2020], 'Internet of things (Iot), applications and challenges: A comprehensive review', *Wireless Personal Communications* 114, 1687–1762.

[18] Kumar, A., Dhanagopal, R., Albreem, M. A. and Le, D.-N. [2021], 'A comprehensive study on the role of advanced technologies in 5G based smart hospital', *Alexandria Engineering Journal* 60(6), 5527–5536.

[19] Li, W., Chai, Y., Khan, F., Jan, S. R. U., Verma, S., Menon, V. G., & Li, X. [2021]. 'A comprehensive survey on machine learning-based big data analytics for IoT-enabled smart healthcare system', *Mobile Networks and Applications* 26(1), 234–252.

[20] Mathew, P. S., Pillai, A. S. and Palade, V. [2018], Applications of Iot in healthcare, in '*Cognitive Computing for Big Data Systems Over IoT*', Springer, pp. 263–288, edited by Arun Kumar Sangaiah, Arunkumar Thangavelu, Venkatesan Meenakshi Sundaram, ISBN: 978-3-319-70688-7, NY, US.

[21] Mishra, S. S. and Rasool, A. [2019], Iot healthcare monitoring and tracking: A survey, in '*2019 3rd International Conference on Trends in Electronics and Informatics (ICOEI)*', IEEE, pp. 1052–1057.

[22] Mourya, A. K., Idrees, S. M. et al. [2020], Cloud computing-based approach for accessing electronic health record for healthcare sector, in *'Microservices in Big Data Analytics'*, Springer, pp. 179–188, edited by Anil Chaudhary, Chothmal Choudhary, Mukesh Kumar Gupta, Chhagan Lal, Tapas Badal, ISBN: 978-981-15-0128-9, NY, US.

[23] Mukherjee, S. and Biswas, G. [2018], 'Networking for Iot and applications using existing communication technology', *Egyptian Informatics Journal* 19(2), 107–127.

[24] Pradhan, B., Bharti, D., Chakravarty, S., Ray, S. S., Voinova, V. V., Bonartsev, A. P. and Pal, K. [2021], 'Internet of things and robotics in transforming current-day healthcare services', *Journal of Healthcare Engineering* 2021, 1–15.

[25] Pradhan, B., Bhattacharyya, S. and Pal, K. [2021], 'Iot-based applications in healthcare devices', *Journal of Healthcare Engineering* 2021, 1–18.

[26] Qadri, Y. A., Nauman, A., Zikria, Y. B., Vasilakos, A. V. and Kim, S. W. [2020], 'The future of healthcare internet of things: A survey of emerging technologies', *IEEE Communications Surveys & Tutorials* 22(2), 1121–1167.

[27] Rehman, H. U., Asif, M. and Ahmad, M. [2017], Future applications and research challenges of Iot, in *'2017 International Conference on Information and Communication Technologies (ICICT)'*, IEEE, pp. 68–74.

[28] Robel, M. R. A., Bharati, S., Podder, P. and Mondal, M. R. H. [2020], 'Iot driven healthcare monitoring system', *Fog, Edge, and Pervasive Computing in Intelligent IoT Driven Applications*, 161–176.

[29] Saji, M., Sridhar, M., Rajasekaran, A., Kumar, R. A., Suyampulingam, A. and Prakash, N. K. [2021], Iot-based intelligent healthcare module, in *'Advances in Smart System Technologies'*, Springer, pp. 765–774, edited by P. Suresh, U. Saravanakumar, Mohammed Saleh Hussein Al Salameh, ISBN: 978-981-15-5029-4, NY, US.

[30] Selvaraj, S. and Sundaravaradhan, S. [2020], 'Challenges and opportunities in Iot healthcare systems: A systematic review', *SN Applied Sciences* 2(1), 1–8.

[31] Singh, P. [2018], 'Internet of things based health monitoring system: Opportunities and challenges', *International Journal of Advanced Research in Computer Science* 9(1), 224–228.

[32] Solanki, A. and Nayyar, A. [2019], Green internet of things (G-Iot): Ict technologies, principles, applications, projects, and challenges, in *'Handbook of Research on Big Data and the IoT'*, IGI Global, pp. 379–405, edited by Gurjit Kaur and Pradeep Tomar, ISBN13: 9781522574323, Hershey, Pennsylvania.

[33] Sun, L., Gupta, R. K. and Sharma, A. [2021], 'Review and potential for artificial intelligence in healthcare', *International Journal of System Assurance Engineering and Management*, 13(1), 1–9.

[34] Verma, V., Chowdary, V., Gupta, M. K. and Mondal, A. K. [2018], Iot and robotics in healthcare, in *'Medical Big Data and Internet of Medical Things'*, CRC Press, pp. 245–269, edited by Aboul Hassanien, Nilanjan Dey, Surekha Borra, ISBN: 9781351030380, FL, US.

[35] Yadav, V., Kundra, P. and Verma, D. [2021], Role of Iot and big data support in healthcare, in *'Advances in Computational Intelligence and Communication Technology'*, Springer, pp. 445–455, edited by Xiao-Zhi Gao, Shailesh Tiwari, Munesh C. Trivedi, Krishn K. Mishra, ISBN: 978-981-15-1275-9, NY, US.

[36] Yew, H. T., Ng, M. F., Ping, S. Z., Chung, S. K., Chekima, A. and Dargham, J. A. [2020], Iot based real-time remote patient monitoring system, in *'2020 16th IEEE International Colloquium on Signal Processing & its Applications (CSPA)'*, IEEE, pp. 176–179.

[37] Zemmar, A., Lozano, A. M. and Nelson, B. J. [2020], 'The rise of robots in surgical environments during covid-19', *Nature Machine Intelligence* 2(10), 566–572.

[38] Zgheib, R., Kristiansen, S., Conchon, E., Plageman, T., Goebel, V. and Bastide, R. [2020], 'A scalable semantic framework for Iot healthcare applications', *Journal of Ambient Intelligence and Humanized Computing*, 1–19.

[39] Zou, N., Liang, S. and He, D. [2020], *'Issues and Challenges of User and Data Interaction in Healthcare-Related Iot: A Systematic Review'*, Library Hi Tech, Bingley, UK.

2 Applications of i-IoT for Smart Healthcare Systems

Rohit Mittal
Manipal University Jaipur

Vibhakar Pathak
Arya College of Engineering & I.T.

Amit Mithal
Jaipur Engineering College & Research Centre

CONTENTS

2.1   INTRODUCTION

Artificial intelligence is becoming more prevalent in Internet of things (IoT) applications and deployments. The amount of money invested in IoT start-ups that use artificial intelligence (AI) has increased dramatically. The IoT connects physical devices to the internet, allowing data to be delivered and received via the web. Sensors, computer vision, real-time analysis, as well as embedded devices have all grown into and from the IoT notion. It is all about the smart hospital idea and other equipment that are connected to the internet via wired or wireless connections [1]. In order to do the desired work, smart gadgets can acquire and share data in everyday life. Smart cities, cars, electronics, entertainment systems, residences, and interconnected healthcare

DOI: 10.1201/9781003326182-2

all benefit from IoT applications [2]. IoT deployment in the medical industry relies on a variety of sensors, medical equipment, machine intelligence, and diagnosis, including modern imaging technologies. In both old and modern industries and communities, these devices boost overall productivity. For its capacity to swiftly extract insights from data, AI is playing a prominent role in IoT. Reinforcement learning is an AI technology that allows smart sensors and gadgets to intelligently discover patterns and identify abnormalities in data [1]. When it comes to evaluating IoT data, machine learning has several advantages over traditional business intelligence tools, including the ability to generate functional estimates up to 20 times faster and with more accuracy than cut-off point monitoring devices. In the health sector, a rising number of studies have been undertaken on employing IoT technology to capture data everywhere, analyze data quickly, and disseminate data wirelessly, with incorporated AI functionalities such as machine learning-based statistics [3,4]. In upcoming sections, the authors discuss the idea behind combining IoT with AI along with sensors, applications, and network architecture depicted.

2.2 i-IoT IN THE HEALTHCARE INDUSTRY

The IoT is a novel network that provides communication among billions of smart devices. Moreover, an intelligent system adapts from the patterns it forms by imitating how humans execute tasks. This self-improvement method is significantly used in AI. AI, in general, has several advantages to the IoT. It is defined as AI software that is incorporated into IoT-connected systems to supplement fog or edge computing solutions and add intelligence to IoT [2].

There is a good chance that combining AI and IoT in the medical industry will improve operational efficiency. Tracking, monitoring, scheduling, optimization, and mechanization are critical steps for the fast and creative implementation of AI algorithms in IoT devices (modeling and predicting). The classification of the healthcare system is depicted in Figure 2.1.

They can reduce the operational stress on clinical staff when they collaborate [5]. Medical officers will also be able to spend more time with people because of improved clinical workflows, resulting in a more patient-centric approach to healthcare service delivery.

Rural patients, health staff, and big-city professionals employ IoT technologies to facilitate primary healthcare. M-health, which is identified as mobile computing, biomedical sensors [6], and communication technologies for healthcare, is attracting an increasing number of academics who are using fourth-generation (4G) wireless communication systems and IoT in healthcare [7]. In terms of omnipresent data accessing medical services, the uses of IoT technology present both opportunities and concerns [8]. The development of universal data accessing solutions to obtain and process data in decentralized data sources has received more attention.

2.3 i-IoT IN COVID-19

The IoT connects all computational, industrial, and innovative electronics to transport data over the internet without any need for human contact. During the COVID-19

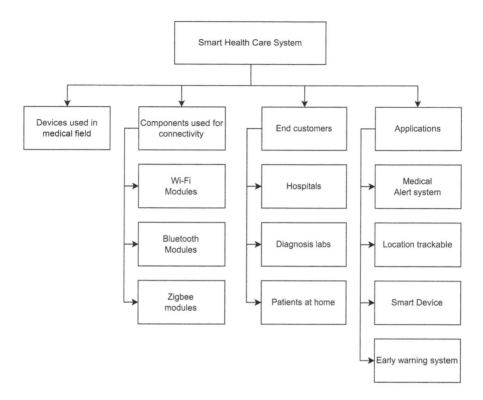

FIGURE 2.1   Overview of the smart healthcare system.

outbreak, this technique has been blooming in terms of monitoring healthcare. In today's world, many people die as a result of inaccurate and timely health information. Using a sensor, such technology can instantly alert users to health-related risks. All COVID-19 customer data is kept in the cloud [9], which can aid in providing appropriate care. This device can monitor a person's everyday activities and send out alerts if there is a health problem.

In the healthcare industry, it is critical to have the right equipment in order to run a successful surgery. IoT has a strong capability for performing successful operations and analyzing results afterward. During the COVID-19 outbreak, the use of IoT has resulted in better care delivery. IoT allows for real-time surveillance, which saves lives from a variety of conditions such as hypertension, heart failure, asthma attacks, high cholesterol, and so on. Intelligent health devices are linked to a cell phone to seamlessly communicate essential patient data to a physician. These gadgets also capture information on oxygen levels, blood pressure, weight, and sugar levels, among other things.

During an epidemic, trustworthy electronic information is a vital barrier in the healthcare industry, which IoT can easily address. Analyzing the innovations in use and potential benefits, including associated important applications to meet increased efficiency criteria is difficult. According to its expanded ability, it can tackle a variety of problems by delivering novel knowledge during an epidemic. With the support of breakthrough technologies, IoT has a strong ability to produce high-quality outputs. This becomes a true future in healthcare as an original concept that delivers quality inspection to COVID-19 patients and executes accurate surgery. During the ongoing pandemic, complicated situations are readily handled and regulated digitally. IoT creates outstanding support networks for clinicians, therapists, and customers by tackling new difficulties in the medical profession. Flying ad-hoc networks (FANETs) were also utilized to perform several tasks (i.e., inspection, surveillance, communication, spraying, delivery of items, temperature monitoring, etc.) during the COVID-19 pandemic [10].

2.4 CORE ELEMENTS AND SENSORS USED IN i-IoT FOR REMOTE MONITORING

Identification, localization, detection, and networking are the core elements of medical systems. Paramedics, smart computing, sensors, lab on chips, remote patient monitoring, wearables, connected devices, and big data are all examples of intelligent medical systems [11]. Through telehealth systems, IoT systems are associated with embedded sensors. They incorporate equipment with unique types of nodes that detect frequent differences in patient data; sensors can detect data for various measurements that contribute to the ventilation process of a room in order to assess the ventilation conditions for patients in rooms. Heat, pressure, and humidity, as well as other critical environmental parameters, are all measured by such sensors, which are designed to analyze data in a variety of ranges [12,13].

These solutions allow for remote monitoring of the patient's condition. The device can deliver hospital reports on a regular basis and keep track of the patient's medical history. The data can be viewed by hospital staff, who can then construct a therapy process for patients under surveillance. Wireless Sensor Networks are one of the most popular gadgets used in IoT medical systems [14]. From the perspective of remote patient control and reporting, the issue is more complex than in the previous scenario. In some cases, IoT is the most dependable and cost-effective solution, and the link between various devices including interactive communication systems still needs further formal investigation.

Intelligent IoT (i-IoT) makes it a lot easier to track a person's health and provide data to healthcare professionals such as physicians, paramedics, and experts. Specialists would benefit from employing the store-and-forward approach to keep and retrieve patient data so that it may be accessed at any time. The function of IoT in modern healthcare is portrayed, as well as the services it provides. Smart healthcare, smart dustbins, and vehicle parking are all examples of i-IoT approaches. Because the patient's health is tracked via a screen, it is indeed difficult to evaluate the patient at all times. As a result, sensors [15] can be used to assess the patient's present status, such as pulse rate, temperature, body posture, blood glucose, and echocardiogram.

The sensors are connected to Arduino UNO sensors [16], which collect data and send it to the server when connected to the core Arduino board which is shown in Figure 2.2. The information is transferred from this website to the doctor who provides medical advice.

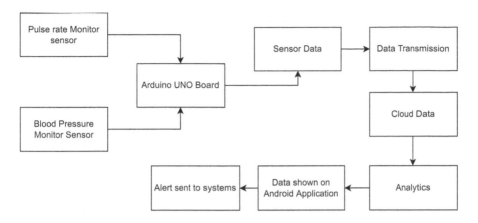

FIGURE 2.2 Flow diagram of i-IoT.

2.5 i-IoT APPLICATIONS IN THE HEALTHCARE SECTOR

IoT applications, parallel to IoT services, demand further attention. It is worth noting that solutions are utilized to create apps; however, apps are used immediately by customers and patients. As a result, services are developer-focused, whereas apps are user-focused. These goods can be thought of as IoT advancements that could lead to a variety of healthcare solutions.

2.5.1 DIABETES

Diabetes is a set of biochemical illnesses characterized by persistently elevated blood glucose (sugar) content. Individual patterns of blood glucose variations are revealed by blood glucose monitoring, which aids in the scheduling of meals, exercises, and medication timings.

On a factual basis, an medical-IoT customization approach for non-invasive glucose detection is proposed. Patients' sensors are connected to appropriate healthcare providers using IPv6 connectivity in this technique [2,13]. The utility model reveals a transmission device that uses IoT networks to transmit gathered human data on blood glucose. A blood glucose collector, a cell phone or laptop, and background processing are all included in this gadget.

2.5.2 ELECTROCARDIOGRAM (ECG)

Observing the ECG, or the electrical impulses of the heart as captured by electrocardiography comprises determining the fundamental rhythm and measuring the simple heart rate, as well as diagnosing complex arrhythmias, myocardial ischemia, and prolonged QT intervals. The usage of IoT in electrocardiography can provide a wealth of data and can be exploited to its full potential. IoT-based ECG monitoring has been discussed in several research. An IoT-based ECG monitoring system consists of a built-in Bluetooth procurement transmitter as well as a wireless reception processor described in [17]. The system includes a search auto-mation mechanism for detecting anomalous data, allowing for real-time identifica-tion of heart function.

2.5.3   INTERNAL BODY TEMPERATURE

As internal body temperature is a crucial vital sign in order to maintain homeostasis, body temperature measurement is an important aspect of medical care. The m-IoT idea is demonstrated in [18] utilizing a body temperature sensor incorporated in the TelosB mote, as well as a typical sample of acquired body temperature changes dem-onstrating the successful operation of the built m-IoT system. Reference [19] pro-poses an IoT-based temperature measurement system depending on an access point. Using infrared sensing, the access point (gateway) sends the user's body temperature. Reference [20] proposes another IoT-based temperature measurement solution. The radiofrequency identification (RFID) module as well as the module for detecting body temperature is the major system hardware liable for temperature collection and transmission.

2.5.4   GLOBAL POSITIONING SYSTEM (GPS)

The IoT is now widely employed in the healthcare industry. Medicines, for example, are barcoded so that they can be supplied to patients more accurately, whereas para-medics are linked to the global positioning system (GPS) as well as RFID tags so that they will be identified more rapidly. As a result, sharing medical data during the procurement of medical services becomes both a significant and a problematic issue for specialists and administrators in medical centers, as it is such a procedure that necessitates close cooperation. IoT notes link many items together to give medical activities to patients. To communicate with IoT, such IoT messages must adapt. To help clinicians and administrators easily access datasets, a descriptive and adaptable data framework is formulated to facilitate heterogeneous data exchange, particularly in the big data environment of IoT applications. The semantic data paradigm will be self-explanatory, allowing for diversified and decentralized data storage as well as convenient and dynamic data sharing. Moreover, data must be accessible at any time and from any location for healthcare services to be effective.

2.6   NETWORK ARCHITECTURE OF i-IoT

Qualified healthcare institutions such as clinics, emergency rooms, and the drug supply chain are directly linked to a **smart healthcare service layer**. Clinicians, for example, can effectively handle a big group of patients. Doctors can examine a patient's clinical information, conduct a deeper analysis of a questionable area of the patient's bio-signals (e.g., ECG), and issue a new e-prescription as a result [21].

Moreover, clinicians can conduct an overall evaluation of a patient group using specialized software that examines the variability in a particular individual's overall state or position, such as 1 week or 1 month. As a result, doctors can quickly identify which patients' medical situation has improved and inform them of their progress.

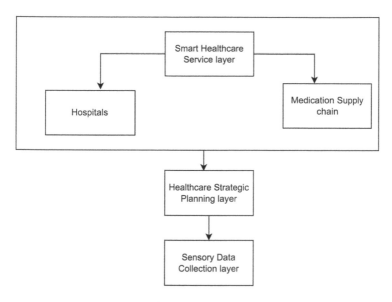

FIGURE 2.3   Network architecture of i-IoT.

The **healthcare strategic planning layer** serves as a changeover auxiliary layer, assisting the iHome system's smooth operation by efficiently administering and managing medical resources. Cloud technology and services are made accessible to health and life science institutions at this tier, ensuring that data security and patient privacy are protected in an effective manner. The **sensory data collection layer** is the network's foundation which is shown in Figure 2.3. Information sensing as well as collecting devices, remote computing and data units, storage media, and wired/ wireless transmission modules all make up the system.

It is a multi-standard WSN architecture that can work with a variety of wired and wireless protocols, including Gigabit, RFID, Zigbee, Wi-Fi, NFC, and 3G/4G networks. Communication between healthcare personnel and home-stay patients can easily take place on-demand or on a regular basis with this three-layer iHome Health-IoT system [22].

2.7   CONCLUSION

The recent study investigates a variety of i-IoT system elements. This chapter has covered in detail the architecture of an i-IoT system, its aspects, and how these components communicate with one another. The existing healthcare systems where IoT-based solutions have been investigated are also included in this study. The i-IoT has assisted healthcare practitioners in monitoring and diagnosing a variety of health concerns, measuring a variety of health factors, and providing diagnostic facilities in remote places by utilizing these principles. Due to this, the healthcare sector has changed from being primarily focused on hospitals to one that is more patient-centric.

REFERENCES

[1] K. Natarajan and B. Prasath, "Smart health care system using internet of things", *Journal of Network Communications and Emerging Technologies*, 6, 3, 37–42, 2016.

[2] Bikash Pradhan, Saugat Bhattacharyya, Kunal Pal, "IoT-based applications in health-care devices," *Journal of Healthcare Engineering*, 2021, 1–18, 2021.

[3] Y. Yuehong, "The internet of things in healthcare: an overview," *Journal of Industrial Information Integration*, 1, 3–13, 2016.

[4] K. K. Goyal, A. Garg, A. Rastogi, and S. Singhal, "A literature survey on internet of things (IOT)," *International Journal of Advanced Networking and Applications*, 9, 6, 3663–3668, 2018.

[5] Z. Ali, M. S. Hossain, G. Muhammad, and A. K. Sangaiah, "An intelligent healthcare system for detection and classification to discriminate vocal fold disorders," *Future Generation Computer Systems*, 85, 19–28, 2018.

[6] G. Yang, L. Xie, M. Mantysalo et al., "A health-IoT platform based on the integration of intelligent packaging, unobtrusive bio-sensor, and intelligent medicine box," *IEEE Transactions on Industrial Informatics*, 10, 4, 2180–2191, 2014

[7] L. Syed, S. Jabeen, M. S., and A. Alsaeedi, "Smart healthcare framework for ambient assisted living using IoMT and big data analytics techniques," *Future Generation Computer Systems*, 101, 136–151, 2019.

[8] G. Marques and R. Pitarma, "An indoor monitoring system for ambient assisted living based on internet of things architecture," *International Journal of Environmental Research and Public Health*, 13, 11, 1152, 2016.

[9] S. T. U. Shah, "Cloud-assisted IoT-based smart respiratory monitoring system for asthma patients," in *Applications of Intelligent Technologies in Healthcare*, pp. 77–86, Springer, Berlin, Germany, 2019, edited by Fazlullah Khan, Mian Ahmad Jan, Muhammad Alam.

[10] Devi, M., Maakar, S.K., Sinwar, D., Jangid, M. and Sangwan, P., "March. Applications of flying ad-hoc network during COVID-19 pandemic," in *IOP Conference Series: Materials Science and Engineering* (Vol. 1099, No. 1, p. 012005). IOP Publishing, 2021.

[11] A. Raji, "Respiratory monitoring system for asthma patients based on IoT," in *Proceedings of the 2016 Online International Conference on Green Engineering and Technologies (ICGET)*, pp. 1–6, Coimbatore, India, 2016

[12] Z. J. Guan, "Internet-of-Things human body data blood pressure collecting and transmitting device," Chinese Patent 202 821 362 U, Mar. 27, 2013.

[13] T. J. Xin, B. Min, and J. Jie, "Carry-on blood pressure/pulse rate/blood oxygen monitoring location intelligent terminal based on Internet of Things," Chinese Patent 202 875 315 U, Apr. 17, 2013.

[14] R. S. H. Istepanian, S. Hu, N. Y. Philip, and A. Sungoor, "The potential of Internet of m-health Things 'm-IoT' for non-invasive glucose level sensing," in *Proc. IEEE Annu. Int. Conf. Eng. Med. Biol. Soc. (EMBC)*, pp. 5264–5266, Boston, MA, USA, 2011.

[15] Z. Jian, W. Zhanli, and M. Zhuang, "Temperature measurement system and method based on home gateway," Chinese Patent 102 811 185 A, Dec. 5, 2012.

[16] A. J. Jara, M. A. Zamora-Izquierdo, and A. F. Skarmeta, "Interconnection framework for mHealth and remote monitoring based on the Internet of Things," *IEEE Journal on Selected Areas in Communications*, 31, 9, 47–65, 2013.

[17] A. Dohr, "The internet of things for ambient assisted living," in *Proceedings of the 2010 Seventh International Conference on Information Technology: New Generations*, pp. 804–809, Las Vegas, NA, USA, April 2010.

[18] R. S. H. Istepanian, S. Hu, N. Y. Philip, and A. Sungoor, "The potential of Internet of m-health Things 'm-IoT' for non-invasive glucose level sensing," in *Proc. IEEE Annu. Int. Conf. Eng. Med. Biol. Soc. (EMBC)*, pp. 5264–5266, Boston, MA, USA, 2011.

[19] Z. Jian, W. Zhanli, and M. Zhuang, "Temperature measurement system and method based on home gateway," Chinese Patent 102 811 185 A, Dec. 5, 2012.

[20] Z. L. In, "Patient body temperature monitoring system and device based on Internet of Things," Chinese Patent 103 577 688 A, Feb. 12, 2014.

[21] P. P. Ray, "Home health hub internet of things (H³ IoT): an architectural framework for monitoring health of elderly people," in *Proceedings of the 2014 International Conference on Science Engineering and Management Research (ICSEMR)*, pp. 1–3, Chennai, India, November 2014.

[22] G. Shanmugasundaram and G. Sankarikaarguzhali, "An investigation on IoT healthcare analytics," *International Journal of Information Engineering and Electronic Business*, 9, 2, 11, 2017.

3 Technological Shift of the Healthcare System Using IoT

*Gauri Shanker Gupta, Shishir Singh Chauhan,
Mrinal Pathak, and Rakesh Kumar Sinha*
Birla Institute of Technology

CONTENTS

3.1 INTRODUCTION

Enough research has been conducted in the healthcare industry to use the Internet of things (IoT) technology to collect data everywhere, process data quickly, and wirelessly disseminate data [1,2]. Ambient assisted living (AAL) is described in [3] as a method of assisting older persons in carrying out their everyday tasks as independently as feasible. IoT technology is utilized in [4] to help medical discussions

DOI: 10.1201/9781003326182-3

between rural patients, health professionals, and specialists in larger cities. mHealth, which is described as medical sensors, mobile computers, and wireless communications for healthcare, is attracting a growing number of academics utilizing fourth-generation (4G) mobile telecommunications and the IoT in healthcare [5]. It investigates software adaptation solutions in ubiquitous computing that allow resource-constrained devices to respond to changes in user demand proactively and transparently [6].

The rise of the IoT has sparked interest in various health practices aimed at improving population health [7,8]. Semantic devices, eHealth, wearable devices, AAL, cellphones, mobile health, and community-based health care are just a few of the IoT services and applications that have lately been investigated in health care [9]. They provide the ability for medical practitioners to remotely track and assess health gains, increase self-management of chronic medical disorders, and aid in early identification. These services can help with a variety of ailments quickly.

Effect detection and medical diagnosis provide early treatment and effectively contribute to prescription medicines [10]. These apps can better use healthcare resources while providing high-quality, low-cost medical treatment.

During the COVID-19 pandemic, the technology of IoT has flourished in healthcare monitoring. Many people today die as a result of erroneous and timely health information [11]. With sensors, this innovation can instantly alert users to health-related risks. The cloud stores all COVID-19 patient data, which may aid in proper care. This device can monitor a person's everyday activities and send out alerts if there are any potential health issues [12].

IoT is becoming an increasingly important part of our lives, and it can be felt all around us. As depicted in Figure 3.1, the invention of the IoT brings together a diverse set of intelligent applications, architectures, sensors, and intelligent gadgets. Furthermore, it uses nanotechnology and quantum in storage, processing speed, and sense, which were previously unknown [13].

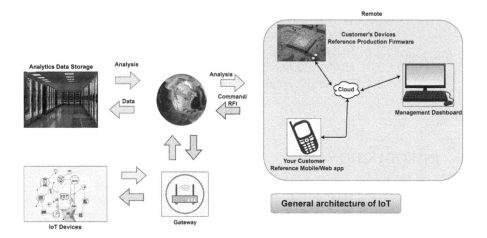

FIGURE 3.1   General architecture of IoT.

3.2   RESEARCH METHODOLOGY

The problem of just inside or outdoor patient monitoring or the elderly is complicated; incorporating both indoor and outdoor situations, particularly in the case of
IoT, is far more complex. As a result, we suggest systematizing the design process
to complete the design of such a system. Figure 3.2 depicts the proposed design
approach, divided into two stages: issue formulation and product development, each
with three phases. Furthermore, at each step of the design process, the stakeholder's,
future users', and designers' views are taken into account to avoid excluding any critical components of the planned system.

Problem formulation: The three stages of problem formulation are (i) demand
definition, (ii) demand formulation, and (iii) feasibility evaluation. Because all project participants, including consumers, potential users, and designers, are required to

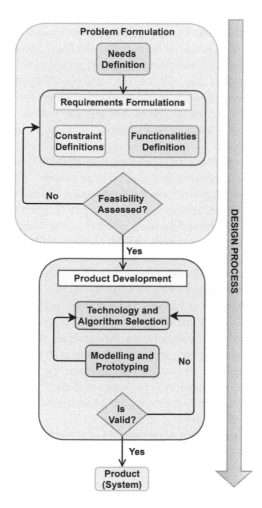

FIGURE 3.2   Flowchart of the proposed DM.

participate in the proposed design methodology (DM), each of them may contribute to the problem definition. Their aims and expectations for the proposed network, however, may differ. The user, for example, may be concerned with comfort, security, and confidentiality, and the medical staff, on the other hand, maybe possibly worried about the system's dependability, simplicity of operation, maintenance, and the value of the data acquired. The stakeholders consider the product's financial and marketing implications well before designers focus on the design development tools and their experience and knowledge.

Needs definition: The designers are introduced to the concept and the overall challenge, which begins with the design process. This step of the planned DM should be completed in collaboration with potential users to incorporate their demands. Using this method, consumers and prospective users can convey their demands and expectations for the working system's output. Users should not focus on specific needs at this point but rather on the system's broad goals so that designers can assess whether the task is feasible given their resources.

Requirements formulation: The suggested DM relies heavily on developing prerequisites. Stakeholders and potential users define the characteristics of the planned system at this step, such as fall detection and tracked person position. In addition, the created system's restrictions, such as price, size, and needed lifetime, are discussed. The functionality and limits in each investigated environment must be defined in the event of multi-environmental usage. These features and limitations are the designers' needs, contributors, and prospective consumers that may indirectly influence the medical system's structure.

Feasibility assessment: Designers must assess the feasibility of contributors' and potential users' general expectations and specific requirements. They must also determine whether the present alternative solutions can resolve the problems identified and whether the demands and needs are even achievable. The designers must also consider the limits imposed by the intended working settings. If the designers have difficulty fulfilling the specifications, future users and stakeholders will be requested to adjust the requirements to meet their needs. After that has been determined, all requirements may be completed, and the production phase of development can commence.

Product development: Selection of relevant technologies and algorithms is usually made in three steps: Choosing techniques and methods, modeling and development, and finally, solution validation due to the complicated trade-offs and heterogeneity of desirable features and limits. Furthermore, stakeholders and prospective users are included throughout this design phase; yet the designers should drive the conversation with all participants. During product development, the principal responsibility of future consumers and stakeholders is to ensure that all of their needs and criteria are met. The future essential enhancements can be imagined when the functionality and limitations have been verified.

Technologies and algorithms selection: The designer presents methods and algorithms that adhere to the intended functionality and constraints expressed by stakeholders and potential users during the issue formulation stage. Therefore, the limits deriving from the intended system's environment must be addressed when selecting technologies and algorithms, such as indoor/outdoor or high humidity. Furthermore, the appropriate technologies and algorithms must be considered in light of the price limitation. Only a few alternative solutions would remain after the first elimination; hence, the price may suggest the ultimate option. If no acceptable solutions meet the criteria or current solutions lack some features or limitations, the designers must guide and build new solutions or modify existing ones.

Modeling and prototyping: The designers' primary responsibilities are to model and prototype the system. These tasks take the most incredible time and may require the participation of specialists from many professions. However, both designers and potential users must agree on the models and prototypes in user-centered design. It is a step-by-step procedure. The designers assess the solution's performance, and prospective users confirm that the functionality and limits are satisfied. If anything is missing or improved, the designers must eliminate bugs and correct any flaws. The procedure is repeated until all contributors are happy. The final result must then be validated.

Validation: The stakeholders and the designers must verify that all of the system's demands and specifications have been met. It can now also check the product's expenses and accept the pricing. Assume that the anticipated objectives and the designed and developed multi-environmental health information system do not meet expectations. In that situation, the developers must return to the beginning of the product development stage and revisit the suggested technologies and algorithms. Nonetheless, if both stakeholders and experts approve of the results, the technology is ready to be launched and provided as a service.

3.3   BACKGROUND OF AN IoT TECHNOLOGY

As we approach the 21st century, more devices are connected to the web than ever before, and this trend is expected to continue unabated. More than 2.7 trillion devices will be linked to the web and the rest of the globe by 2020, up to fivefold from only 4 years ago [14]. The technology of IoT enables securely recognized commodities (or things) to connect to the internet and gather, transmit, preserve, and collect information in its most basic form [15]. The IoT in medical services refers to devices that accumulate health and well-being data from patients, such as computers, mobile phones, smart bands and wearable technology, cloud-based medications, surgically implanted medical tools, and other handheld devices that can evaluate health data and can interlink with the network [16].

The emergence of IoT technology has inspired several public health programs [17]. Mobile health [mHealth], eHealth, supported environmental living, semantic devices, wearable technology, cellphones, and societal medical services are one of the most recent IoT applications and goals in healthcare coverage [16].

The ability for healthcare experts to track and identify health advancements remotely, facilitate early screening and diagnosis, quick side effect appreciation and pharmacological diagnosis and treatment, deliver the proper intervention, and improve adherence to pharmaceutical drugs are just a few of the application areas of all of these services [18]. These apps can better use healthcare resources while offering high-quality, low-cost medical care.

With the support of breakthrough technologies, the IoT has a significant ability to provide high-quality results. It has become a new medical reality as an original

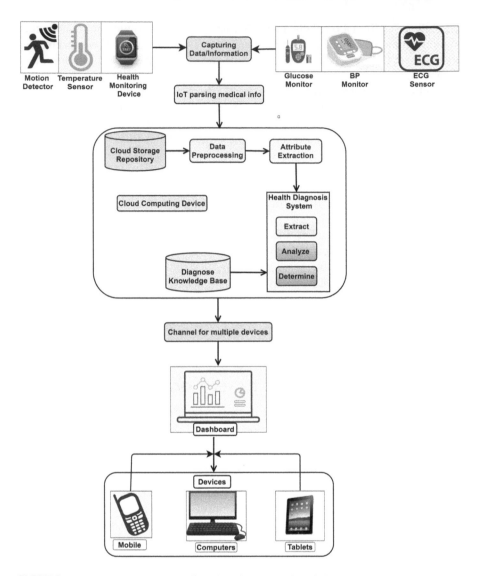

FIGURE 3.3　IoT implementation flowchart in the medical field.

concept that delivers the most outstanding service to COVID-19 patients while executing precision surgery [19]. During the current pandemic, complicated situations are conveniently handled and monitored digitally. The IoT creates unique support systems for surgeons, patients, and doctors by solving new difficulties in the medical industry.

The various process processes are meticulously defined for efficient IoT deployment. The IoT procedure in the medical field is depicted in Figure 3.3. Sensors detect and capture a patient's health and illness information and receive critical data. The internet connects all physical things (networked), and gadgets monitor constantly. Confident clinicians are given essential medical knowledge based on their needs.

3.4 EMERGENCE OF IoT-BASED HEALTHCARE DURING THE COVID-19 PANDEMIC

The IoT has a noticeable impact on healthcare, benefiting millions of people. It identifies illness and keeps a watchful eye on the healthcare system. It helps individuals by providing them with specific attention. During the COVID-19 pandemic, IoT technology could remind people about engagements, exercises, calorie tracking, heart rate, disease condition, and more [20]. Table 3.1 displays one of the most popular IoT applications in the healthcare sector during COVID-19. During the COVID-19 pandemic, IoT has a new use in the medical profession to spur innovation. The most efficient approach to track patients and personnel, resulting in shorter wait times. It introduces a variety of devices to aid the patient's relaxation. Blood gas analyzers, thermometers, intelligent beds, glucose meters, ultrasounds, and X-rays are innovative technologies that have improved inpatient care.

The IoT has the potential to replace or enhance biological systems. During the COVID-19 pandemic, applications including clinical operations, drug delivery, linked imaging, medication administration, patient monitoring, and laboratory analysis have increased. Doctors and nurses can deliver the best possible care to their patients because of the IoT [21,22]. It provides a centrally governed system at a hospital where all acts are electronically logged, and it might be used to address issues during the COVID-19 pandemic. This device can easily monitor patients' health and make precise decisions [23]. It alerts potential future problems and provides a solution for their avoidance by continuously monitoring the health situation. It assists in the timely identification of an asthma attack and the timely treatment of the condition.

3.5 HEALTHCARE ARCHITECTURE

The architecture of IoT is extensive and unlimited; thus, to implement it, classification is required. In the preliminary stage of the study, the three-layer architecture is *delineated* as follows [41].

3.5.1 THE THREE-LAYER ARCHITECTURE

The three-layer architecture as depicted in Figure 3.4 defines the fundamental paradigm of IoT, yet it is not adequate to model the complex structure of IoT. Thus, in subsequent years of research, more such layers were established.

i. **Perception layer:** IoT's physical layer comprises sensors and actuators to sense information and gather physical environment data. This layer can also detect other intelligent appliances connected to the network.
ii. **Network layer:** The network layer consists of data transfer devices like routers and gateways, which help connect with other intelligent devices in

TABLE 3.1

COVID-19 Pandemic: IoT-Enabled Healthcare Approaches

S. No.	Different Approaches	Description	References
1	COVID-19 patient treatment	• IoT with real-time location service provided the best treatment for COVID-19 patients. • Nebulizers, scales, wheelchairs, pumps, and other medical devices are used for monitoring in the IoT framework.	[24]
2	Smart hospital	• Using a connected network infrastructure and controls, IoT creates an intelligent hospital. • The software delivers accurate information on the patient's ongoing problems. • The intelligent hospital offers essential information with comprehensive system automation, minimizing the patient's waiting time.	[25]
3	Obtain information from a variety of sources and devices	• IoT in healthcare gives a variety of sources and devices that may be automatically analyzed. • COVID-19 patients' data is automatically collected, reported, and stored via an IoT device.	[26,27]
4	Making accurate decisions	• This technology records data and makes an exact and quality judgment due to the many types of communication essential for proper surgery. • It helped gather accurate COVID-19 patient data, which used to be traditionally difficult for clinicians to get.	[28]
5	COVID-19 is an illness that should be avoided	• This technology warns humans of COVID-19 sickness in life-threatening conditions and allows for real-time tracking. • It sends out alerts to consumers via linked devices promptly. • Provide more accurate real-time alerts, on-time treatment, and tracking.	[29,30]
6	Appropriate medication	• It records the COVID-19 patient's medication and their protein and nutritional consumption. • Examine and track the patient's progress in daily life.	[31,32]
7	Appropriate facilities	• During the COVID-19 pandemic, IoT can simply automate the patient process to offer convenient healthcare services. • It appears to be the most effective method for better using high-quality resources and improving complex surgical planning.	[33,34]
8	An asthma attack is detected	• It detects asthma symptoms before they turn into an attack. • The assault was reported, and guidance on avoiding it was provided.	[35,36]
9	Smart bed	• IoT applications aim to develop a smart bed that can alter its height to meet the demands of COVID-19 patients. • The pressure and support for patients can be automatically adjusted with this intelligent bed.	[37,38]
10	Emergency case	• IoT analyses the distance and retrieves patient information before approaching a facility/hospital in emergency cases. • As a result, emergency care has improved, and related losses have decreased.	[39,40]

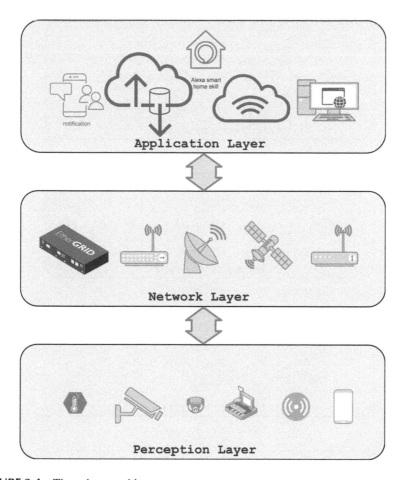

FIGURE 3.4   Three-layer architecture.

the network. This layer helps to process and transfer data collected by the
sensors.

iii. **Application layer:** It encompasses servers and the cloud, which helps to
convey processed data transmitted by the network layer to the IoT like innovative healthcare services, smart homes, etc.

3.5.2   THE FIVE-LAYER ARCHITECTURE

The five-layer architecture as depicted in Figure 3.5 was developed to model the
overall structure of the IoT [42]. The application and perception layers are equivalent
to the three-layer architecture. The new layers which are further added are described
below:

i. **Transport layer**: With the use of network gateways, this layer assists in the
data flow from sensors to the process layer and vice versa.

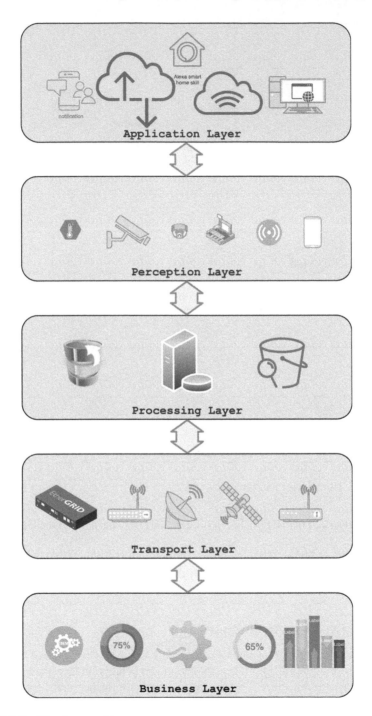

FIGURE 3.5 Five-layer architecture.

ii. **Processing layer**: This is the middle layer in this architecture that helps process (storing, classification, merging) vast amounts of data collected by the sensors. It takes the help of various datasheets, distributed and parallel computing techniques, machine learning techniques, etc.
iii. **Business layer**: It helps maintain the integrity of the IoT framework by providing client and server protection and develops a model for the benefit of the business. It is also known as the external layer.

3.6 APPLICATIONS

3.6.1 SINGLE CONDITION APPLICATION

3.6.1.1 Glucose-Level Sensing

Continuous increases in glucose levels in the blood can lead to diabetes, one of the human metabolic diseases. Thus, it is an essential factor which is to be monitored by us to plan our diets and medications. A non-invasive sensing module is used in an IoT-based glucose-level sensor to provide real-time tracking of blood glucose levels [43]. This IoT model displays glucose levels and includes components such as a blood sugar collector, a CPU, and a mobile phone or computer [44]. It can be used to manage the flow of glucose as needed, automatically adjusting the insulin dose to keep it within safe limits.

3.6.1.2 Blood Pressure Monitor

Blood pressure monitoring can also be measured with the help of the IoT. Generally, a communication module is shared between the healthcare center and post by which the doctors continuously monitor blood pressure [45]. A device [46] collects these data and transmits them to the remote data collection center through an IoT channel. An intelligent IoT-based blood pressure monitoring system can also be equipped with a location tracking facility which consists of an apparatus with a communication interface [47].

3.6.1.3 Body Temperature Monitoring

In healthcare facilities, monitoring body temperature is vital as the body's temperature is a sign of preserving homeostasis [48]. An IoT-based m-IoT device consists of a temperature sensor enclosed in the Telos-B module [43]. The samples of the temperature variations are collected and transferred to the healthcare center through the communication module. The IoT-based temperature measurement system consists of a home gateway module that collects and transmits the data with the help of infrared sensors. Temperatures are recorded and transmitted through the radiofrequency identification module [49].

3.6.1.4 Oxygen Saturation Monitoring

Pulse oximetry is the continuous monitoring of the amount of oxygen present in the blood. IoT-based pulse oximetry is a modern application for healthcare systems [50]. Nowadays, wearable pulse oximeters [51] are available in the market, which are quite helpful for oxygen saturation monitoring. This device comes with Bluetooth connectivity which continuously takes oxygen-level data through the sensor and sends the data directly to the mobile application platform. This IoT-based device constantly monitors the patient's vital signs through an IoT network.

3.6.1.5   Electrocardiogram Monitoring

An electrocardiogram (ECG) monitors the heart's electrical activity, recorded by a technique known as electrocardiography. This device detects myocardial ischemia, arrhythmias, and prolonged QT intervals by measuring the patient's heart rate and determining the heart's basic rhythm [52]. Integrating the IoT with ECG monitoring is a technological breakthrough that will benefit the healthcare sector. A portable wireless acquisition transmitter and a receiving processor make up an IoT-based ECG monitoring device [53]. The system's algorithm detects aberrant cardiac function data and allows for real-time analysis. The process is automated, and the data acquired in samples can be sent via the communication module.

3.6.2   CLUSTER CONDITION APPLICATION

3.6.2.1   Wheelchair Management System

Researchers have identified an urgent need to monitor the health condition and safety of wheelchair patients in modern healthcare systems. IoT-based, fully automated wheelchair-based healthcare systems have been proposed for physically disabled people [54]. A wireless body area network (WBAN) is used in this system, consisting of many sensors that continuously monitor patients' vital signs [55]. The information gathered can be sent to a data center for analysis and risk management. In an emergency, the global positioning system module attached to the wheelchair can track the person's whereabouts.

3.6.2.2   Rehabilitation System

The rehabilitation system is developed mainly to restore and improve the life quality of physically disabled people. The potential of IoT in this field is also vast, and it has the potential to improve the lives of the elderly. A rehabilitation method based on the IoT [56] consists of a service layer linked directly to medical care units such as the medicine supply chain, emergency healthcare centers, and hospitals. We can remote access the rehab system through an active platform for proper diagnosis through IoT. It can be helpful in hemiplegic patients, smart city medical systems, and childhood autism patients [57].

3.6.2.3   Healthcare Solutions Using Smartphones

Modern medication systems and healthcare facilities require substantial financial support for proper maintenance and usage. By incorporating the IoT into the medical system, this problem can be solved in the long run at a low cost. A modern IoT-based medical management system [58] requires a few smartphone sensor modules and software to gather and analyze data. The interactive packing (I2Pack) module and intelligent pharmaceutical box are two available modules (iMedBox). These modules use wearable sensors to capture various medically essential data, which is then used to diagnose diseases and monitor patients' vital signs. As a result, it significantly improves the quality of life for the aged, physically challenged, and sick people.

3.6.2.4 Healthcare Solutions Using Music as a Therapy

If we talk about healthcare management, music as a therapy is evolving rapidly. Music therapy is a more modern method of assisting medical professionals. It helps a person calm down the brain waves, and IoT is a concept where interaction between machines and the human world happens. Data is collected without any human intervention. The element of music, or samgiita, which consists of a multitude of bháva (idea), sur (melody), chanda (rhythm), and bhasa (lyrics), is used to explore the various expressions of human life. Music has something to do with our inner nature and how we express ourselves. Music is a medium for communication. Music therapy can reduce anxiety and help patients cope with stress in an inpatient setting, as Timoney et al. (2020) explained [59].

It's a popular method for resolving mental health issues such as anxiety, depression, and hypertension. If we take the case of stress, music helps a lot in its management, and these sensors can be used to measure stress parameters. Through these sensors, records can be taken in real time. The effect of music on the person can be recorded with the help of graphs and data received from the sensors. The internet of musical things (IoMT) is a subset of the IoT that focuses on music-related technologies (IoMusT) [60]. Although this field is still in its infancy, it has the potential to develop into multi-person virtual music systems, intelligent and wearable instruments, and overall network interactive music performances. Analyzing a specific arrangement might lead to the fine skill of sound comprehension.

"The silent sound of our vibrations, which we may overlook but which is the musical core within all of us, resides deep within us."—Yehudi Menuhin. The value of music and its impact on the mind were recognized by ancient Indians, who established science around it. It is mentioned in the Sama Veda, which is among the four Vedas related to musical compositions. It contains a detailed account of tunes and chants and their effect on humans' minds, bodies, and souls depicted in Figure 3.6.

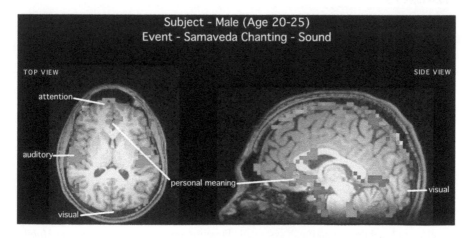

FIGURE 3.6 The impact of different receptions on the human brain in other places [61].

It also includes musical renditions of lines from the Rig Veda. Indian music is thought to have originated from Sama Veda. It teaches us about various chants that have a tremendous influence on our body, mind, and soul at varying times of the day. Ragas impacts the emotions of a human being by changing the resonance of the human body. We know that everything in our world has a resonant structure if we look at it through the eyes of applied sciences. Something can be worked on if this resonating structure is met, and energy can be transmitted, either taken or given. Nowadays, for people of any age, smartphones and apps have become part and parcel of life. As a pilot project, we may use influential music and computing technique of machine learning tools to embed music as the background sound of applications, whether an online shopping app or a typical reading app, and collect the data. Music improves mood strength, just like a motor accelerates you significantly faster than your feet.

3.7 CONCLUSION

The current study looked into several facets of the healthcare IoT system. The structure of a healthcare IoT system, its components, and the communication among these components have been addressed in-depth here. In addition, this article gives information on current healthcare services that have investigated IoT-based technology. IoT technology has aided healthcare practitioners in monitoring and diagnosing various health concerns, measuring multiple health factors, and providing diagnostic facilities in remote places by leveraging these principles. Consequently, the healthcare business has shifted from a hospital-centric to a patient-centric model.

We also spoke about the several uses of the healthcare IoT system and its current trends. Additionally, readers interested in starting their research and making breakthroughs in the field of healthcare IoT devices will find thorough, up-to-date information on the subject.

REFERENCES

1. Wang L, Yang G-Z, Huang J, Zhang J, Yu L, Nie Z, et al., A wireless biomedical signal interface system-on-chip for body sensor networks. *IEEE Trans Biomed Circuits Syst.* 2010; 4(2):112–117.
2. Agarwal R and Sonkusale S. Input-feature correlated asynchronous analog to information converter for ECG monitoring. *IEEE Trans Biomed Circuits Syst.* 2011; 5(5):459–468.
3. Dohr A, Modre-Osprian R, Drobics M, Hayn D, Schreier G. The Internet of things for ambient assisted living. In *2010 Seventh International Conference on Information Technology: New Generations*, Las Vegas, Nevada, USA, 2010, pp. 804–809.
4. Adewale OS. An internet-based telemedicine system in Nigeria. *Int J Inf Manag.* 2004; 24(3):221–234.
5. Istepanaian RSH, Zhang Y-T. Guest editorial introduction to the special section: 4 G health—The long-term evolution of m-health. *IEEE Trans Inf Tech Biomed.* 2012; 16(1):1–5.
6. Nazir S, Ali Y, Ullah N, García-Magariño I. Internet of things for healthcare using effects of mobile computing: a systematic literature review. *Wireless Commun Mobile Comput.* 2019; 2019:1–20.

7. Kakousis K, Paspallis N, Papadopoulos GA. A survey of software adaptation in mobile and ubiquitous computing. *Enterp Inf Syst.* 2010; 4(4):355–389.

8. Saarikko T, Westergren UH, Blomquist T. The internet of things: are you ready for what's coming? *Bus Horiz* 2017; 60(5):667–676.

9. Dang LM, Piran MJ, Han D, Min K, Moon H. A survey on Internet of things and cloud computing for healthcare. *Electronics* 2019; 8(7):768.

10. Yin Y, Zeng Y, Chen X, Fan Y. The Internet of things in healthcare: an overview. *J Ind Inf Integration* 2016; 1:3–13.

11. Singh S, Bansal A, Sandhu R, Sidhu J. Fog computing and IoT based healthcare support service for dengue fever. *Int J Pervasive Comput Commun.* 2018; 14(2):197–207.

12. Alqahtani FH. The application of the Internet of things in healthcare. *Int J Comput Appl.* 2018; 180(18):19–23.

13. Gatsis K, Pappas GJ. Wireless control for the IoT: power spectrum and security challenges. In *2017 IEEE/ACM Second International Conference on Internet-of-Things Design and Implementation (IoTDI)*, Pittsburg, PA, USA, 18–21 April 2017. INSPEC Accession Number: 16964293.

14. Internet of Things (IoT) in Healthcare. Research Markets. 2019. URL: https://www.medicaldevice-network.com/comment/bringing-internet-things-healthcare/ [accessed 2020-10-02].

15. Mitchell-Box K, Braun KL. Fathers' thoughts on breastfeeding and implications for a theory-based intervention. *J Obstet Gynecol Neonatal Nurs.* 2012; 41(6):E41–E50. [doi: 10.1111/j.1552-6909.2012.01399.x] [Medline: 22861175].

16. Dang LM, Piran MJ, Han D, Min K, Moon H. A survey on Internet of things and cloud computing for healthcare. *Electronics* 2019; 8(7):768. [doi: 10.3390/electronics8070768].

17. Saarikko T, Westergren UH, Blomquist T. The internet of things: are you ready for what's coming? *Bus Horiz* 2017; 60(5):667–676. [doi: 10.1016/j.bushor.2017.05.010].

18. Yin Y, Zeng Y, Chen X, Fan Y. The Internet of things in healthcare: an overview. *J Ind Inf Integration* 2016 Mar; 1:3–13 [doi: 10.1016/j.jii.2016.03.004].

19. Siriwardhana Y, De Alwis C, Gür G, Ylianttila M, Liyanage M. The fight against the COVID-19 pandemic with 5G technologies. *IEEE Eng Manag Rev.* 2020; 48(3):72–84.

20. Ye J. The role of health technology and informatics in a global public health emergency: practices and implications from the COVID-19 Pandemic. *JMIR Med Inf.* 2020; 8(7):e19866.

21. Basatneh R, Najafi B, Armstrong DG. Health sensors, smart home devices, and the internet of medical things: an opportunity for dramatic improvement in care for the lower extremity complications of diabetes. *J Diabetes Sci Technol.* 2018; 12(3):577–586.

22. Farahani B, Firouzi F, Chang V, Badaroglu M, Constant N, Mankodiya K. Towards fog-driven IoT eHealth: promises and challenges of IoT in medicine and healthcare. *Future Generat Comput Syst.* 2018; 78:659–676.

23. Ali Z, Hossain MS, Muhammad G, Sangaiah AK. An intelligent healthcare system for detection and classification to discriminate vocal fold disorders. *Future Generat Comput Syst.* 2018; 85:19–28.

24. Arun M, Baraneetharan E, Kanchana A, Prabu S. Detection and monitoring of the asymptotic COVID-19 patients using IoT devices and sensors. *Int J Pervasive Comput Commun.* 2020; 18(4):407–418.

25. Lin H, Garg S, Hu J, Wang X, Piran MJ, Hossain MS. Privacy-enhanced data fusion for COVID-19 applications in intelligent Internet of Medical Things. *IEEE Internet of Things J.* 2020; 8(21):15683–15693.

26. Kato S, Ando M, Kondo T, Yoshida Y, Honda H, Maruyama S. Lifestyle intervention using Internet of Things (IoT) for the elderly: a study protocol for a randomised control trial (the BEST-LIFE study). *Nagoya J Med Sci.* 2018; 80(2):175–182.

27. Swayamsiddha S, Mohanty C. Application of cognitive Internet of medical things for COVID-19 pandemic. *Diabetes Metabol Syndr: Clin Res Rev.* 2020; 14(5):911–915.

28. Abdulkarim A, Al-Rodhaan M, Ma T, Tian Y. PPSDT: a novel privacy-preserving single decision tree algorithm for clinical decision-support systems using IoT devices. *Sensors.* 2019; 19(1). https://doi.org/10.3390/s19010142. PII: E142.

29. Catherwood PA, Steele D, Little M, Mccomb S, Mclaughlin J. A community-based IoT personalized wireless healthcare solution trial. *IEEE J Transl Eng Health Med.* 2018; 6:2800313. https://doi.org/10.1109/JTEHM.2018.2822302.

30. Kolhar M, Al-Tudjman F, Alameen A, Abualhaj MM. A three-layered decentralised IoT biometric architecture for city lockdown during COVID-19 outbreak. *IEEE Access.* 2020; 8:163608–163617.

31. Palani D, Venkatalakshmi K. An IoT based predictive modelling for predicting lung cancer using fuzzy cluster-based segmentation and classification. *J Med Syst.* 2018; 43(2):21. https://doi.org/10.1007/s10916-018-1139-7.

32. Hossam A, Magdy A, Fawzy A, Abd El-Kader SM. An integrated IoT system to control the spread of COVID-19 in Egypt. In: *International Conference on Advanced Intelligent Systems and Informatics.* Springer, Cham, 2020, pp. 336–346.

33. Park A, Chang H, Lee KJ. Action research on development and application of Internet of Things services in hospital. *Healthc Inform Res.* 2017; 23(1):25–34.

34. Ashraf MU, Hannan A, Cheema SM, Ali Z, Alofi A. Detection and tracking contagion using IoT-edge technologies: confronting COVID-19 Pandemic. In: *2020 International Conference on Electrical, Communication, and Computer Engineering (ICECCE).* IEEE; 2020:1–6.

35. Fan YJ, Yin YH, Xu LD, Zeng Y, Wu F. IoT-based smart rehabilitation system. *IEEE Trans Ind Inf.* 2014; 10(2):1568–1577.

36. Kumar A, Sharma K, Singh H, Naugriya SG, Gill SS, Buyya R. A drone-based networked system and methods for combating coronavirus disease (COVID-19) pandemic. *Future Generat Comput Syst.* 2020; 115: 1–9.

37. Veda SS, Fotovvat A, Mohebbian MR, et al. COVID-SAFE: an IoT-based system for automated health monitoring and surveillance in post-pandemic life. *IEEE Access.* 2020; 8:188538–188551.

38. Siripongdee K, Pimdee P, Tuntiwongwanich S. A blended learning model with IoT based technology: effectively used when the COVID-19 Pandemic? *J Educ Gifted Young Sci.* 2020; 8(2):905–917.

39. Xu B, Xu LD, Cai H, Xie C, Hu J, Bu F. Ubiquitous data accessing method in IoT based information system for emergency medical services. *IEEE Trans Ind Inf.* 2014; 10(2):1578–1586.

40 Ishimaru Y, Takahashi T, Souma Y, et al. Innovation in surgery/operating room driven by Internet of Things on medical devices. *Surg Endosc.* 2019. https://doi.org/10.1007/s00464-018-06651-4.

41. Miao W, Ting L, Fei L, ling S, Hui D. Research on the architecture of internet of things. In: *3rd International Conference on Advanced Computer Theory and Engineering (ICACTE),* Chengdu, 20–22 August 2010, 1–15. https://doi.org/10.1109/ICACTE.2010.5579493.

42. Zhang HD, Zhu L. Internet of things: key technology, architecture and challenging problems. *2011 IEEE International Conference on Computer Science and Automation Engineering,* Shanghai, 10–12 June 2011, 3–12. https://doi.org/10.1109/CSAE.2011.5952899.

43. Istepanian, RS., Hu, S., Philip, NY., & Sungoor, A. The potential of Internet of m-health Things "m-IoT" for non-invasive glucose level sensing. In *2011 annual international conference of the IEEE engineering in medicine and biology society,* 2011, August, pp. 5264–5266. IEEE.

44. Lijun Z. Multi-parameter medical acquisition detector based on Internet of Things. Chinese Patent 202 960774 U, 2013.

45. Puustjarvi J, Puustjarvi L. Automating remote monitoring and information therapy: an opportunity to practice telemedicine in developing countries. In: *2011 IST-Africa Conference Proceedings*, Gaborone, Botswana, 2011, p. 1–9.
46. Guan ZJ. Internet-of-Things human body data blood pressure collecting and transmitting device. Chinese Patent 202 821 362 U, 2013.
47. Xin TJ, Min B, Jie J. Carry-on blood pressure/pulse rate/blood oxygen monitoring location intelligent terminal based on internet things. Chinese Patent 202 875315 U, 2013
48. Ruiz MN, Garcia JM, Fernandez BM. Body temperature and its importance as a vital constant. *Revista Enfermeria*. 2009; 32(9):44–52.
49. In ZL. Patient body temperature monitoring system and device based on Internet of Things. Chinese Patent 103 577688 A, 2014.
50. Larson EC, Goel M, Boriello G, Heltshe S, Rosenfeld M, Patel SN. Spiro smart: using a microphone to measure lung function on a mobile phone. In: *Proceedings of the 2012 ACM Conference on Ubiquitous Computing*, Pittsburgh Pennsylvania, 2012, pp. 280–289.
51. Larson EC, Lee T, Liu S, Rosenfeld M, Patel SN. Accurate and privacy preserving cough sensing using a low-cost microphone. In: *Proceedings of the 13th International Conference on Ubiquitous Computing*, Beijing China, 2011, p. 375–384.
52. Drew BJ, et al. Practice standards for electrocardiographic monitoring in hospital settings. *Circulation*. 2004; 110(17):2721–2746.
53. Liu M-L, Tao L, Yan Z. Internet of Things-based electrocardiogram monitoring system. Chinese Patent 102 764118 A, 2012.
54. Yang L, Ge Y, Li W, Rao W, Shen W. A home mobile healthcare system for wheelchair users. In: *Proceedings of the 2014 IEEE 18th International Conference on Computer Supported Cooperative Work in Design (CSCWD)*, Hsinchu, Taiwan, 2014, pp. 609–614.
55. Dr. Hawking's Connected Wheelchair Project. [Online]. http://www.intel.co.kr/content/www/kr/ko/internet-of-things/videos/dr-hawkings-connected-wheelchair-video.html [accessed 28 Jan 2008].
56. The Mimo Kimono: How it Works. [Online]. http://mimobaby.com [accessed 28 Jan 2008].
57. Lin DY. Integrated Internet of Things application system for prison. Chinese Patent 102 867236 A, 2013.
58. Pang Z, Tian J, Chen Q. Intelligent packaging and intelligent medicine box for medication management towards the Internet-of-Things. In: *16th International Conference on Advanced Communication Technology*, Pyeongchang, 2014, pp. 352–360. https://doi.org/10.1109/icact.2014.6779193.
59. Timoney J, Yaseen A, Mcevoy D. The potential role of the internet of musical things in therapeutic applications. In: *Proceedings of the 10th Workshop on Ubiquitous Music (UbiMus 2020)*. g-ubimus, 2020, pp. 35–47.
60. Pingle Y. IOT for music therapy In: *2016 3rd International Conference on Computing for Sustainable Global Development (INDIACom)*, 2016, pp. 1453–1455, Coimbatore, India.
61. https://www.hubbardfoundation.org/meditation.

4 IoT-Based Healthcare System
Cloud Data Governance

Shantha Visalakshi Upendran
Ethiraj College for Women

CONTENTS

DOI: 10.1201/9781003326182-4

4.1   INTRODUCTION

This chapter is concerned with the application of big data management and information security using cloud data governance in the Internet of things (IoT)-based smart healthcare systems (SHCS). Big data management is a class of solutions for batch cum real-time processing, interactive exploration of big data, and predictive analytics with a view to assess their effects on the SHCS as a whole. In the past decade, several traditional data management strategies for any web-based application have shown increased attention to competence and growth by using inventive secured data management approaches. The aim of this chapter is to present big data management for analysis and reporting and to govern the storage and retrieval of data using cloud data governance in an enhanced secured way by applying the phases of the information security life cycle. For the past few years, there continues to be a notable increase in many IoT-based smart applications in different areas of IoT applications such as smart cities, IoT retail shops, smart grids, industrial IoT, and SHCS.

Normally, this study is shaped as a prototype case for the progress of a formal model that provides a data management mechanism for the big data generated by the "things" interconnected. It provides an analysis of data storage implications, cloud storage, and data governance exposed themes for effective data management strategies that distinguish the growth of secured data processing with an exclusive design, the conciliation of what counts as a suitable elucidation, an instinctive theory of wrapping big data analytics, and a cognitive reorganization about designing and fine-tuning of the data management in IoT-based SHCSs. Implications of these ideas for moving forward in building an IoT SHCS model are discussed in this work; in addition to that, information security life cycle phases comprised in this model have been observed to be due to the need of the current scenario.

Providing secured data management mechanisms over the "things" connected in IoT SHCSs is one of the vital tasks for both the service provider and acquirer. The occurrence of security vulnerabilities is increasing due to the emergence of more data sources and the adoption of modernized technological advancements associated with the rapid use of smart devices. Contemporary enterprises need to be agile and dynamic in nature to support much of the decision-making processes taken at various levels. Therefore, to achieve this, sensitive business information needs to be available at the right point in a timely manner and in the required form.

4.1.1 Technologies for IoT SHCS

As stated earlier, this chapter deals with three domains, namely, the IoT SHCS model, information security, and cloud data governance with big data analytics. Other technologies have been incorporated for realizing IoT SHCSs, wireless body area networks (WBANs), embedded systems, communication technologies, fog computing, edge computing, and autonomic computing (Naresh, 2020) as given in Figure 4.1. This study is carried out to analyze secured data management from the perspective of big data analytics and cloud data governance only and not any other technologies covered in the IoT SHCS environment. In addition to data management with respect to Data Analytics and Cloud Storage, phases of Information Security having applied in this work for secured data analysis.

4.1.1.1 Big Data Management

Governance of big data comprises the facets like people, process, policy, technology, automation, and strategy as depicted in Figure 4.2 where reliability and

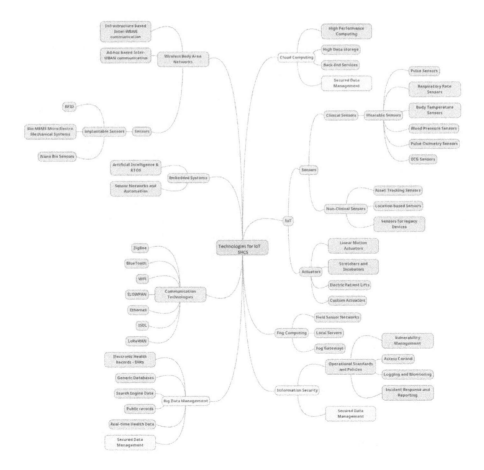

FIGURE 4.1   Technologies for IoT SHCS.

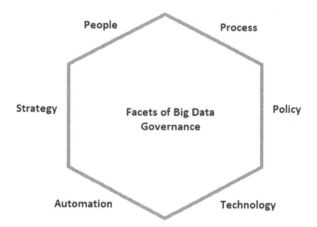

FIGURE 4.2   Facets of big data.

integrity are the prime challenges as it deals with the smart healthcare sector. In addition to that, the objective of big data is used to investigate medical research activities to improve the efficacy of diagnosis and further-level medication which will improve the value, quality, and timeliness. Data in healthcare can be captured from machines or "things," for example, electrocardiogram (ECG), blood pressure (BP) reading, patient-ventilator reading, and all other electronic medical health records. Along with these technologies, various data management stages like data generation, data acquisition, data validation, data storage, data processing, data remanence, and data analysis have been taken into consideration for IoT-based SHCS.

Hence, it is obvious that authorized healthcare service providers ought to maintain a secured database with high capacities so as to store and retrieve sensitive data for further levels of medications and for better decision-making. Healthcare service providers have to share medical data, such as medical history, medications, and treatment used, to the cloud-based database with an assurance that only authorized data analysts can enter and can have access to confidential data stored. The diverse nature of service providers and acquirers may have different data structures and content organization which demands a careful intense way of sharing among authentic partners.

4.1.1.2   Information Security

In networking, like any other systems interconnected, an IoT-based SHCS is also affected by security risks or cyber-attacks where the intruder tries to make a system or network entity unavailable to its authorized users by temporarily or indefinitely disrupting the services of a host connected to the internet. With the sensitive medical data which transits in a large network with the "things" or devices interconnected, the risk of having a wider range of vulnerabilities has also increased in exponential growth if adequate countermeasures have not been incorporated. Continuous monitoring and regular and periodic audit plans

FIGURE 4.3   Goals of system information security.

have to be applied to make the IoT SHCSs always safe from any attacks. The basic security requirements such as authentication, authorization, confidentiality, integrity, availability, and non-repudiation must be provided to the IoT SHCSs as stated in Figure 4.3.

As stated earlier, numerous things and communicable devices have been interconnected, and in the IoT SHCS environment, it is noticeable that the system is vulnerable to security risks and attacks like Denial of Service (DoS), Man in the Middle (MITM) attacks, location-based attacks, Structured Query Language (SQL) injection attacks, etc., which will lead to mismanagement of data results with the end of the precious life of the patients. It is recommended to have secured storage and management, stronger protocols, upgrades in operating systems and firmware applications, and system hardening would definitely mitigate the security threats expected in IoT SHCS.

4.1.1.3   Cloud Data Governance

The striking demand associated with the SHCS considers medical data as a business asset and therefore is placed as a prime element of the IoT SHCS model (data as a service) that will sustain the horizontal and vertical digitalization of the smart healthcare service providers. The big volume of data that the IoT SHCS generates, its heterogeneity and complexity, and the reusability for the futuristic processes need granulated policies, standards, and protocols with formulated directives for its apt governance.

Having considered the exchange and the exploitation of the information generated at each level of the IoT SHCS model, it is necessary to develop and implement methodologies, tools, and technologies that coincide with the actual data managerial requirements of IoT SHCS as portrayed in Figure 4.4, which assures to have high computing power in any ubiquitous and wireless environments. The capacity to cope with big volumes of data generated by the "things" and devices interconnected in real time and process them, the dynamic scaling of the change in workload fluctuations and load balancing strategies adopted, the responsive interaction with intelligent

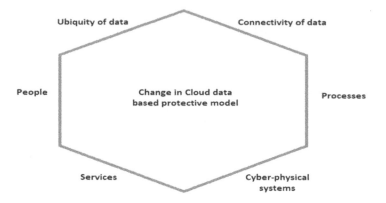

FIGURE 4.4   Cloud data protective model.

application environments and social media, and the prompt adaptive interface with artificial intelligence and machine learning.

4.1.2   Issues and Challenges

There are several challenges that persist in IoT SHCS including the following:

1. Resource limitations comprising energy, data capacity, memory, and device lifetime are to be taken into consideration and to be monitored periodically.
2. Sensors kept at various positions due to multi-path and mobility leading to the increase in complexity.
3. IoT devices are often made to work with low power consumption and have limited processing ability.
4. Organizations are destined to share data, credentials, software applications, code, and other infra with "trusted" partners. Hackers utilize such opportunities to gain unauthorized access to the loosely protected network of service providers.
5. Appropriate selection, authentication, and attestation of cryptographic platforms have to be incorporated.
6. Some of the network-related issues like fault tolerance, latency, energy efficiency, interoperability, and availability must be clearly addressed.

4.1.3   Summary

This section discusses the three giant technologies associated with data management and governance required for IoT SHCS. Furthermore, this section reviews in detail big data management, information security, and cloud data governance. This study focuses on the complete phase-by-phase implementation of the above-said technologies to transform the heterogeneity in raw data to secured and structured data; thereby, better decisions can be derived for better diagnosis.

4.2 DATA MANAGEMENT

4.2.1 WHY DATA MANAGEMENT FOR IoT SHCS?

Data management in IoT-based systems is a sensitive task as it comprises many numbers of data sources such as sensors, radiofrequency identification (RFID) tags, embedded systems, and smart gadgets. Query operations involved are numerous and expected to be versatile in nature. In order to adapt to the diverse data types and prompt queries generated by the "things" connected, the innovative dynamic applications and services require location and context awareness knowledge. The design primitives associated with IoT data management involved are data collection, database system design, and processing.

4.2.2 SOURCES OF IoT DATA

IoT data come from various sources like control systems, business application systems, wearables, sensors and devices, web data and online open data sources, other media data like photos, videos, and audio data, and location-based dynamic data by which the IoT SHCS model can enable smarter decision-making and faster responses across the domain as given in Figure 4.5. Based on the nature of IoT data communication, data sources can be classified as follows:

1. **Data from passive**: which has the ability to consume data from sensors that do not actively communicate.
2. **Data from active**: where the streaming data have been tossed off from the sensors.
3. **Data from dynamic**: where the data from the sensors with a complete set of abilities like to have a change in produced data, change in data format,

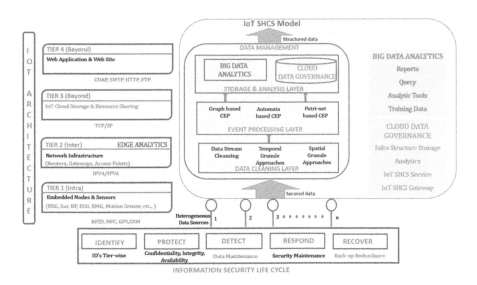

FIGURE 4.5 Data management for IoT SHCSs.

change in frequency, and even to deal with security issues to provide better automated software updates and to deal with the issues in a cognitive way.

While building IoT SHCSs, all these IoT data types have to be mixed to meet the demanding requirements of the model. In addition to this, the data life cycle needs to be considered with three predominant criterions, namely, adequate metadata management, data quality, and risk management (Yebenes, 2019).

4.2.3 Design Primitives for Data Management

With the advent of the growth of the IoT, data management systems have to consolidate the data online while allocating storage, logging, and auditing facilities for offline analysis. In continuation with the data management from online to offline storage, query processing, and transaction-oriented activities, the stages of IoT data decomposition need to be examined.

The decomposition stages of the IoT system are represented in Figure 4.6 which proceeds from data generation to acquisition, validation, storage, and pre-processing,

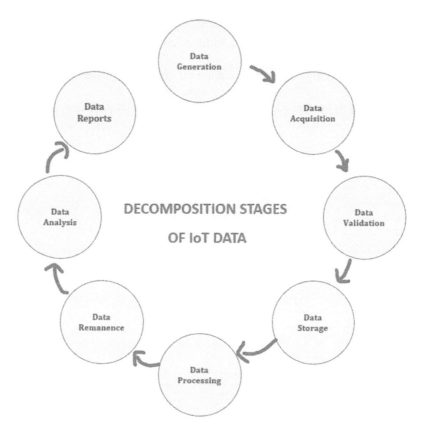

FIGURE 4.6   Data decomposition stages.

remanence, querying, and analysis which results in the reports. Elkheir (2013) outlined the components of a complete IoT data management framework with core data and sources, layers, and support for federated architecture for a two-way, cross-layered approach that meets the query analysis and service needs.

4.2.3.1 IoT Data Collection

Data can be collected in two ways. One is a temporal method which involves collecting data from all "things," whereas the modal method involves collecting data from specific elements. The predominant two properties, device portability and user mobility, associated with the "things" or devices connected, session-based synchronization for data exchange, storage, and forwarding mechanisms for data organization, and publisher–subscriber-based systems for notification-based data delivery have to be ensured.

4.2.3.2 IoT Database System Design

The "things" in IoT generate and maintain data in a vast manner; it needs to be organized and overseen by means of federated database systems to provide interoperability and linking features specific to the service providers, for which service-oriented architecture (SOA) can be deployed. SOA assures a well-established set of design primitives that ensure systematic development and integrate components for the distributed "things" linked.

4.2.3.3 IoT Data Processing

With the added advantage of SQL for data access, variants like TinySQL for sensors and StreamSQL for stream processing can be incorporated for the abundant data process/access associated with IoT-based services. Query processing enables efficient and scalable data management in the ever-increasing data generation rate, resulting in intricacies sensed with the analysis of data.

4.2.3.4 IoT with Big Data Characteristics

There are seven characteristics associated with IoT with Big Data.

   i. **Number of IoT devices (Velocity)**: IoT deals with numerous data sources wherein vast data will be generated for further-level processing.
   ii. **Multiple IoT devices (Variability)**: It describes the status of a diverse set of IoT-based communicable devices.
   iii. **Data types (Variety)**: IoT handles different properties in various data types including semi-structured and unstructured data.
   iv. **Data quality/nature (Veracity)**: Unambiguous data acquired out of the IoT model always result in better quality.
   v. **Upgrade frequencies (Velocity)**: In order to make the entire process as quick as it moves, upgraded frequencies are incorporated.
   vi. **Content data (Validity)**: It refers to the degree of the data demand for smart processing.
   vii. **Historical data (Volatility)**: It deals with the scope of the IoT data and the rate of change of the data.

4.2.4 IoT Data Management Reference Model

On inspecting the above-mentioned characteristics, the three-layered reference model can be built exclusively for data management in the IoT SHCS as given in Figure 4.7. To manage the volume, velocity, and variety of data in "smart" systems, cloud data governance is a suitable platform to handle and process such big data (Ruithe, 2016).

The roles and responsibilities associated with each layer are elaborated as follows.

4.2.4.1 Data Cleaning Layer

One of the challenging and toughest tasks is data cleaning due to the enormous quantity of data and heterogeneous sources of errors from data remanence which third parties may recover with, to process the real-time processing involved. It is clear that with a well-cleansed data set, accurate interpretation and better analysis can be achieved, and thereby, intelligent business decisions can also be derived. As different data can be taken from diverse nature of data sources, it is obvious to have different types of cleaning too. That is, data cleaning can be initiated with the removal of unwanted observations (fixing up with relevant data), then fixing up with structural errors (with data remanence – tiny data lead to noisy data), managing unnecessary outliers (rare usage data with no demand), and handling missing data (monitoring data lost during transmission if any).

Stream data cleaning: An active pipeline architecture comprising the phases such as point, smooth, merge, arbitrate, and virtualize has been incorporated into extensible sensor stream processing to clean the sensor data. In the first phase, point filters the single data value for ensuring quality like outliers. The second and third phases, smooth and merge, hold the responsibility of processing data in the temporal and spatial granules. In the fourth phase, arbitrate eliminates the logic fault, and in

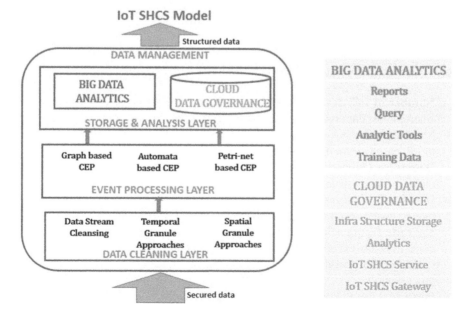

FIGURE 4.7 Data management reference model.

the fifth phase, virtualize, data from heterogeneous sources are fused. For better boosting performance, a few of the data mining approaches like unnecessary observation prevention and filtering outliers can be bagged. Approaches used to reduce and eliminate data quality issues are the stream data cleaning framework and the temporal granule approach (Ma, 2013).

Temporal granule approach: This approach utilizes time-series smoothing and outlier detection that deals with plenty of series in a vectorized way. Time-series smoothing is useful for a reason that it can provide pre-process steps such as denoizing removal and safeguarding the temporal pattern present in the raw data. The raw time series have to be separated into equal windowed items which can be smoothed individually. Technically, this temporal granule approach can very well be mapped into the second phase, smooth, of the ESP framework. Based on statistical characteristics, the data can be cleansed using this approach.

Spatial granule approach: The temporal granule approach falls under the low-level cleansing technique; hence, improved spatial and logic need to be wrapped up to attain higher-order data cleansing techniques for better results. This approach can be correlated with the third phase merge of the ESP framework as its prime function is to clean and consolidate data from different sources. This approach requires the maximum possible inter-device communication and adequate system topology control measures so as to cope with the striking needs of data cleansing.

The data cleansing tools like Openrefine, Trifacta Wrangler, TIBCO Clarity, Cloudingo, and IBM Infosphere Quality sage can also be built along with IoT SHCS as an individual or as a mixture of any combo according to the requisite.

4.2.4.2   Event-Processing Layer

The cleansed data coming out with the criterion's reliability and usability may not meet the need of the hour the IoT SHCS model looking for. The event-processing layer holds the functionality to transmute the raw data into structured data having applied with higher-level intelligent business logic. With the name itself, it is clear that the event-processing layer is built to react to events from the environment which follows the event-driven architecture. In IoT SHCSs, cleansed data can be viewed as primitive events. The complex semantic events have been extracted from bottom-level primitive events to back up higher-level events known as complex event processing (CEP). This CEP can be deployed to come out with appropriate data patterns for rendering services such as event detection, monitoring, and response.

The CEP models can be classified as follows:

1. **Graph-based CEP model:** In this model, complex semantic events can be expressed as a tree structure with primitive events as leaf nodes. The detection of the event based on the operation mechanism commutes from the leaf node to the upper nodes in descending order of node levels as implemented in READY and YEAST (other CEP systems based on the graph model).
2. **Automata-based CEP model:** As the name suggests that an event can be constructed as an automata-based model, i.e., a set of states and transition functions. When an automaton reaches an accept state then the complex event is successfully detected.

3. **Petri-net-based CEP model:** In this model, the complex model has been represented as a Petri-net-based model where the input node is designated as a primitive node and the output node is an occurrence of complex events. When all the input nodes are marked, then transition will occur and complex events will be detected whenever the output node has been reached as it is implemented in SAMOS.

4.2.4.3 Storage and Analysis Layer

With the cleansed data and the appropriate data patterns required for intelligent business logic, an IoT SHCS has to offer services to cater to the needs and to store them with a suitable schema. Such a structured schema must compress the amount of data and support the data analysis in a variety of hierarchies. In that way, data storage and analysis layer have to be implemented with data exchange, storage, compression, and mining for IoT-based SHCSs. To meet the challenges wrapped up with the IoT big data, i.e., providing horizontal scalability, availability, and performance, the alternatives of big data storage NoSQL and NewSQL came into existence. NoSQL – "Not only SQL" ensures to provide the schema flexibility and effecting scaling over live streaming data on large scale. NoSQL offers powerful data processing capabilities and different approaches for providing querying abilities. However, NoSQL lacks advanced indexing and optimizing.

1. **Big data analytics:** To derive the discovered patterns, data relations, and newly extracted knowledge from IoT SHCS, big data analytics can be merged. The provision of handling both structured and unstructured massive data, various MapReduce techniques can be taken, for example, Apache Hadoop, Skynet, Sailfish, and FileMap. The technical strengths in connection with BDA are the storage and processing of large volumes of immutable data and monitoring data collected from different sources.
2. **Cloud data governance:** In order to assign decision-related rights and duties to handle IoT SHCS data as a sensitive asset, cloud data governance (CDG) has to be defined, i.e., to plan, monitor, and enforce the IoT SHCS data assets, so thereby accurate business decisions can be taken. CDG has to orchestrate fixing the decision-making rights and responsibilities in the IoT SHCS processes related. CDG ought to be coherent with the norms and regulations imposed by IoT SHCS so as to manage IoT data as a strategic asset, offer quality control, protect access management, and oversee the maintenance activities for the sake of improving the competitive advantage of IoT SHCS.

In parallel, CDG policies must have coverage over data security, metadata management, and quality of the data. These policies explicitly define the way in which IoT SHCS cloud data is governed at the different levels such as edge, fog, and cloud. In addition to the CDG policies, the inclusion of service level agreements (SLAs) has to be signed among the third parties (cloud carriers, cloud agents, and cloud providers) and cloud actors. To ensure compliance, the transformation of data policies into processes and procedures has to be carried out. Some of the top data governance tools are Infogix, Informatica, SAP, and OneTrust.

4.2.4.4 Issues and Challenges

In SHCSs, the quality of the data plays a vital role as any discrepancy may lead to very serious effects on human lives. Even though there is a wider usage of big data in various business logic and in health sectors, there are a few pitfalls associated with medical data management as they are very sensitive and deal with the privacy of individual human beings. Hence, this leads to data misuse if the data have not been managed and governed properly. Appropriate measures have to be applied for balanced security and privacy concerns (Tse, 2018).

4.2.5 SUMMARY

This section provides brief coverage of data management for IoT SHCSs, sources of data, design primitives of data management, and IoT data management reference model in a broader manner. Furthermore, studies of layers present in the reference model and its functionalities have been discussed. The roles of NoSQL and NewSQL were also discussed.

4.3 INFORMATION SECURITY

Information security is implemented in IoT SHCS using CDG and data management so as to mitigate security threats and breaches by adapting the phases involved and identifying and monitoring risks through pre-defined policies and standard protocols. This work analyses the governance and security wrapped up with the cloud computing layer which concentrates on services like IoTaaS, SaaS, Paas, and IaaS, cloud deployment models such as public, private, community, and third parties, namely, cloud providers, cloud agents, cloud auditor, and the cloud data management strategies involved as stated in Figure 4.8.

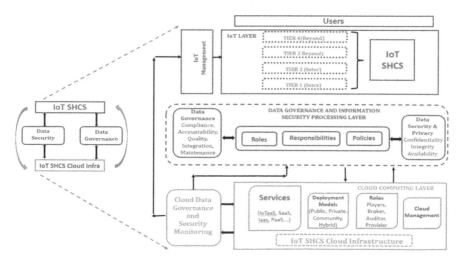

FIGURE 4.8 IoT CDG and information security for IoT SHCSs.

4.3.1 IMPORTANCE OF SECURITY IN IoT SHCS

As the data generated by various sources such as sensors, RFID tags, mobile devices, laptops, embedded chips, GPS-enabled vehicles, and other intelligent communicable smart gadgets are tangled in the IoT SHCS model, and the number of threats and attacks against "things" connected are also on the increase as well. IoT SHCS deals with lives and societies on a large scale, and it is necessary to wrap up enhanced security with an urge to comprehensively understand the threats and risks on the IoT SHCS infrastructure. The tools utilized by the hackers are also more effective and efficient toward the misuse of data. Thus, the IoT SHCS is expected to assure data protection and access control policies with complete potential and efficacy.

4.3.2 INFORMATION SECURITY LIFE CYCLE

Cyber security threats could be launched against any "things" or entities present in the IoT SHCS model that causes impairment to the system resources itself and disables the entire system operation, which ends with severe economic losses to the service providers. Consider the scenario of a smart healthcare model comprising attacks on itself, taking control of sensitive medical records, physical security systems, utility systems, etc., to mesh up with the ongoing meticulous process, resulting in a negative impact on lives and societies at a large scale. Ensuring the security measures for the protection of "things" and services offered and avoidance of unauthorized access from within the devices connected and overall. In SHCS, it is a crucial systematic approach for security and privacy considerations that must be incorporated into device manufacturing, interconnecting things, communication, and data handling and storage (Karunarathne, 2021).

In IoT SHCS, data access can be gained not only by the users but also by authorized objects. This scenario requires two prime aspects for consideration.

1. Access control and authorization mechanism – (Provider side)
2. Authentication and identity management – (Acquirer side)

To achieve the implementation of efficient IoT SHCS security, the predominant phases of the life cycle of information security should be embedded as stated in Figure 4.9. The information security life cycle phases involved are (i) **Identify**, (ii) **Protect**, (iii) **Detect**, (iv) **Respond**, and (v) **Recover**.

4.3.2.1 Identity

The IoT SHCS model comprises more communicable resources with different abilities. Such resources have to be uniquely identifiable for assessing risks associated with and for applying proper data governance. The possible identifiers by which the end-point devices can be uniquely identified are TagIDs and RFIDs and, similarly, network entities such as routers, gateways with unique IP addresses, etc. In CDG, the cloud access and user grants are monitored by cloud identity and access management (CIAM). Web applications maintain an access control list (ACL) for login restrictions and system access permissions.

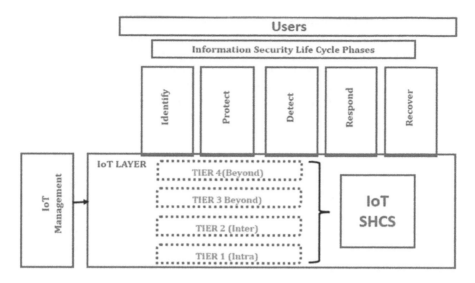

FIGURE 4.9 Information security life cycle and IoT SHCSs.

4.3.2.2 Protect

This phase concentrates on the absolute protection of data and resources by implementing safety and security measures to fortify the system elements and entities against threats and risks. The supervisory control measures such as protected access, awareness and training, and identity management are covered in this phase.

4.3.2.3 Detect

This phase deals with the detection of any anonymous activity attempted in IoT SHCSs. Appropriate alert notifications with the remedial actions will be sent promptly once when any unusual attempt is detected. The built-in cloud security can monitor user access and the overall security features can protect the software running on the cloud.

4.3.2.4 Respond

Soon after the alert notification is received, the IoT SHCS model must respond with appropriate actions against the issue raised. With the right mixture of planning, communication, analysis, and mitigation the system can be able to respond. The right choice of deep learning strategies can also be included for having improved security policies derived from past experience and to combat newly encountered threats.

4.3.2.5 Recover

Even being applied with the above-said phases, the IoT SHCS model ought to withstand in case of any critical situations and lend the readiness to meet our emergency needs. Resilience and system recovery are the prime focus in this phase so as to avoid collision on every single node and the ability to recover in a speedy way.

4.3.2.6 Issues and Challenges

One of the major constraints seen in implementing information security features is that the heterogeneous "things" connected in SHCS have to run on different operating systems with diverse needs and varied capabilities. These "things" may not have uniform security controls such as strong authentication and authorization mechanisms, system configuration controls, encryption, protocols, and updated firmware.

4.3.3 SUMMARY

This section gave insight into the updated guidelines and information security phases at all layers of the IoT SHCS model; periodical governance of risks, risk evaluation, and strategic management for mitigation of threats are discussed, and the precautionary measures to deal with any unusual activity attempted and pre- and post-remedial actions to be applied whenever suspicious activity is sensed are also covered.

4.4 IoT SHCS MODEL

4.4.1 SIGNIFICANCE OF THE IoT SHCS MODEL

IoT-based SHCSs have emerged from conventional means of visiting hospitals and continuous monitoring. The exclusive features of IoT such as sensing through sensors, processing, and communicating through communicable "things" with both physical and biomedical entities are present in the IoT SHCS model. This model interlinks the physicians, patients, and people whoever in the medical field through intelligent devices which have the predominant characteristics of "user mobility" and "device portability". Because of these features with all the smart gadgets, every entity can roam without losing the services with 24×7 support.

Although the IoT SHCS model has the capability of interconnecting patients with specialists across the globe, the model is concerned with certain issues too. They are

    i. Critical treatment situations,
    ii. Personalized health check-ups,
    iii. Regular medication,
    iv. Remote treatments by means of smart "things",
    v. Personal health record transfer over the cloud.

In order to ensure the above-said issues, it is suggested to have the deployment of IoT SHCS with the three technology giants, namely, **Big Data Management** for improved data analytics, thereby deriving better diagnostic results with an intensive study over the historical medical data, **Information Security** for the assurance of transferring sensitive data over the cloud and "things" without any misuse of data, and **CDG** for the smooth functioning of the entire IoT SHCS activities by imposing the roles and responsibilities to the people connected with IoT SHCS and by generating the policies which are best suited for the structure of the organization to which the model intended for.

4.4.2   WBAN FOR IoT SHCSs

WBANs allow the provision of wearing the autonomous nodes on the clothes, under the skin, or even on the body. Through the support of wireless communication channels, the nodes can be connected and passed on to the medical reading values. WBANs ensure the communication between ultra-low-power smart sensors or "things" that are worn on the human body or engrained internally in the human body as represented in Figure 4.10. The fifth generation of communication technologies supports IoT technologies in various applications in smart healthcare. It ensures 100 times higher wireless bandwidth with power saving and massive storage usage by applying big data analytics (Riaz, 2017).

All the wearables ought to communicate with the control unit or regulatory device which has been placed closer to the human body's vicinity; thereby, the physiological health data collected by radio-enabled or wireless sensors can be shared with the nodes in the IoT SHCS model. In addition to that, wearable sensors allow for various **Medical/Physiological Monitoring,** for example ECG, temperature, respiration, Heartbeat rate, and BP, **Disability Assistance** for the needy, and **Human Performance Management** in general.

The WBAN communication as given in Figure 4.11 has been designed with three essential components, namely,

    i. Tier 1: Intra-BAN communication
    ii. Tier 2: Inter-BAN communication
    iii. Tiers 3 and 4: Beyond BAN communication

4.4.2.1   Tier 1: Intra-BAN Communication

This kind of intra-BAN communication's coverage ranges within the limit of a 2 m area coverage closer to the human body. Direct communication between the portable

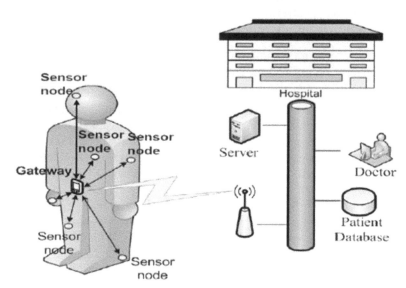

FIGURE 4.10   WBAN-based IoT SHCSs.

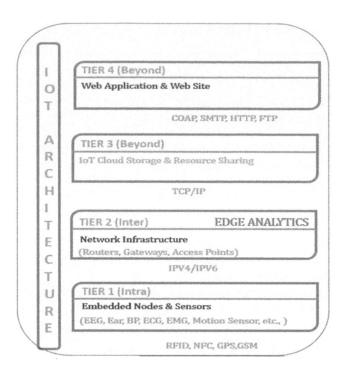

FIGURE 4.11 IoT SHCS architecture.

personal server and the body sensors enables the prompt delivery of appropriate alerts. Every WBAN on a human body with sensors, computing devices, and electronic wearables can be considered an independent autonomous network. Within this network, regular routing algorithms like OSPF, Link state, and Dijkstra's algorithm can be implemented to find the optimal path between any two nodes.

4.4.2.2 Tier 2: Inter-BAN Communication

In this type of inter-BAN communication, two autonomous bodies are connected through virtual links which run on their own networking and routing logic. That is, access points (APs), personal servers (PSs), cellular nodes, and internet networks are the autonomous bodies that communicate with each other. All nodes are connected using dynamic routing protocols such as OSPF – Open Shortest Path Link State routing protocol. As in wireless communication, both Infrastructure (decentralized) and ad-hoc based (centralized) connectivity can be established with BAN communication.

4.4.2.3 Tiers 3 and 4: Beyond BAN Communication

Any communicable device which can function as a gateway is used to generate a link between inter-BAN and beyond BAN communications. With the able support of the communication standards like Blue Tooth, GPRS, GPS, and internet, IoT SHCS can be employed in different systems to achieve authorized healthcare personnel to access medical records remotely. Beyond BAN communication has a database with a complete set of medical records for further reference. Therefore, a physician can monitor the patient along with appropriate alert notification to the "in case of emergency" ICE contacts of the person. In addition to this, beyond BAN communication offers extended user-specific services like sending alerts through short message service (SMS) or through electronic mail, consultation through video, and voice conferencing.

4.4.2.4 Issues and Challenges

While realizing the WBAN architecture, it is quite important to look into the environmental challenges, i.e., WBANs are affected by high path loss due to body absorption. In pursuit of wireless communication, the networking criteria such as multi-paths, multi-hop links, and antenna design lead to more challenging issues. Also, due to the limited radio resources in terms of processing power, memory, and energy, the existing security measures need to be improved furthermore. It is recommended to wrap up with efficient retransmission, error detection mechanisms, and secured correction methods to be embedded for enhanced uninterrupted service.

4.4.3 Summary

In this section, three types of WBAN communication have been discussed. The first and foremost thing to be decided is which level of communication needs to be deployed. Inter-BAN communication between body sensors and master node, intra-BAN communication between the master node and APs, and beyond BAN communication for maintaining personalized medical health records and providing remote consultation to patients by means of cellular and internet networks.

4.5 CONCLUSION

In recent times, IoT-based solutions have become a key part of SHCSs. The IoT SHCS has made medical-related activities possible anywhere anytime. Innovations in information technology have made a very great impact on the IoT SHCS, resulting in the construction of an IoT SHCS model with big data management, information security, and CDG to enhance the secure way of storing and retrieving health records. From these characteristics, the important thing to be noted is eventual consistency, which means that strict or immediate consistency is not anticipated, but consistency is achieved over the threats bounded during sensitive data retrieval.

Durability refers to the impact of a committed transaction that cannot be undone in case of a data transmission failure; that is, even after a failure, the system should go forward and not backward by retransmitting the data in the available route. The route or path in which the packets need to get forwarded must be determined in prior. Hence, it is required to include the path determination component along with the beyond BAN communication.

Overall, this IoT SHCS model highlights the need for a three-way, cross-layered design approach which can meet the demanding needs in both real-time and archival query analysis and service requirements. It has also been taken into consideration that to provide the source of information regarding the different fields of application of IoT intending to assist future researchers who have the passion to contribute more and achieve in the field to gain knowledge in SHCSs. Additional considerations of data security and privacy have been imposed in the dynamic, heterogeneous environment. The roles and responsibilities associated with CDG ensure the smooth processing of business logic. Along with secured data management and big data analytics, IoT SHCSs can provide the finest services at a large scale.

REFERENCES

Abu-Elkheir, M., M. Hayajneh, and Najah Abu Ali. 'Data management for the internet of things: Design primitives and Solution.' *Sensors (Basel, Switzerland)* 13, 11, 15582–15612, 2013. 10.3390/s131115582.

Al-Ruithe, M., Siyakha Mthunzi, and Elhadj Benkhelifa. 'Data governance for security in IoT & cloud converged environments.' 1–8, 2016. 10.1109/AICCSA.2016.7945737.

Karunarathne, S., N. Saxena, and M. Khan, 'Security and privacy in IoT smart healthcare *IEEE Internet Computing* 25, 4, 37–48, 2021. 10.1109/MIC.2021.3051675.

Ma, M., P. Wang, and C.-H. Chu, 'Data management for internet of things: Challenges, approaches and opportunities', *IEEE International Conference on Green Computing and Communications and IEEE Internet of Things and IEEE Cyber, Physical and Social Computing*, pp. 1144–1151, 2013. 10.1109/GreenCom-iThings-CPSCom.2013.199.

Naresh, Vankamamidi Srinivasa, Pericherla Suryateja, Pilla Sita, and Sivaranjani Reddi, 'Internet of things in healthcare: Architecture, applications, challenges, and solutions.' *Computer Systems Science and Engineering* 6, 411–421, 2020. 10.32604/csse.2020.35.411.

Riaz, Muhammad Hussnain, U. Rashid, Muhammad Ali, and L. Li, 'Internet of things based wireless patient body area monitoring network.' *2017 IEEE International Conference on Internet of Things (iThings) and IEEE Green Computing and Communications (GreenCom) and IEEE Cyber, Physical and Social Computing (CPSCom) and IEEE Smart Data (SmartData)*, IEEE, 970–973, 2017. 10.1109/iThings-GreenCom-CPSCom -SmartData.2017.180.

Tse, Daniel, C.-k. Chow, T.-p. Ly, C.-y. Tong, and K.-w. Tam, 'The challenges of big data governance in healthcare.' *17th IEEE International Conference on Trust, Security and Privacy in Computing and Communications/ 12th IEEE International Conference on Big Data Science and Engineering (TrustCom/BigDataSE)*, New York, 1632–1636, 2018. 10.1109/TrustCom/BigDataSE.2018.00240.

Yebenes, Juan, and Marta Zorrilla, 'Towards a data governance framework for third generation platforms.' *Procedia Computer Science*, 614–621, 2019. 10.1016/j.procs.2019.04.082.

10+ Data Governance Tools To Fulfill Your Data Needs In 2022, Updated on: May 6, 2022. https://www.softwaretestinghelp.com/data-governance-tools/.

5 Information Security and Data Management for IoT Smart Healthcare

Maram Bani Younes and Nameer N. El-Emam
Philadelphia University

CONTENTS

5.1 INTRODUCTION

International legislation and health authorities urge and promote healthcare providers to adopt meaningful use of becoming network integrated. As a result, healthcare services are intelligently provided using the Internet of things (IoT)-based principle. However, transiting healthcare providers and organizations to electronic-based systems are vulnerable to information security attacks and cybercrimes [1]. Information security techniques protect information and systems from illegal and unauthorized admission, usage, disclosure, interference, or conversion. This is accomplished by processing the three main elements: confidentiality, integrity, and availability of information. Confident information is available or disclosed only to legal processes and only by authorized people from a healthcare perspective. Therefore, only authorized users can modify and control the integrity and protection of electronic data.

DOI: 10.1201/9781003326182-5

Therefore, besides the availability guarantee upon demand, electronic health information is accessible and usable [2].

Cybercrime appeared as a real threat to information technology; it follows the digital world's revolution. Cybercrime starts as simple as spam threats for gathering data and advertising boniness. However, with time, it developed into viruses and malware. It is becoming more sophisticated, more synchronized, and more dangerous. Attackers and intruders are attracted to the health industry because it contains sensitive personal and financial information [1].

Moreover, cybercriminals can sell the medical and billing information of the patients and use it for insurance fraud purposes. More importantly, internet-connected medical devices such as pacemakers or intensive care unit (ICU) respirators are susceptible to interference. Thus, medical data can be very sensitive and they directly affect patients' lives [3]. They can also lock down patient care systems and take advantage of lucrative ransom payments. Interestingly, often sociopolitical issues are linked with medical data records of political candidates' backgrounds.

Popular health organizations and vital governments have been victims of ransomware. For example, in the United States of America, the year 2015 was a record year for healthcare data breaches [4]. More than 113 million patient and health plan member records were exposed or stolen, of which 78.8 million were stolen in a single cyber-attack. However, these cases have been broken several times until now. In addition, several unexpected and severe attack cases are reported daily in vital smart hospitals and healthcare centers [4].

This work aims to investigate information security in healthcare systems and its importance. In the beginning, we define the general healthcare systems identifying all included sections there. Then, we discuss smart IoT-embedded devices and how they can help patients instantly. After that, the threats and pre-defined security solutions are explored regarding smart healthcare systems and IoT-embedded devices. Then, several comprehensive platforms that adopt information security requirements in healthcare systems are reviewed, and general remarks are generated. Finally, data management requirements are investigated for smart healthcare systems.

5.2 HEALTHCARE SYSTEMS

Healthcare systems usually exist in hospitals, clinics, or community health agencies. Each system contains several entities and different categories to handle: types of hospital systems, patient care, insurance, healthcare providers, and legal issues. In any healthcare system, several separate databases are generated for the healthcare team workers, patients, insurance companies, supply and demand materials, etc. These databases should be created for each department in the system accurately and individually. A relational database can be used to connect different departments. Figure 5.1 illustrates the main contents of healthcare systems.

All tables in the healthcare database are important and should be protected from unauthorized disclosure and modification. However, each table has special nature and requires specialized data entry and a reader (i.e., a nurse or a doctor). For example, the tables that contain details regarding the patients require extra protection compared to the tables that contain details regarding the healthcare system team.

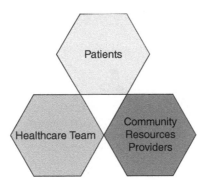

FIGURE 5.1   The contents of the healthcare system.

This is to keep the privacy of patients and their diagnostic situation. Moreover, the health insurance tables require a financial audit to guarantee a high level of accuracy.

In general healthcare systems, data are gathered directly from patients, healthcare teams, or suppliers. Moreover, the diagnostic and medical treatment details are inserted directly by doctors or nurses into the system. Any mistake in these inserted details can lead to a catastrophic scenario, including a wrong diagnosis, repeating the medical treatment, and increasing medical doses.

5.2.1   PATIENT CARE

The core of any healthcare system is the patients. All services and processes are dedicated to helping, diagnosing, and healing patients. There are different types of care for patients, depending on their needs. In this section, we review a set of the most important types of patient care [5]:

- **Primary care**: The first place patients go for medical care is a general clinic.
- **Specialty care**: This is for patients with health problems or illnesses requiring special knowledge of specific diseases or organ systems.
- **Emergency care**: This includes diagnosing and treating life-threatening illnesses or injuries that need immediate attention.
- **Long-term care**: A combination of medical, nursing, and social care. It can be provided to a patient who cannot perform daily living activities.
- **Mental care**: Include medication and psychotherapy to assist patients who need help with a mental illness or emotional crisis.

5.3   SMART HEALTHCARE SYSTEMS

The more advanced the technology used in the system, the less the human being interacts with the system, and the smarter it becomes. The healthcare field is required to be smart to reduce the direct interaction between patients and healthcare teams. Thus, reducing the high probability of infection among the healthcare team. During the high expansion of COVID-19, we have seen several countries, hospitals, and

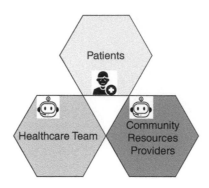

FIGURE 5.2   Smart healthcare system.

agencies using robots to diagnose and heal patients. This has reduced the speed of the disease's spread and saved lives among the healthcare team [6].

Figure 5.2 illustrates an abstract example of a smart healthcare system. Comparing it with the regular healthcare system in Figure 4.1, we can infer that robotic devices are used instead of specialized people in healthcare teams and community resource providers. Advanced technologies and sophisticated devices provide these services to patients remotely inside the smart healthcare center.

5.3.1   Healthcare Team (Medical Robots)

First, smart healthcare systems require smart and robotic devices to replace the healthcare team. These devices can read the temperature, measure blood pressure, and the sugar level and perform other diagnostic operations on patients. Moreover, they insert these reads directly into the patient's database and connect it to the smart diagnostic center. This requires smart devices connected to computer systems to gather the basic data regarding the situation of the patient and his/her tests [6]. In the advanced smart healthcare system, robotic devices can also determine the patient's disease. Then, it can contact the healthcare center to determine the best medicine or medical treatment. This is according to the acquired data from the patient and the pre-trained information regarding several diseases.

Furthermore, smart robotic medical devices can benefit patients in ICUs. For example, patients can take instant action when the oxygen or heart rate level is dangerously decreased [5]. Moreover, for long-term care and mental care cases, advice, instructions, and remote surveillance could be provided for patients timely and accurately by expert system technologies. Figure 5.3 illustrates the smart healthcare team's main functionalities for different types of patients without human interactions.

5.3.2   Community Resources Providers

On the other hand, the community resources providers are responsible for supplying the required materials and medical equipment. They also construct and follow insurance contracts between insurance companies and patients. Moreover, these providers handle cleaning and maintenance responsibilities as a main part of the healthcare

FIGURE 5.3   Functionalities of the smart healthcare team.

FIGURE 5.4   Parts of community resource providers.

system. Several companies and departments have been created to provide these services and requirements to the healthcare system. However, smart robotic devices can easily accomplish all of these missions. Figure 5.4 illustrates the main jobs classified among community resource providers.

5.4   IoT-ENABLED SMART HEALTHCARE SYSTEMS

Smart healthcare systems save lots of time and effort. Smart machines, instead of people, take regular checkups and continuous surveillance. Moreover, urgent medical treatments and scheduled medicine are accurately prepared and given to the patients by machines and smart equipment. The IoT technology plays a key role in enabling smart healthcare systems.

5.4.1   INTERNET OF THINGS (IoT)

A set of connecting devices that communicate with each other and make decisions without any human interaction or notification is the main principle of the IoT. The

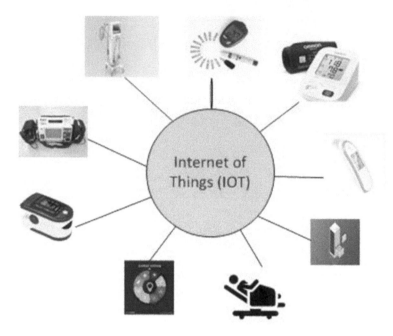

FIGURE 5.5 IoT-enabled healthcare system.

smart environment of IoT is gained by using several technologies such as sensors, cameras, embedded processors, and connecting networks. The global positioning system and cloud networks form the backbone of IoT services and applications.

5.4.2 IoT-Enabled Healthcare System

Enabling IoT technology in healthcare systems is promising to reduce human interaction errors. The diagnostic devices are connected with the medical treatment devices to apply the most suitable procedure. This is also connected directly to the historical database related to that patient. Moreover, an expert system trained to tackle most diseases and injury cases is also connected to the system to instantly recommend the required medicine and treatment for each case. Figure 5.5 illustrates an example of connected devices and equipment in a smart healthcare system using the technology of IoT. As we can see in the figure, the cloud servers are required to record the historical database regarding the patients and obtain the expert system's recommendations. Some devices are connected as input devices to read the patients' conditions. However, other devices exist to apply the recommended procedure.

5.5 INFORMATION SECURITY FOR IoT-ENABLED SMART HEALTHCARE SYSTEMS

Information security for smart healthcare systems is a significant issue to investigate. In this section, first, we define the general information security threats in healthcare systems. Second, the general perspectives on applying information security technologies in healthcare are discussed. Finally, several healthcare cybersecurity solutions are presented and investigated.

5.5.1 INFORMATION SECURITY THREATS

In general, threats that can face information security in health systems can be categorized into three main classes [2]:

- **Intentional threats**: These involve manipulating and destroying data, software, or hardware. Malicious codes such as viruses or worms, theft, and fraud create these threats. This is due to vulnerabilities in network management (e.g., the resilience of routing), lack of firewall, and old used versions of the operating system.
- **Environmental threats**: Threats are caused by external factors such as natural disasters, **earthquakes, fires, floods, and storms. The chance of a natural disaster affecting the** organization depends on the location of its processing facilities and the procedures used to store data. Robust backup systems usually defeat these threats.
- **Accidental threats**: Represent errors and omissions by employees. Accidental threats might cause damaging network cabling or loss of network equipment. This is due to the lack of redundancy and backups, poor network management, and lack of proper implementation of communication cabling or handling [2,7].

5.5.2 INFORMATION SECURITY TECHNOLOGIES APPLIED IN HEALTHCARE

The advanced and sophisticated threats that aim to attack information systems have been developed and controlled using various advanced mechanisms and technologies. However, to maintain the successful security of healthcare information systems, authentication, encryption, data masking, and access control should be satisfied. Figure 5.6 summarizes the main information security technologies applied in the general healthcare systems.

Authentication aims to guarantee that all existing data in the electronic health record is correct and has been entered and processed only by authorized responsible members of the healthcare team. Moreover, the corporate networks of the healthcare organization are crucial to be secured. Moreover, the identities of the legal users in the system should be completely protected. These requirements are usually satisfied in any information system using the advanced technology of cryptography. All cryptographic procedures contain an endpoint authentication mechanism that aims mainly to prevent active and passive man-in-the-middle attacks.

Secondly, encryption is used to prevent unauthorized access to sensitive data. Encryption mainly avoids exposure to breaches such as theft of storage devices. It also protects and maintains data ownership from the data center to the endpoint devices and the cloud environment. This includes mobile devices and applications that healthcare providers and administrators use. Therefore, healthcare organizations

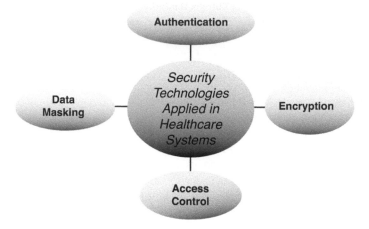

FIGURE 5.6   Applied security technologies in healthcare.

should use an efficient encryption scheme. Indeed, choosing the most suitable encryption algorithms to enforce secure storage in these situations remains a complex problem [8,9].

Thirdly, data masking is the technology of replacing sensitive data elements with unidentifiable values, so the original value becomes masked. It removes the identity of the information; in other words, it masks personal identifiers such as name and social security number or generalizes identifiers like zip codes or birth dates. Data masking is called data anonymization, where the data becomes completely unknown. K-anonymity is a technique by which data is anonymized where the identity of an entry can only be narrowed to a set of k-individuals [10]. Another anonymization method occurs by adding noise to the data, swapping cells within columns, and replacing groups of K records with K copies of a single representative. Data masking reduces the need for applying additional security controls on that data since it is unidentified to the reader [8,11,12].

Finally, access control is where users can process the information system but under a governed access control policy based on the privilege and right of each authorized patient or a trusted third party. It also provides sophisticated control to ensure users can perform only certain permitted activities such as data access or cluster administration. Role-based and attribute-based access control are the most used access control models for EHRs. However, they have shown some limitations in the medical system [13,14]. Some healthcare systems have used cloud-oriented dynamic access control schemes based on symmetric encryption algorithms (i.e., advanced encryption systems) [8,15,16].

5.5.3 HEALTHCARE CYBERSECURITY SOLUTIONS

For the application of health informatics, organizations usually do not use high-priced services. They mainly rely on internet connections and cloud network services. The connectivity of the internet is done via a standard TCP/internet protocol (IP) suite of protocols. Thus, the internet is a shared network that introduces several security vulnerabilities. The transferred data on the internet is subjected to spying, manipulation, and deception.

Moreover, there is no guarantee of quality in internet security. Its connections are susceptible to traffic congestion link failures or even an unresponsive host. Some solutions for cybersecurity in healthcare and medical systems are summarized without the need for connecting to the traditional internet or cloud network. In this section, we investigate two recent advanced technologies [17]:

- **Site-to-site virtual private networks**: Assuring the encryption, data integrity, and authentication requirements can be achieved using the technology of a virtual private network (VPN). At the server source, data should be stored in an encrypted manner. Then, a compressed secure version should be generated at the server upon request from the destination points (i.e., hospital or clinic). A secure virtual channeling occurs between the server as a source of data and the requested point. Moreover, the decompressing and decryption procedures are determined and handled at the requested destination points.

    The technology of VPNs enables remote users to operate in a network as secure as the local user. The VPN technology can organize any used application regardless of its implementation without the need to design the application in certain settings or following special requirements. Besides, healthcare organizations can connect multiple services and departments, each with its network over the public internet. This is accomplished by using dedicated equipment and standards robust encryption mechanisms. A site-to-site VPN is defined by the scenario where one or more remote locations are connected to a single private network using the internet.

    Recently, site-to-site VPNs using the public internet are becoming very common in healthcare organizations [18–20]. A certain VPN can be expanded to accommodate many users and different far-located destinations. Firewalls can be used besides VPN technology to increase security measures. This is by terminating the VPN sessions and restricting the open ports on the established connection. Firewalls also determine the allowed type of packets and protocols on the initiated VPN [21].

- **Internet protocol security virtual private networks**: The main vulnerability in the TCP/IP protocol is the lack of native encryption. The default solution was to extend the IP suite into IP security (IPSec). IPSec is defined as a collection of protocols that provides encryption and authentication at the third layer of the open system interconnect (OSI) network model. IPSec has been incorporated by the internet engineering task force (IETF) using IP version 6 (IPv6) [21].

    Another sophisticated security solution for the smart healthcare system has been developed by connecting the technologies of IPSec and VPNs. The IPSec VPNs enhance the security features via comprehensive authentication principles. IPSec has two main algorithmic encryption modes: tunnel and transport. The tunnel mode encrypts the header and payload of each transmitted packet; meanwhile, the transport mode only encrypts the payload and transmits an unencrypted header [21].

5.6   DATA MANAGEMENT FOR IoT-ENABLED SMART HEALTHCARE SYSTEMS

In the health domain, a huge transfer occurs from traditional, paper-based documents to electronic records stored in database systems applying information systems such as:

- **Healthcare management, the general practice of medicine**: Working in the healthcare system requires a high level of responsibility and a professional attitude. Any information regarding the patient's historical situation and previous medical treatment is vital for accurate diagnosis and determining the medical treatment. On the other hand, the various gathered information from large groups of real cases increases medical data accuracy and size. This assists in remote patient monitoring and tracking, remote examinations, and medical treatment. Moreover, remote surgery is based on the automation of treatments based on remote prescription and dispensing and based on improved accessibility [22].
- **Medical information distribution and EHRs**: This is the leading innovation in health informatics, storage, and distribution of precise and recent information. This facilities health professional practice and improves the daily lives of individuals. It mainly allows healthcare providers to deliver better patient care [22].
- **Research results**: Several experimental and theoretical analyses obtain optimal medical treatments for specific diseases. However, health informatics prevents the use of outdated information and resources that lack critical real-world facts and leftovers and opens doors to reach reliable information analysis. Real-time data and analytical tests using various connected instruments and devices should be available and correctly declared for professionals in the healthcare system.
- **Medical devices**: These are essential to the healthcare system. Without professionally trained staff, this equipment is useless. However, for the IoT-enabled smart devices, no stuff is required since these devices can completely treat patients. Health informatics fills the gaps between healthcare delivery and equipment by creating a system not only just a tool. It reveals patterns and missing elements in healthcare devices such as pacemakers or chemotherapy drug delivery pumps [17].
- **Emergency care**: Emergency services have always suffered from being disconnected from the base facility and limited resource information. This is mainly due to the importance of the time factor in dealing with these cases and the required latency time for processing the patient's historical record. Fortunately, the advanced available technology, automation systems, and health informatics allowed emergency cases to be analyzed immediately or

from far distances. This could happen even before an ambulance arrives so that critical care is delivered to the patients [17].

- **Remote diagnostics and management**: Health applications installed on smartphones and health wearable devices can be used to diagnose patients remotely. It is helpful to have these tools connected directly to the expert medical system or professional healthcare staff [17].

5.7 CONCLUSION

This chapter investigated the importance of information security and data management for IoT-enabled smart healthcare systems. First, we investigated the main components of healthcare systems and how its different than IoT-enabled smart healthcare systems. Then, we explored the main threats and vulnerabilities in this system. After that, some recent and sophisticated security solutions have been introduced to tackle these issues. Finally, we discussed the data management of several scenarios in smart healthcare systems.

REFERENCES

[1] Kruse, C. S., Frederick, B., Jacobson, T., and Monticone, D. K. Cybersecurity in healthcare: A systematic review of modern threats and trends. *Technology and Health Care,* 25(1), 1–10, (2017). DOI: 10.3233/THC-161263

[2] Ahmad, R., Samy, G. N., Ibrahim, N. K., Bath, P. A., and Ismail, Z. Threats identification in healthcare information systems using genetic algorithm and cox regression. In *2009 Fifth International Conference on Information Assurance and Security* (Vol. 2, pp. 757–760). IEEE, (2009). DOI: 10.1109/IAS.2009.313

[3] Loughlin, S. A. Roundtable discussion: Safeguarding information and resources against emerging cybersecurity threats. *Biomedical Instrumentation and Technology*, 48, 8, (2014). DOI: 10.2345/0899-8205-48.s1.8

[4] Argaw, S. T., Troncoso-Pastoriza, J. R., Lacey, D., Florin, M. V., Calcavecchia, F., Anderson, D., and Flahault, A. Cybersecurity of hospitals: Discussing the challenges and working towards mitigating the risks. *BMC Medical Informatics and Decision Making,* 20(1), 1–10, (2020). DOI: 10.1186/s12911-020-01161-7

[5] Coventry, L., and Branley, D. Cybersecurity in healthcare: A narrative review of trends, threats and ways forward. *Maturitas*, 113, 48–52, (2018). DOI: 10.1016/j.maturitas.2018.04.008

[6] Saranya, A., and Naresh, R. Efficient mobile security for E health care application in cloud for secure payment using key distribution. *Neural Processing Letters*, 53(1), 1–12, (2021). DOI: 10.1007/s11063-021-10482-1

[7] Ryan, J. J., and Ryan, D. J. Proportional hazards in information security. *Risk Analysis: An International Journal,* 25(1), 141–149, (2005). DOI: 10.1111/j.0272-4332.2005.00573.x

[8] Hathaliya, J. J., and Tanwar, S. An exhaustive survey on security and privacy issues in Healthcare 4.0. *Computer Communications*, 153, 311335, (2020). DOI: 10.1016/j.comcom.2020.02.018

[9] Singh, S., Rathore, S., Alfarraj, O., Tolba, A., and Yoon, B. A framework for privacy-preservation of IoT healthcare data using federated learning and blockchain technology. *Future Generation Computer Systems* 129: 380–388, (2022). DOI: 10.1016/j.future.2021.11.028

[10] Mahanan, W., Chaovalitwongse, W., and Natwichai, J. Data privacy preservation algorithm with k-anonymity. *World Wide Web*, 24(5), 1551–1561, (2021). DOI: 10.1007/s11280-021-00922-2

[11] Abouelmehdi, K., Beni-Hssane, A., Khaloufi, H., and Saadi, M. Big data security and privacy in healthcare: A review. *Procedia Computer Science*, 113, 73–80, (2017). DOI: 10.1016/j.procs.2017.08.292

[12] Awotunde, J. B., Jimoh, R. G., Ogundokun, R. O., Misra, S., and Abikoye, O. C. Big data analytics of IoT-based cloud system framework: Smart healthcare monitoring systems. In *Artificial Intelligence for Cloud and Edge Computing*, pp. 181–208. Springer, Cham, (2022). DOI: 10.1007/978-3-030-80821-1_9

[13] Cruz, J. P., Kaji, Y., and Yanai, N. RBAC-SC: Role-based access control using smart contract. *IEEE Access*, 6, 12240–12251, (2018). DOI: 10.1109/ACCESS.2018.2812844

[14] Kore, A., and Patil, S. Cross layered cryptography based secure routing for IoT-enabled smart healthcare system. *Wireless Networks*, 28(1), 1–15, (2022). DOI: 10.1007/s11276-021-02850-5

[15] Li, N., Wang, Y., Xu, X., and Liu, X., A CP-ABE Al-gorithm based HDFS distributed storage data security solution. In *IOP Conference Series: Materials Science and Engineering* (Vol. 768, No. 7, p. 072011). IOP Publishing, (2020). DOI: 10.1088/1757-899X/768/7/072011

[16] Babbar, H. The role of emerging technologies in smart healthcare. *IoT-Enabled Smart Healthcare Systems, Services, and Applications,* (2022). DOI: 10.1002/9781119816829. ch1

[17] Venkatachalam, K., Prabu, P., Almutairi, A., and Abouhawwash, M. Secure biometric authentication with de-duplication on distributed cloud storage. *PeerJ Computer Science,* 7, e569, (2021). DOI: 10.7717/peerj-cs.569

[18] Shepard, C. L., Doerge, E. J., Eickmeyer, A. B., Kraft, K. H., Wan, J., and Stoffel, J. T. Ambulatory care use among patients with spina bifida: Change in care from childhood to adulthood. *The Journal of Urology,* 199(4), 1050–1055, (2018). DOI: 10.1016/j. juro.2017.10.040

[19] Usak, M., Kubiatko, M., Shabbir, M. S., Viktorovna Dudnik, O., Jermsittiparsert, K., and Rajabion, L. Health care service delivery based on the internet of things: A systematic and comprehensive study. *International Journal of Communication Systems,* 33(2), e4179, (2020). DOI: 10.1002/dac.4179

[20] Rajamohan, K., Rangasamy, S., Nayak, S., Anuradha, R. and Chellasamy, A., Revolutionizing healthcare: Decentralized data management of iot devices using blockchain technology. In *Blockchain Technology in Healthcare Applications* (pp. 153–174). CRC Press, (2022). DOI: 10.1201/9781003224075

[21] Alsubaei, F., Abuhussein, A., and Shiva, S. Security and privacy in the internet of medical things: Taxonomy and risk assessment. In *2017 IEEE 42nd Conference on Local Computer Networks Workshops (LCN Workshops)* (pp. 112–120). IEEE, (2017). DOI: 10.1109/LCN.Workshops.2017.72

[22] Keshta, I., and Odeh, A. Security and privacy of electronic health records: Concerns and challenges. *Egyptian Informatics Journal*, 22(2), 177–183, (2021). DOI: 10.1016/j. eij.2020.07.003

6 AI-Assisted Big Data Analytics for Smart Healthcare Systems

Akruti Sinha, Devika Sapra, Gaurav Srivastava,
Mahin Anup, and Deepak Sinwar
Manipal University Jaipur

CONTENTS

6.1   INTRODUCTION

The recent COVID-19 pandemic severely strained the entire world's healthcare system, exposing flaws in our traditional healthcare system that were previously overlooked. It exemplified many of the issues plaguing the healthcare system. The most serious issues were the high cost of healthcare and the lack of access to high-quality care. One of the major reasons for this is the complexity of the healthcare system. It is a highly interconnected system, which is something that can be exploited by hackers. The interconnectedness of the system also increases the data volume exponentially

DOI: 10.1201/9781003326182-6

with each patient, and the number of patients is growing at the moment. There are solutions to these issues, and the ongoing wave of innovation has demonstrated that artificial intelligence (AI) and big data analytics (BDA) are the two fundamental components with the potential to lead the smart healthcare transformation.

While AI can assist with predictive analysis, intelligent judgements, and creative solutions to age-old problems [1], BDA can assist with the first part of the problem, that is, mining information and extracting meaningful data from the massive amount of available data [1] that is growing exponentially by the minute.

Despite its recent popularity, there have not been many foolproof frameworks, and platforms that use the power of both BDA and AI to provide a better smart healthcare system (SHCS) in terms of reliability, security, access, and other important features. There are several challenges to properly deploying such a framework in today's ever-changing, interconnected healthcare systems. First and foremost is the problem of unstructured data. Healthcare is an industry that generates a lot of data, but a lot of that data is not easily consumable. This is primarily because of the variety of different formats in that data is stored. For example, the medical notes of patients, doctors' reports, images, and various other types of documents. As the authors of [2] have stated, the problems of unstructured data, which brings its own set of problems such as correlated and redundant data, result in the consumption of more energy and bandwidth by networks, which are already quite constrained in terms of the resources they can access. This eventually leads to network congestion.

The rest of the chapter is organised into different subsections. Section 6.2 deals with an overview of a few related works. The background of AI and big data is presented in Section 6.3. Section 6.4 deals with the importance of AI and BDA for SHCSs. Common methods and their implications are discussed in Section 6.5. Section 6.6 discusses the most used frameworks in the field of SHCSs that integrate both AI and BDA. Emerging trends in big data and AI with reference to the SHCS are presented in Section 6.7. Section 6.8 discusses various challenges and issues followed by a conclusion in Section 6.9.

6.2   RELATED WORKS

Scholars in the field of healthcare have published numerous papers that integrate both AI and BDA to propose architectures and frameworks that can be implemented at a higher level to create a smart and efficient healthcare system. The authors of [3] have meticulously compiled a comprehensive survey that not only reviews but also enumerates the strengths and weaknesses of all such proposed frameworks and architectures. They have also identified a few challenges and unresolved issues as we have done later in the chapter as well. Reference [3] has provided excellent insight for all scholars and aids in keeping up with current trends in the field.

The authors of [3] hold [4] in high regard, and it is entirely feasible that it deserves such praise. The authors of [4] proposed a one-of-a-kind system that derives its power and functionality from that of the Internet of things (IoT) to not only recognise an emergency but also aid in the quick communication of healthcare personnel amongst themselves. As the authors correctly point out, one of the benefits of such a system is that it significantly reduces the possibility of human errors caused by individuals' delayed reaction time. It also provides doctors and physicians with more time to make accurate decisions.

While the idea is admirable in every way, and the architecture is nearly flawless, it should be noted that the results generated by [4] may vary greatly depending on person to person and situation to situation. In this case, testing with a large dataset is recommended.

In [5], one finds a very lucid explanation of the crucial areas of BDA needed for successful implementation in the healthcare sector. Reference [5] also discusses the challenges that usually encompass the applications of BDA in the field of healthcare organisations. Due to issues like confidentiality, privacy, and unstructured data, the authors of [5] suggest three major components of BDA that have a significant impact on it:

a. **Data validation**: This ensures the validity of data and checks to see if it is corrupted or not to ensure its accuracy. The Hadoop Distributed File System (HDFS) is used for the validation process.
b. **Process validation**: This component ensures that the business logic is correct and that the key-value pair that is created is accurate.
c. **Output validation**: This final one determines whether the data has been distorted after it has been processed in the repository. The data is validated by comparing it to an HDFS file.

As [6] correctly points out, BDA can be applied in varied ways. According to the authors of [6], the various sources of BDA include patient demographics, treatment history, and diagnostic reports. This information can give healthcare providers a more complete picture of their patients and allow them to customise treatment. It can also be used to enhance the quality of care patients receive. For example, a patient with a history of cancer may require a different type of treatment than a patient without such a history.

According to the authors of [7], advanced analytics must be used to gather important information from electronic health records (EHRs) because BDA can reveal important patterns that can improve the overall value of the healthcare system. Reference [7] also suggests that in the future, artificial neural networks may be used in conjunction with BDA. These algorithms can be trained to recognise patterns that indicate fraud or other problematic behaviours. This can help to reduce fraud and improve healthcare security and reduce the time spent on detecting fraud and other problematic behaviours.

GEMINI [8] is one of the most extraordinary proposals for a real-time service that provides health services. GEMINI begins by extracting data from different types of sources, which includes both structured and unstructured data, for each patient and storing it for future use. The stored information forms a patient's profile graph, allowing it to provide a detailed view of the health information of the patient. In addition, the profile graph enables GEMINI to infer and extract information that may not be easily understood to perform predictive analysis. Another notable part of the proposed model is that it gives a "self-learning knowledge base" [8], which also keeps all medical professionals in the loop to determine findings and conclusions.

While innovations in the field of BDA and AI are constantly being developed, it is equally important to ensure their dependability and trustworthy use. The authors of [9] propose a few possible solutions. As a first step, it has been suggested that a clear and effective data governance framework be developed. To ensure that the design and frameworks are human-centred, all steps must be taken. The following step is to define a clear process that explains how, why, and which information can be used. The third step should focus on empowering those whose data is being used by understanding and enforcing strict rules for how this data can be managed and governed more effectively. As a fourth and final step, all government agencies must collaborate to ensure that the process is not only transparent but also accurate.

The steps outlined above can be used effectively to ensure that trustworthiness and equality continue to exist in the field of healthcare [9]. Reliability is especially important in the field of healthcare due to the very sensitive nature of the data. The misuse of medical data can wreak havoc on the healthcare system because it can lead to discrimination and has the potential to cause serious harm to individuals.

6.3   AI AND BIG DATA BACKGROUND

6.3.1   BIG DATA IN HEALTHCARE

According to [10], big data encompasses several statistical techniques for data evaluation and assessment [11,12]. "Big Data" has been a phrase often coined to define huge data obtained through data interchange across diverse systems [13,14]. Even though it is indicated as a "huge" database, its relevance has been driven by the ability to gather little information regarding the given issue under investigation [15,16]. Reference [17] outlined the features of big data with "seven Vs", that is, "Volume, Variety, Velocity, Veracity, Value, Variability, and Valence". With the progressively increasing quantity of big information inside the given environment, data analysing applications within medical services are steadily developing [18,19]. Diverse inferences, such as patient characteristics [20], clinical history [21], and examination results, are among the potential big data origins in the health sector [22]. Such information, according to [23], might be organised (for example, genome, phenotype, or genomics data) or unstructured. Patient information frequently necessitates the development and collection of high-quality actual statistics [24,25]. Experienced professionals in medical institutions may use big data to get useful insights and take measures [25,26]. Technology is being used by medical institutions to cope with the different intricacies of data processing [27,28]. Furthermore, big data in medical services may be used to integrate diverse sectors to further investigate a condition holistically [29]. In conclusion, all the aforementioned features of big data may be observed in the case of health care.

When leveraging big data, observational, prospective, and adaptive statistical tools may be used to upgrade the effectiveness of many areas of medical care [30]. Clinical diagnostics, universal healthcare, clinical observation, and clinical management are some of the opportunities presented by big data in the health industry.

6.3.2   AI in Healthcare

According to [31], one of the most attractive prospect sectors for the implementation of automated systems is healthcare [32]. Doctors can now diagnose cancers more quickly and sooner than ever before, detect illnesses before they emerge, and discover genetic problems that may harm us in the future. Similarly, analytics can improve backroom procedures, enhancing the patient hospital experience while also reducing expenses by decreasing inefficiencies and money that can then be spent on improving patient outcomes. Nevertheless, in the medical industry, technologies must adhere to the legislation, norms, and security standards in ensuring that technology serves the public good. Technology can help not only in the discovery of valuable medications but also in enhancing the efficiency of current products. Even though AI systems in medical services are now limited, the health and financial benefits are too tremendous to ignore. High-cost industries will become opportunities for forward-thinking healthcare organisations to adopt cutting-edge technology and maintain their competitive advantage over their competitors. These are only a few instances of what is possible when AI is implemented in health systems to its utmost advantage. The opportunities are limitless, and coordination between government and private-sector entities is vital to accomplishing goals. As worldwide societies remain healthy and the prevalence of acute illness grows, the costs of medical care will continue to be a focal area amongst healthcare entities.

The use of AI for medical services is both exciting and desirable. Collaboration between physicians and robots might mark a watershed moment in our abilities to combat ailments and enhance human health. The advantages will undoubtedly be essential, ranging from accuracy and focused treatment to backend administration and simpler procedures, from assistance for transitional housing for the aged to advanced testing abilities.

It might be time to seek the assistance of computers. In spite of the fantastic innovations, they should be examined in the context of our current medical transition. The arrangement of modern healthcare has a huge influence on the medical industry, and the actions we take now will impact fairly long ramifications according to how we treat patients.

6.4   IMPORTANCE OF AI AND BDA IN SHCSs

As previously stated and by researchers in [33], the current wave of innovation will be one of the most crucial for the global healthcare system, owing to the increased potential of tools that will enable us to address the most pressing concerns in the healthcare sector. These tools will include novel, affordable, and easy-to-use devices that will deliver diagnostics and therapeutics to the patient faster than ever before.

AI and BDA have long been considered potential solutions to the problems that currently plague the healthcare system. However, as the authors of [34] correctly point out, at this point, we have the required technology including a large AI talent pool, making this future not only plausible but also likely. The impact on healthcare sustainability is difficult to predict, but one thing is certain: change is coming, and it is coming soon.

The improved tools at our disposal only increase BDA's ability to provide better results and not only assist healthcare personnel in their daily tasks of documentation and others but also provide better, clear, accurate image analysis, patient monitoring, and perhaps even fully automated life-supporting devices used extensively in SHCSs. However, it is not all that easy. The most difficult task, and one that has long been a source of concern, is an accurate interpretation of data in the form of an image or video [33]. The challenge, of course, is much greater for images taken in poor lighting conditions or a noisy environment. However, there have been many innovations in the current era, and with an increased number of professionals in the industry, BDA used cautiously and diligently can solve this issue in the coming days as well.

When we shift our focus to BDA, we find that it is just as critical as, if not more important than, AI. First and foremost, BDA can be defined as "the process of analysing a huge amount of data from various sources of data and different formats to convey the perception of enabling a decision-making process in real-time" [35].

Many people were unsure what role BDA could play in the healthcare industry other than "analysing" patient data. BDA can do much more than that, thanks to the massive amount of data being appended every passing second. BDA applications in the smart healthcare industry today include managing, storing, and examining clinical data from doctors and prescriptions. BDA can also help organise and interpret computed tomography (CT) scans, magnetic resonance imaging (MRI) images, X-rays, laboratory data, Electronic Patient Records (EPR) data, and other types of data. When implemented intelligently and utilised, BDA can also aid in the analysis of accurate and meaningful data from drugstore documents, insurance-related files, and other sources. This data can then be used to enhance healthcare services, ensure lower expenses, and increase efficiency. Even though scientists have access to a large amount of data, they have not been able to develop a suitable framework to aid in the achievement of all of the aforementioned applications [35].

As previously stated, this decade will be very eventful for the healthcare field, especially because we now have improved tools to help us solve problems that were once thought unsolvable. With increased efficiency comes new challenges such as security, interoperability, and other issues, but with BDA on the scene to assist, the SHCS is poised for a bright future.

6.5 COMMON METHODOLOGIES AND THEIR IMPLICATIONS

There have been instances where certain common techniques in the domains of IoT and information analysis were recommended for the creation of advanced medical systems. According to [36], a predictive model known as ViSiBiD may correctly detect harmful clinical events using patient monitoring based on data gathered from various patients with similar symptoms. (i) efficient and scalable data acquisition in all parameters combining "Pearson's correlation coefficients" and "wavelet transform", as well as quick metrics; (ii) using numerous data mining tools, such as "random forest (RF)", "J48 Decision Tree (J48)", as well as "sequential minimal optimisation (SMO)" [37], can improve initial clinical irregularity prediction.

Intel has launched the "A-wear" initiative, which is centred on a portable gadget that connects predictive analysis and portable tech. "Apple" has been striving for analysing blood sugar levels through tears, as well as creating motion medical equipment for blood tracking through the skin. Google is focusing on cancer detection, imminent strokes, and cardiovascular problems, among other things. Samsung is collaborating with medical doctors from the "University of California, San Francisco" to accelerate the development and commercialisation of sensor technologies, computations, as well as medical technology. The given measures sparked rivalry in the business for wearable technology, as well as technological advancements that have energised the sensors and wearable business [38].

A medical scheme based on power harvesting calculation for monitoring systems and the deployment for information analysis throughout medicare was proposed. Resource harvesting and generation of data, pre-processing, data analysis, as well as data application, are the three levels of the strategy. It highlighted the efficacy of the medical IoT with power generation, as well as reliable samples that have been utilised through the "Hadoop server" for method standardisation using threshold limit values (TLVs) [39]. Wearable technology systems to constantly monitor individuals' conditions have been built using a semantic centralised database to incorporate diverse wearable medical datasets [40]. Wearable biosensors enable personalised mHealth and eHealth, making it easier for healthcare professionals to provide personalised and premium services [41].

The following are some of the issues of massive data and data analytics in healthcare [42–46]: (i) data with a massive quantity, several dimensions, or a wide range of formats; (ii) unbalanced data, inconsistent data, and data of low performance and durability; (iii) Healthcare professionals (particularly hospitals) who are responsible for aggregating and analysing fragmented or siloed data; (iv) Unstructured or semi-structured data aggregation and analysis; (v) filtering and analysing continuous data streams, particularly rapidly moving data streams; (vi) algorithmically difficult jobs in genetic data analysis; (vii) massive data visualisation; and (viii) data ownership, information management, confidentiality, and cybersecurity are all important considerations. Even if privacy protection is guaranteed, many healthcare professionals are unwilling to disclose their information owing to market rivalry. Preserving an optimal balance between safeguarding patient data and maintaining information availability or integrity of data is often challenging. There are problems with public access, formalisation, and the incorporation of usable and legible data [44].

6.6 TYPES OF AI-BDA FOR SHCSs

6.6.1 Recommendation Systems

Numerous recommendation systems use the power of AI, BDA, and IoT to recommend either an appropriate diagnosis or steps for disease monitoring. Other types of recommendation systems exist as well.

The authors of [47] proposed a rather viable recommendation engine for personalised IoT solutions provided to any individual. The engine's process, as proposed by the authors of [47], is as follows: first, the diseases to which a person is predisposed are identified. This is accomplished by considering their medical history and analysing this unstructured data using text mining, as well as taking into account their lifestyle attributes. These two elements are then fed into a machine learning (ML) classification algorithm, which predicts the disease. The next step is to map these diseases to the lifestyle attributes that were initially considered to monitor them. As a final step, the authors created a mathematical optimisation model for recommending wearable devices and IoT-inspired solutions for the individual. This is an impressive framework proposed by the authors; however, as the authors have stated, more work must be done in the direction of considering the individual's choices before recommending an appropriate wearable device.

In [48], the authors presented a "type-2 fuzzy ontology-aided recommendation system" for not only monitoring the patient but also recommending appropriate diets that include drugs in addition to food. As a first step, the system gathers details about the patient's risk factors. The following step involves the use of wearables to determine the health status of the patient and, finally, the recommendation of a diet involving medicines and food. While the integration of T2FL or "Type-2 Fuzzy Logic" with the fuzzy ontology has demonstrated a significant increase in disease prediction accuracy as well as diet recommendation accuracy, this collaboration needs to be further investigated and implemented in the real-world setting.

Authors in [49] presented ProTrip, another such food recommendation system. The distinction between this and other recommendation systems is that this is a health-centric ontology-based tourism recommender framework that derives its power from the hybrid filtering mechanism that it employs. The trip can provide a semantic understanding of the system in the tourism domain, which is unprecedented. Truly, ontology aids in better, more efficient classification; however, because ProTrip employs both implicit and explicit information, it is susceptible to varying accuracy rates depending on the location and surroundings of its implementations. It can be seen that the recommendations generated are based not only on demographic data but also on user preferences, which is a commendable achievement. While there is no doubt that the authors' claim that the website is user-friendly is correct, the more pressing concerns are the permissions related to accessing location: some users may not want to share their location. One of the more commendable aspects of the proposed framework is that the recommendation system is evaluated using an IoT-based real-time healthcare support system.

6.6.2 PREDICTION SYSTEMS

The authors of [47] proposed a novel framework for the purpose of analysing and forecasting the occurrence of COVID-19 that makes use of both the IoT and Big Data. The paper's most impressive feature is that the authors used four types of analysis to predict COVID-19: "descriptive analysis, diagnostic analysis, predictive analysis, and prescriptive analysis". In [47], the framework focuses on the various COVID-19 symptoms and applies them to a real-world data set to test the efficacy of the same framework. The data set in question is a compilation of real-crime data gathered from various hospitals in Khyber-Pakhtunkhwa, Pakistan. The descriptive analysis entailed investigating a wide range of attributes from the data set chosen by the authors. The relationship between the attributes has also been investigated using data visualisation methods. The authors used a neural network-based model for predictive analysis, which not only predicts the occurrence of COVID-19 but also compares the results to other ML algorithms. The authors claim that the neural network has a 99% accuracy rate and that it performs significantly better than ML-based algorithms. The splitting of the entire framework into four different analysis modules may perform better at this stage, but when additional analyses are added to the framework, this can cause problems.

In [48], a novel model is presented that employs the power of AI and IoT to diagnose diseases. This model is primarily used for the diagnosis of heart disease and diabetes, with the various stages referred to as "data acquisition, pre-processing, classification, and parameter tuning". The authors' AI-IoT convergence techniques for the aforementioned purpose were very well utilised in the paper as the AI techniques use data that has been seamlessly collected by IoT devices like sensors and wearables for disease diagnosis. The proposed model employs a "Crow Search Optimisation algorithm-based Cascaded Long Short Term Memory (CSO-CLSTM)" model for diagnosing diseases. One of the authors' impressive decisions was to use CSO to tune both the weight and bias parameters of the CLSTM mode. This contributes to more efficient medical data classification. To remove outliers, the iForest or isolation forest technique is used. The authors claimed a maximum accuracy of 96.16% in the diagnosis of heart disease and 97.26% in the diagnosis of diabetes, implying that the use of CSO was effective. While the paper appears to be flawless overall because the techniques were used correctly, several other problems can be solved using other techniques. Figure 6.1 shows the methodology of the CSO-CLSTM method used in [48].

Mobile edge computing and deep learning (DL) are rarely used in SHCSs, but [49] has proposed a framework that uses B5G or Beyond 5th generation networks to diagnose COVID-19. Because of its less latency and higher bandwidth, the 5G network has been used. The authors propose a distributed DL model in which each of the COVID-19 edges has its own local DL framework. In three stages, these local frameworks that run on edge nodes reconcile with the global framework that runs on a cloud environment. The advancement of B5G has greatly benefited local frameworks, which aids in providing an accurate result. The model proposed in [49] aims to add semantics to existing DL models to assist human healthcare practitioners in gaining insights and making faster and more accurate decisions. The authors claim that the test results are promising. An intriguing aspect of the framework is that DL models can be deployed effectively at both the edge and cloud DL environments. The "explainability layer" for each algorithm is a commendable addition to the framework to reveal semantics that will eventually be required by healthcare professionals for the diagnosis of COVID-19. However, the actual implementation of this model cannot be verified. The authors must now deploy this model in local hospitals to validate the model's results in a real-world setting.

Reference [50] is another such paper, though it is less well known. Similarly, References [48,50] aid in the diagnosis of diseases by utilising the power of big data and ML. Data on a variety of diseases is collected and then pre-processed for classification. The framework's primary goal is to recommend various ML methods to medical healthcare professionals to assist them in diagnosing diseases using the best

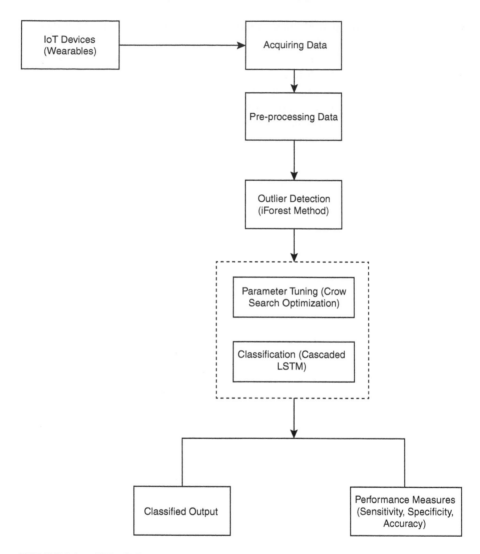

FIGURE 6.1   CSO-CLSTM method proposed by [48].

classifiers. The framework is divided into three major sections. The first segment is concerned with the input of patient information as well as the output of results. The second section focuses on BDA and data management, while the final section focuses on ML analysis and disease prediction algorithms. While the intention is commendable, more work needs to be done to improve the accuracy.

6.6.3   SYSTEMS THAT AGGREGATE DATA

The SHCS's goal continues to provide care to individuals in remote locations as well as to ensure ongoing diagnostics that send statistical information for crucial choice processes via infinite connectivity functionality offered by IoT gadgets. Deep convolutional networks are utilised for achieving higher standards in performance for important aspects like final reaction rate, cost, as well as precision if the medical business is to prosper in the transition from end-to-end clinical information processing. Depending on the real-time data, the authors of [51] present the "Gray Filter Bayesian Convolutional Neural Network (GFB-CNN)", a comprehensive "Deep Neural Network-driven" IoT intelligent healthcare technique in this research. They present a comprehensive Intelligent IoT-based eHealth structure on the basis of the "Gray Filter Bayesian Convolutional Neural Network" in this research, which reduces critical service qualitative factors including duration and expense along with greater precision. An extensive mobile HEALTH (MHEALTH) dataset is used to test the technique's practicality.

The "GFB-CNN" approach has been meant to improve the rate of efficiency of clinical data processing while consuming the least amount of time and resources possible, therefore advancing to a smarter civilisation in medical services. The use of the "Volume Align Softmax CNN" model achieves the target of the "GFB-CNN" approach. By integrating efficient and robust pre-processing attributes for SHCSs, the suggested GFB-CNN approach boosts the computational efficiency with the number of instances accurately evaluated as to whether normal cardiac signal or harmful cardiac signal with minimum time in comparison to current research. In addition, as opposed to ordinary works, the suggested GFB-CNN approach reduces the workload by storing and accessing attributes inside the platform through virtualised infrastructure using necessary function mappings. Moreover, as opposed to existing methods, the suggested GFB-CNN technique minimises the final reaction time just by maintaining the ideal individual behaviour using the Bayesian Logistic Sigmoid activation function. The suggested GFB-CNN technique's efficiency is assessed in terms of transmission time, overhead, and accuracy for various numbers of occurrences, and it is in contrast to two past projects. Whenever contrasted to previous research, computational outcomes depict that the suggested GFB-CNN approach outperforms them. The suggested GFB-CNN technique, on the other hand, fails to consider healthcare analysis of data in terms of data security. The suggested method should be expanded for secured health data analysis and prediction by including an additional security methodology.

The entire workflow of the suggested GFB-CNN approach in clinical data processing is depicted in Figure 6.2. The suggested technique's input layer consists of unprocessed input data obtained from smart gadgets. Subject chest "Schist", right wrist "Srw", and left ankle "Sla" are among the IoT devices employed in the presented architecture for cardiac monitoring. In addition to the input nodes, the proposed approach uses a grey filtering model using convolution to apply filtration on the input data obtained from a smart detector, resulting in a function space which encapsulates the source's pre-processed properties.

6.6.4 Systems That Provide Living Assistance

Communities have emerged because of the growing usage of smart gadgets in localities. The authors of [52] introduce the "Big Data-Enabled Smart Healthcare System Framework (BSHSF)", which provides visual depictions of revenue models in the medical environment. Similarly, modern technology and intelligent machines have

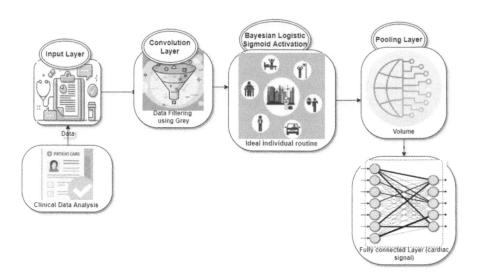

FIGURE 6.2   Complete procedure proposed by [51].

the power to transform health services as they already have in other sectors. In the frame of reference of data, cities, and medical services, this article [52] investigated how technology and solutions are changing. This evolution is a radical transformation that helps individuals to learn how to solve a variety of challenges via enhanced administration and new visions. The authors of [52] also looked at many sophisticated 3T technologies in this research that have grown in prominence in recent times as a goal for motivating productivity and growth, as well as delivering automatic, effective care coordination and city infrastructure. As big data and intelligent systems grow increasingly significant in healthcare services, challenges including secure data sharing, safeguarding the integrity, maintaining assurance and management, and constantly improving tools and techniques will be more vital.

Even though big data-enabled intelligent medical systems provide several benefits to healthcare organisations, they are currently underutilised in practice owing to inadequate technical assistance and poor safety [53]. Furthermore, in the medical business, several smart technologies and big data systems need a significant amount of computing, which the average end user may lack. Because smart systems and data analysis in health services are still relatively new, administrative legislation concerns such as lawful authority, data protection, personal and institutional privacy, and regulations are still to be resolved. In the medical business, the aforementioned issues are undeniably important negatives, necessitating proper exchange [54]. Consequently, to effectively tackle the difficulties, new comprehensive approaches are required.

6.7   EMERGING TRENDS IN BIG DATA AND AI IN TERMS OF SHCSs

According to [55], as medical companies embrace the statistics approach of systemic transformation, data analysis has now become a key area for healthcare technology development. Big data is quickly becoming a key metric for achieving economic and therapeutic progress.

Most suppliers are still seeking resources and devices that will allow them to engage in fundamental big data operations such as risk classification, healthcare systems, and cost control. Cutting-edge software engineers, on the other hand, are now moving past this initial phase of acceptance and into a world where large data is no longer a problem

The following listed below are a few new tactics, information systems, as well as infrastructural initiatives which are expanding frontiers over how data analytics integrates into the medical industry.

1. Various analytical possibilities using visual analysis

   Evaluating X-Rays, CT scanners, and MRI scans have mainly been the domain of competent doctors who specialise in detecting anomalies and documenting observations since the dawn of imaging techniques. However, as computational power improves and analytical programmes grow more adept at analysing patterns in digital pictures, these test findings are bringing in new significance for the diagnostic process – and widening the possibilities for employing this information for other parts of treating patients.

   The possibility of visualising insights, which becomes a critical part of the battle to reduce cost by reducing redundant or unwanted facilities, has already ignited numerous collaborative initiatives and billions in financing for promising programmers providing methodologies that can compress additional money out of the system.

2. Patient care is being revolutionised by wearable gadgets

   Consumers are buying wearable gadgets, residential tracking systems, and eHealth applications at an alarming rate, putting patient-centred healthcare on the cusp of transformation.

   Specialists in patient involvement are attempting to translate fantastic factors of smartwatches and eHealth applications into better chronic illness administration, patient happiness, and community health.

   Although the IoT has yet to find a reliable position in the healthcare IT environment, unlocking the secret to dealing with the chaotic, unorganised, and unmanageable data generated by devices and applications might help to swiftly tackle a variety of many other big data problems.

3. Medical decisions will be transformed by cognitive technologies

   The use of methodologies that "train" analytical platforms to spot trends in big information is known as cognitive computing. The models were trained to establish connections in the same way that the human brain may deduce links between dissimilar things using a set of standards.

   Some medical organisations are still using the management of the information systems' semantic computational capacity and unlimited internet platforms, and many others are prepared to do so in the coming years, altering the manner people are monitored, and the threat is evaluated and handled.

4. Precision medicine incorporates genetic knowledge into the diagnosis procedure

Automation, wireless sensor networks, as well as visual processing are all primed to unite genome decoding with computational chemistry that ignites one of healthcare's most exciting trends: precision healthcare.

The "Precision Medicine Initiative (PMI)" has been counting upon the sector's increasing contentment with big data to lay the groundwork for every coordinated ability to collect health information into a more central database to be used as well as reprocessed for research, presumably yielding additional insight into Parkinson's disease, Asperger's syndrome, chronic diseases, cardiovascular disease, and other serious conditions.

AI technologies, as it is widely assumed, will aid, and improve human effort rather than supersede the job of doctors and other medical staff [56]. AI is eager to assist health professionals with a wide range of duties, including administrative functions, patient information, and customer engagement, and specialised help in image processing, clinical equipment digitalisation, and monitoring patients. There are a variety of viewpoints on the most useful applications of AI in medical services. Administrative procedures, image processing, robotic technology, virtual agents, and decision support systems are among the most crucial sectors, according to Forbes [57].

6.8   CHALLENGES AND OPEN ISSUES

6.8.1   SECURITY

According to the authors of [58], since data analysis has become more advanced in smart medical care systems, challenges in security have posed a major threat to the medical sector.

Institutional Security Breaches: They would emerge from improper access to medical data by either individuals and firms exploiting their rights or external entities misusing the obligation of data systems as in a staff who retrieves data without a legitimate need or an imposter who intrudes on a company's information architecture to pluck information or retrieve it in an impractical manner.

System hazards develop when an actor in the data-flow network abuses the exposed data for purposes other than those for which it was intended.

Data Security and Synchronisation: Only a few companies maintain health data in a variety of forms. Using a few of the file formats may be a huge roadblock when it comes to exchanging patient records between institutions, as well as medical health research studies.

Legitimate Data Transfer with Information Security: In the medical industry, it is critical to communicate data across organisational boundaries to provide additional security for different stakeholder groups and to assist with challenging public health concerns. However, the publication of clinical information may contain privately traceable data as well as confidential material, which may compromise privacy and have socioeconomic implications for the patient.

Technological advancements have resulted in the integration of medical files from many origins into a unified database that aids scientists working to strengthen public healthcare, treatment protocols, and wellness support schemes.

6.8.2 SCARCITY OF DATA

According to the authors of [59], sensor networks, cell phones, embedded systems, motors, radiofrequency identification (RFID), and ports all have minimum power and cognitive and computing capacity in the IoT [60–62]. Furthermore, the information obtained by these intensively placed, resource-starved sensors currently includes overlapping and duplicative trends. Distributing such associated data from source to destination consumes a huge amount of energy, has a low quality of service, and has limited bandwidth [63,64]. Incorporating the IoT with the cloud infrastructure helps to alleviate significant challenges to a certain degree. It does, however, lead to higher prices and intricacy. Due to the complex characteristics of IoT networks, dynamic resource management issues such as information retrieval, modelling, allocation, scheduling, estimate, and tracking are still a greater potential problem [65]. Moreover, in this regard, tuning within resource provisioning strategies is an issue that should be investigated extensively. Because most current data consolidation approaches are inefficient, it is necessary to develop innovative, compact, and resource-efficient data-gathering strategies based on AI. Furthermore, unique systems that divide the workload amongst different IoT elements should be designed that not only meet the resource shortages of these systems but also provide an appropriate degree of precision [60].

6.8.3 BIG DATA ANALYTICS

The introduction of technological innovations has not yet addressed and resolved all issues. One of the major issues that scholars and researchers face is the need for high-accuracy algorithms to provide an accurate and efficient patient diagnosis [66]. In recent times, there has been a significant increase in research in the field of BDA, owing primarily to the fact that BDA has numerous applications in a wide range of domains.

However, as [67] correctly points out, the challenges that arise in the field of BDA are typical because the majority of the data that BDA deals with is unstructured, which means that the data does not strictly adhere to any predefined schema. This makes it difficult for BDA to build actionable insights from the data. This, in turn, hampers the ability to generate solutions and results.

As previously stated, the sheer volume of data generated every second only adds to BDA's numerous challenges. Also, because the majority of the data is unstructured, adding the step of structuring and then analysing it only makes matters worse. As [68] suggests, in such cases, scholars and researchers are working on optimising operations using ML and DL techniques and algorithms to gain valuable insights. Researchers have also been developing unique BDA tools to manage data extraction and noise removal to enhance the quality of collected data [69]. This will also help to conserve the network's overall energy [69].

In the healthcare sector, the majority of the applications have been deployed using real-time analysis of patient data which also means that the data is monitored in real time. As an open issue, researchers can try developing algorithms in the field of ML and DL that can use this real-time data analysis to further BDA as well [67]. The authors of [67] also suggest that new and unique data aggregation techniques be developed that can detect and reduce outliers. Working on the aforementioned areas and reducing flaws in existing areas will ensure that all of the various healthcare applications are dependable and relevant.

6.9 CONCLUSION

This chapter delves into the role of AI and BDA in improving, sustaining, and introducing a SHCS. There have been significant advancements in the aforementioned fields, and several scholars have already predicted how AI and BDA, when combined, will not only promote personalised healthcare for all but will also improve the healthcare system's functions. For example, the use of AI in the medical industry can help physicians detect illness, administer prescriptions, and even provide medical advice over the phone. Furthermore, BDA, which is essentially the analysis of data, can be used to provide healthcare providers with extensive knowledge of a patient's medical history, thus enabling them to provide better care. We thoroughly discussed the frameworks with the greatest potential among the several proposed frameworks.

REFERENCES

[1] López-Martínez, Fernando, Edward Rolando Núñez-Valdez, Vicente García-Díaz, and Zoran Bursac. "A case study for a big data and machine learning platform to improve medical decision support in population health management." *Algorithms* 13, no. 4 (2020): 102.

[2] Elhayatmy, G, N Dey, and AS Ashour. "Internet of things based wireless body area network in healthcare." In: *Internet of Things and Big Data Analytics toward Next-Generation Intelligence.* Springer, Cham, (2018), pp 3–20. https://link.springer.com/chapter/10.1007/978-3-319-60435-0_1

[3] Li, Wei, Yuanbo Chai, Fazlullah Khan, Syed Rooh Ullah Jan, Sahil Verma, Varun G. Menon, and Xingwang Li. "A comprehensive survey on machine learning-based big data analytics for IoT-enabled smart healthcare system." *Mobile Networks and Applications* 26 (2021): 234–252.

[4] Prajapati, Bharat, Satyen Parikh, and Jignesh Patel. "An intelligent real time IOT based system (IRTBS) for monitoring ICU patient." In: *International Conference on Information and Communication Technology for Intelligent Systems*, pp. 390–396. Springer, Cham, 2017.

[5] Mehta, Nishita, Anil Pandit, and Meenal Kulkarni. "Elements of healthcare big data analytics." In: *Big Data Analytics in Healthcare*, pp. 23–43. Springer, Cham, 2020. https://link.springer.com/book/10.1007/978-3-030-31672-3

[6] Khanra, Sayantan, Amandeep Dhir, AKM Najmul Islam, and Matti Mäntymäki. "Big data analytics in healthcare: a systematic literature review." *Enterprise Information Systems* 14, no. 7 (2020): 878–912.

[7] Austin, Christopher, and Fred Kusumoto. "The application of big data in medicine: current implications and future directions." *Journal of Interventional Cardiac Electrophysiology* 47, no. 1 (2016): 51–59.

[8] Ling, Zheng Jye, Quoc Trung Tran, Ju Fan, Gerald CH Koh, Thi Nguyen, Chuen Seng Tan, James WL Yip, and Meihui Zhang. "GEMINI: an integrative healthcare analytics system." *Proceedings of the VLDB Endowment* 7, no. 13 (2014): 1766–1771.

[9] Ho, Calvin WL, Joseph Ali, and Karel Caals. "Ensuring trustworthy use of artificial intelligence and big data analytics in health insurance." *Bulletin of the World Health Organization* 98, no. 4 (2020): 263.

[10] Khanra, Sayantan, Amandeep Dhir, AKM Najmul Islam, and Matti Mäntymäki. "Big data analytics in healthcare: a systematic literature review." *Enterprise Information Systems* 14, no. 7 (2020): 878–912.

[11] Galetsi, Panagiota, Korina Katsaliaki, and Sameer Kumar. "Big data analytics in health sector: theoretical framework, techniques and prospects." *International Journal of Information Management* 50 (2020): 206–216.

[12] Mergel, Ines, R. Karl Rethemeyer, and Kimberley Isett. "Big data in public affairs." *Public Administration Review* 76, no. 6 (2016): 928–937.

[13] Bahri, Safa, Nesrine Zoghlami, Mourad Abed, and João Manuel RS Tavares. "Big data for healthcare: a survey." *IEEE Access* 7 (2018): 7397–7408.

[14] Khanra, Sayantan, Amandeep Dhir, and Matti Mäntymäki. "Big data analytics and enterprises: a bibliometric synthesis of the literature." *Enterprise Information Systems* 14, no. 6 (2020): 737–768.

[15] George, Gerard, Ernst C Osinga, Dovev Lavie, and Brent A Scott. "Big data and data science methods for management research." *Academy of Management Journal* 59, no. 5 (2016): 1493–1507.

[16] McAfee, Andrew, Erik Brynjolfsson, Thomas H Davenport, DJ Patil, and Dominic Barton. "Big data: the management revolution." *Harvard Business Review* 90, no. 10 (2012): 60–68.

[17] Kitchin, Rob. "The real-time city? Big data and smart urbanism." *GeoJournal* 79, no. 1 (2014): 1–14.

[18] Galetsi, Panagiota, and Korina Katsaliaki. "A review of the literature on big data analytics in healthcare." *Journal of the Operational Research Society* 71, no. 10 (2020): 1511–1529.

[19] Behera, Deepak Kumar, and Umakant Dash. "Healthcare financing in South-East Asia: does fiscal capacity matter?" *International Journal of Healthcare Management* 13, no. sup1 (2020): 375–384.

[20] Malik, MM, S Abdallah, and M Ala'raj. "Data mining and predictive analytics applications for the delivery of healthcare services: a systematic literature review." *Annals of Operations Research* 270, no. 1 (2018): 287–312.

[21] Ozminkowski, Ronald J, Timothy S Wells, Kevin Hawkins, Gandhi R Bhattarai, Charles W Martel, and Charlotte S Yeh. "Big data, little data, and care coordination for medicare beneficiaries with medigap coverage." *Big Data* 3, no. 2 (2015): 114–125.

[22] Amirian, Pouria, Francois van Loggerenberg, Trudie Lang, Arthur Thomas, Rosanna Peeling, Anahid Basiri, and Steven N. Goodman. "Using big data analytics to extract disease surveillance information from point of care diagnostic machines." *Pervasive and Mobile Computing* 42 (2017): 470–486.

[23] Mehta, Nishita, and Anil Pandit. "Concurrence of big data analytics and healthcare: a systematic review." *International Journal of Medical Informatics* 114 (2018): 57–65.

[24] Tang, Valerie, King Lun Choy, George TS Ho, Hoi Yan Lam, and Yung Po Tsang. "An IoMT-based geriatric care management system for achieving smart health in nursing homes." *Industrial Management & Data Systems* 119, no. 8 (2019): 1819–1840. https://doi.org/10.1108/IMDS-01-2019-0024.

[25] Wang, Yichuan, Lee Ann Kung, and Terry Anthony Byrd. "Big data analytics: understanding its capabilities and potential benefits for healthcare organizations." *Technological Forecasting and Social Change* 126 (2018): 3–13.

[26] Prasser, Fabian, Helmut Spengler, Raffael Bild, Johanna Eicher, and Klaus A. Kuhn. "Privacy-enhancing ETL-processes for biomedical data." *International Journal of Medical Informatics* 126 (2019): 72–81.

[27] Harerimana, Gaspard, Beakcheol Jang, Jong Wook Kim, and Hung Kook Park. "Health big data analytics: a technology survey." *IEEE Access* 6 (2018): 65661–65678.

[28] Zhang, Fan, Junwei Cao, Samee U Khan, Keqin Li, and Kai Hwang. "A task-level adaptive MapReduce framework for real-time streaming data in healthcare applications." *Future Generation Computer Systems* 43 (2015): 149–160.

[29] Zhang, Rui, Gyorgy Simon, and Fang Yu. "Advancing Alzheimer's research: a review of big data promises." *International Journal of Medical Informatics* 106 (2017): 48–56.

[30] Kaur, Prableen, Manik Sharma, and Mamta Mittal. "Big data and machine learning based secure healthcare framework." *Procedia Computer Science* 132 (2018): 1049–1059.

[31] Bartoletti, Ivana. "AI in healthcare: ethical and privacy challenges." In *Conference on Artificial Intelligence in Medicine in Europe*, pp. 7–10. Springer, Cham, 2019.

[32] Bartoletti, Ivana "Algorithms may outperform doctors, but they're no healthcare panacea | The Guardian." https://www.theguardian.com/commentisfree/2018/jul/26/tech-healthcare-ethics-artifical-intelligence-doctors-patients (accessed Jan. 19, 2022).

[33] Bohr, Adam, and Kaveh Memarzadeh (Eds.). "The rise of artificial intelligence in healthcare applications." In *Artificial Intelligence in Healthcare*, pp. 25–60. Academic Press, Cambridge, MA, 2020. https://doi.org/10.1016/B978-0-12-818438-7.00002-2

[34] Lee K-F. *AI Superpowers: China, Silicon Valley, and the New World Order.* 1st ed. Houghton Mifflin Harcourt, New York, 2019. https://www.researchgate.net/profile/Kiran-Dhankhar/publication/352750364_Training_Effectiveness_Evaluation_Models_A_Comparison/links/60d642d0299bf1ea9ebe4ac1/Training-Effectiveness-Evaluation-Models-A-Comparison.pdf#page=88

[35] Khan, Z. Faizal, and Sultan Refa Alotaibi. "Applications of artificial intelligence and big data analytics in m-Health: a healthcare system perspective." *Journal of Healthcare Engineering* 2020 (2020): 8894694.

[36] Wang, Lidong, and Cheryl Ann Alexander. "Big data analytics in medical engineering and healthcare: methods, advances and challenges." *Journal of Medical Engineering & Technology* 44, no. 6 (2020): 267–283.

[37] Forkan, Abdur Rahim Mohammad, Ibrahim Khalil, and Mohammed Atiquzzaman. "ViSiBiD: a learning model for early discovery and real-time prediction of severe clinical events using vital signs as big data." *Computer Networks* 113(2017): 244–257.

[38] Wu, Jing, He Li, Sherri Cheng, and Zhangxi Lin. "The promising future of healthcare services: when big data analytics meets wearable technology." *Information & Management* 53, no. 8 (2016): 1020–1033.

[39] Babar, Muhammad, Ataur Rahman, Fahim Arif, and Gwanggil Jeon. "Energy-harvesting based on internet of things and big data analytics for smart health monitoring." *Sustainable Computing: Informatics and Systems* 20 (2018): 155–164.

[40] Bochicchio, Mario A., Alfredo Cuzzocrea, Lucia Vaira, Antonella Longo, and Marco Zappatore. "Multidimensional mining over big healthcare data: a big data analytics framework." In *26th Italian Symposium on Advanced Database System*, SEBD, Castellaneta Marina, Italy, 2018.

[41] Firouzi, Farshad, Amir M. Rahmani, Kunal Mankodiya, Mustafa Badaroglu, Geoff V. Merrett, P. Wong, and Bahar Farahani. "Internet-of-things and big data for smarter healthcare: from device to architecture, applications and analytics." *Future Generation Computer Systems* 78 (2018): 583–586.

[42] Hsieh, Jui-Chien, Ai-Hsien Li, and Chung-Chi Yang. "Mobile, cloud, and big data computing: contributions, challenges, and new directions in telecardiology." *International Journal of Environmental Research and Public Health* 10, no. 11 (2013): 6131–6153.

[43] Najafabadi, Maryam M, Flavio Villanustre, Taghi M Khoshgoftaar, Naeem Seliya, Randall Wald, and Edin Muharemagic. "Deep learning applications and challenges in big data analytics." *Journal of Big Data* 2, no. 1 (2015): 1–21.

[44] White, Susan E. "A review of big data in health care: challenges and opportunities." *Open Access Bioinformatics* 6(2014): 13.

[45] Jagadish, Hosagrahar V, Johannes Gehrke, Alexandros Labrinidis, Yannis Papakonstantinou, Jignesh M. Patel, Raghu Ramakrishnan, and Cyrus Shahabi. "Big data and its technical challenges." *Communications of the ACM* 57, no. 7 (2014): 86–94.

[46] Hofman, Wout, and Madan Rajagopal. "A technical framework for data sharing." *Journal of Theoretical and Applied Electronic Commerce Research* 9, no. 3 (2014): 45–58.

[47] Ahmed, Imran, Misbah Ahmad, Gwanggil Jeon, and Francesco Piccialli. "A framework for pandemic prediction using big data analytics." *Big Data Research* 25 (2021): 100190.

[48] Mansour, Romany Fouad, Adnen El Amraoui, Issam Nouaouri, Vicente García Díaz, Deepak Gupta, and Sachin Kumar. "Artificial intelligence and internet of things enabled disease diagnosis model for smart healthcare systems." *IEEE Access* 9 (2021): 45137–45146.

[49] Rahman, Md Abdur, M. Shamim Hossain, Nabil A. Alrajeh, and Nadra Guizani. "B5G and explainable deep learning assisted healthcare vertical at the edge: covid-I9 perspective." *IEEE Network* 34, no. 4 (2020): 98–105.

[50] Ephzibah, EP, and R Sujatha. "Big data management with machine learning inscribed by domain knowledge for health care." *International Journal of Engineering & Technology* 6, no. 4 (2017): 98–102.

[51] Patan, Rizwan, GS Pradeep Ghantasala, Ramesh Sekaran, Deepak Gupta, and Manikandan Ramachandran. "Smart healthcare and quality of service in IoT using grey filter convolutional based cyber physical system." *Sustainable Cities and Society* 59(2020): 102141.

[52] Pramanik, Md Ileas, Raymond YK Lau, Haluk Demirkan, and Md Abul Kalam Azad. "Smart health: big data enabled health paradigm within smart cities." *Expert Systems with Applications* 87(2017): 370–383.

[53] Sakr, Sherif, and Amal Elgammal. "Towards a comprehensive data analytics framework for smart healthcare services." *Big Data Research* 4(2016): 44–58.

[54] Raghupathi, Wullianallur, and Viju Raghupathi. "Big data analytics in healthcare: promise and potential." *Health Information Science and Systems* 2, no. 1 (2014): 1–10.

[55] "Top 4 emerging tech trends in healthcare big data analytics." https://healthitanalytics. com/news/top-4-emerging-tech-trends-in-healthcare-big-data-analytics (accessed Jan. 22, 2022).

[56] Bohr, A, and K Memarzadeh, "The rise of artificial intelligence in healthcare applications," *Artificial Intelligence in Healthcare* 25 (2020), doi: 10.1016/B978-0-12-818438-7.00002-2.

[57] Marr, Bernard, "How is AI used in healthcare -5 powerful real-world examples that show the latest advances." https://www.forbes.com/sites/bernardmarr/2018/07/27/ how-is-ai-used-in-healthcare-5-powerful-real-world-examples-that-show-the-latest-advances/?sh=3c72ecb15dfb (accessed Jan. 22, 2022).

[58] Saidulu, D, and R Sasikala. "Understanding the challenges and opportunities with big data applications over â [euro] oesmart healthcare systemâ [euro]." *International Journal of Computer Applications* 160, no. 8 (2017).

[59] Li, Wei, Yuanbo Chai, Fazlullah Khan, Syed Rooh Ullah Jan, Sahil Verma, Varun G. Menon, and Xingwang Li. "A comprehensive survey on machine learning-based big data analytics for IoT-enabled smart healthcare system." *Mobile Networks and Applications* 26, no. 1 (2021): 234–252.

[60] Khan, Ibrahim Haleem, Mohd Khan, and Shahbaz Khan. "Challenges of IoT implementation in smart city development." In *Smart Cities—Opportunities and Challenges*, pp. 475–486. Springer, Singapore, 2020. https://link.springer.com/chapter/10.1007/978-981-15-2545-2_40

[61] Ishtiaq, Madeeha, Ateeq Ur Rehman, Fazlullah Khan, and Abdus Salam. "Performance Investigation of SR-HARQ transmission scheme in realistic cognitive radio system." In *2019 IEEE 9th Annual Computing and Communication Workshop and Conference (CCWC)*, pp. 0258–0263. IEEE, 2019.

[62] Hussain, Fatima, Syed Ali Hassan, Rasheed Hussain, and Ekram Hossain. "Machine learning for resource management in cellular and IoT networks: potentials, current solutions, and open challenges." *IEEE Communications Surveys & Tutorials* 22, no. 2 (2020): 1251–1275.

[63] Naha, Ranesh Kumar, Saurabh Garg, Andrew Chan, and Sudheer Kumar Battula. "Deadline-based dynamic resource allocation and provisioning algorithms in fog-cloud environment." *Future Generation Computer Systems* 104 (2020): 131–141.

[64] Zhou, Jun, Zhenfu Cao, Xiaolei Dong, and Athanasios V. Vasilakos. "Security and privacy for cloud-based IoT: challenges." *IEEE Communications Magazine* 55, no. 1 (2017): 26–33.

[65] Ali, Syed Arshad, Manzoor Ansari, and Mansaf Alam. "Resource management techniques for cloud-based IoT environment." In *Internet of Things (IoT)*, pp. 63–87. Springer, Cham, 2020. https://link.springer.com/chapter/10.1007/978-3-030-37468-6_4

[66] Mahindrakar, P., and M. Hanumanthappa. Data mining in healthcare: a survey of techniques and algorithms with its limitations and challenges. *International Journal of Engineering Research and Applications* 3 (2013): 937–941.

[67] Li, Wei, Yuanbo Chai, Fazlullah Khan, Syed Rooh Ullah Jan, Sahil Verma, Varun G. Menon, and Xingwang Li. "A comprehensive survey on machine learning-based big data analytics for IoT-enabled smart healthcare system. " *Mobile Networks and Applications* (2021): 1–19.

[68] Gill, SS, and R Buyya. Bio-inspired algorithms for big data analytics: a survey, taxonomy, and open challenges. In: *Big Data Analytics for Intelligent Healthcare Management*, pp. 1–17. Academic Press, Cambridge, MA, 2019. https://www.science-direct.com/science/article/pii/B9780128181461000015?via%3Dihub

[69] Wan, R, N Xiong, Q Hu, H Wang, and J Shang "Similarityaware data aggregation using fuzzy c-means approach for wireless sensor networks." *EURASIP Journal on Wireless Communications and Networking* 2019, no. 1 (2019): 59.

7 Cloud Computing-Assisted Real-Time Health Monitoring and Tracking

Amro Al-Said Ahmad and Nameer N. El-Emam
Philadelphia University

CONTENTS

7.1 INTRODUCTION

The healthcare systems have become one of the main targets for the health service sector. This increases the pressure on the quality and quantity of healthcare systems [1]. This sector faces many problems, such as insufficient resources and management for the resources and the high cost of providing a good level of healthcare [2]. Furthermore, the pressure on this sector has increased due to COVID-19 as the pandemic put an outstanding load on the health infrastructure, which cannot cope with such scales of health disasters [3]. This situation urged the health sector to transfer

DOI: 10.1201/9781003326182-7

101

to e-health environments immediately. E-healthcare systems are becoming an essential part of health services, especially in COVID-19, as patients need to be remotely monitored and advised.

In the current healthcare system that uses the Internet of things (IoT), sensors and intelligent systems to monitor and track patients are limited or privileged healthcare services [3]. However, such systems still have many challenges with service availability, quality of real-time monitoring, provisioning, scaling, and centralization [3,4].

Through the advent of cloud computing and its services, health real-time monitoring and tracking have become more accessible. Cloud computing delivers accurate medical information faster and more securely through several ready-to-use services. Thus, cloud computing has efficiency, speed, real-time, and data collecting and processing accuracy. In addition, users and consultants can be alerted to any abnormal case in real time if any monitored indicators are alerted. Incorporating cloud computing capabilities with e-health systems will allow consultants and patients to be a part of a better healthcare system.

The rise of using cloud computing in the healthcare sector has grown recently. According to market studies [5], the total market value of healthcare cloud computing is around 24 million US dollars. This is expected to grow by 2,026 to approximately 53 million US dollars with a 14.12% growth rate [5]. The coronavirus pandemic has sped up the adoption rate of cloud computing services in the healthcare sector regarding storage and data access to an on-demand pool of computing resources. In addition to using cloud computing capabilities to access patients' real-time indicators remotely and securely, cloud computing enables the platform to monitor the patients while in quarantine and allows healthcare workers to work remotely from home.

Incorporating cloud computing with IoT, sensors, and 5G monitoring will be beneficial as it can develop medical systems that can be more elastic and scalable in processing, data storage, and ubiquitous access. In addition, this will allow medical staff and patients to access shared health information and infrastructure and collect real-time related indicators [2,6,7].

This chapter discusses how cloud computing services facilitate and assist in real-time health monitoring and tracking. Then, how do cloud computing services and technologies provide individuals and consultants with accurate data?

The remainder of this chapter is organized as follows: Section 7.2 provides an overview of the cloud and its benefits for healthcare. Section 7.3 discusses cloud computing, real-time health monitoring, tracking, and healthcare applications with IoT and fog computing. Next, Section 7.4 introduces the need for cloud computing and healthcare in the COVID-19 era. Finally, we discuss cloud computing in real-time healthcare challenges.

7.2 CLOUD COMPUTING FOR HEALTHCARE

7.2.1 An Introduction to Cloud Computing

Cloud computing provides on-demand services delivered by resources on a cloud computing infrastructure (i.e., physical, hypervisor, and virtual servers) [8]. The cloud-based services are composed of (i) Infrastructure-as-a-Service (IaaS); (ii)

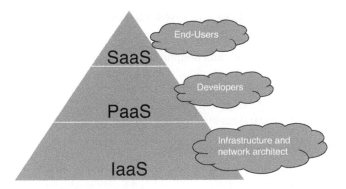

FIGURE 7.1   Cloud service models.

Platform-as-a-Service (PaaS); and (iii) Software-as-a-Service (SaaS) [9]. The software services are expected to scale dynamically with the growing or altering demand for the service, supported by the elastic cloud infrastructure [10]. In general, the development of SaaS is supported by the provision of the underlying PaaS and IaaS cloud-based services [11]. Figure 7.1 illustrates the hierarchy and connections between the three cloud service models.

Cloud services are deployed in four different models based on the type of user; public cloud (e.g., Amazon web service (AWS), IBM Cloud, Google Cloud, and Microsoft Azure), private/corporate cloud, community, and hybrid cloud.

7.2.1.1   Infrastructure-as-a-Service

IaaS provides a pool of on-demand computing resources, such as storage, network, virtual and physical firewalls, load-balancing, virtual local area networks (VLANs), auto-scaling mechanisms, hypervisors, internet protocol (IP) addresses, and virtualization (virtual instances). These services are provided to the consumers with a range of contractual guarantees (in the form of service-level agreement, SLA) by the cloud providers (vendors) about characteristics such as availability, capacity, and performance of the IaaS services.

7.2.1.2   Platform-as-a-Service

The PaaS model provides and facilitates the platforms needed to deploy software applications. The service provides the necessary operating systems, programming languages, web servers, and runtime environments that are necessary to install and host the application. This allows the consumer to deploy customer-owned or SaaS applications using tools provided and offered by the service provider or cloud vendors.

7.2.1.3   Software-as-a-Service

The SaaS model is at the top level of the hierarchy of the cloud computing paradigm. This means that the end users that use this model must outsource and rent both IaaS and PaaS from the same cloud providers. SaaS is a software application available on demand to cloud consumers through the pay-as-you-go model.

7.2.2   Benefits of Cloud Computing for Healthcare

To address the needs of health services and patients, cloud computing with its on-demand services, availability and ubiquitously, low-latency rates, scalability, and high performance. As a result, the cloud has transformed the health sector into a smart healthcare system [12–15]. Figure 7.2 illustrates cloud computing adoption's drivers in the health sector (adopted from [15]).

Some of the main potential benefits the cloud can offer are listed in the following.

7.2.2.1   Collaboration and Data Sharing

Cloud computing simplifies collaboration and data sharing among its users. The health-related information is stored in a centralized location which can be accessed in real time by relevant healthcare stakeholders in a secure way to preserve the required confidentiality of the data [16]. Furthermore, cloud computing facilitates the collecting, processing, and sharing of healthcare information among healthcare management structures [17] and between doctors, consultants, and patients. However, the architecture and design of such systems should focus on security and privacy aspects [15].

7.2.2.2   Scalability and Elasticity

One of the main advantages of the cloud paradigm is scalability and elasticity. Scalability commonly refers to the system's ability to scale and boost

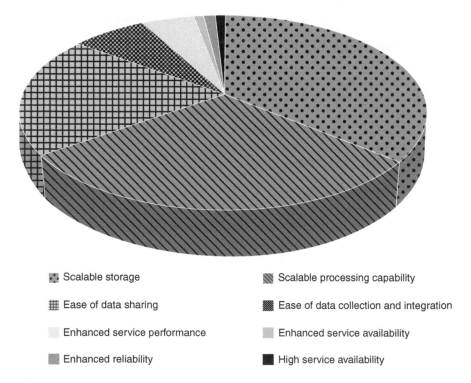

FIGURE 7.2   Cloud computing primary adoption drivers in healthcare.

performance by adding more computing resources at runtime [18]. This will make cloud software services more elastic. Furthermore, elasticity and scalability are supported by cloud computing providers by offering some services such as auto-scaling and load balancers, which enables the system to deal with sudden increases or decreases in demand by adding or removing computing resources at runtime [19].

The abovementioned cloud facilities are compatible to support the changing nature of healthcare systems and sectors. Due to new laws, pandemics, and financial adaptations. Cloud allows those migrated institutions to reconfigure their systems quickly with minimum human intervention. Furthermore, with the extended availability offered by the cloud (24/7, anytime, and anywhere), the system will increase or decrease the needed computing resources as per the need of healthcare stakeholders.

7.2.2.3 Security, Availability, and Reliability

The healthcare sector always has precautions and laws regarding patients, doctors, and health-related data and information. The protection and storage of these data should follow the laws, regulations, and standards for the security of electronic health data. In addition, such data are an attraction to malicious attacks and breaches.

Cloud computing is considered a scalable and elastic repository to store health-related data and information. In addition, cloud providers adopt multiple security mechanisms such as symmetric and asymmetric encryption (public and private key cipher), hashing, digital signature, identity and access management (IAM), cloud-based security groups, and single sign-on (SSO) [20]. Therefore, this will offer a better platform to secure the data stored in cloud-based storage, supporting the confidentiality and security of healthcare-related information.

In terms of reliability and availability, cloud computing provides multiple procedures to support fault tolerance to support reliability, availability, and throughput [21]. For example, cloud computing offers an elastic load balancer service that automatically distributes incoming demand across multiple computing resources (i.e., virtual machines). This service supports the SaaS fault tolerance capabilities by providing more scalable services [22]. In addition, the cloud offers redundancy techniques, automatic backups, and disaster recovery options [23].

7.2.2.4 Cost and Speed

Cloud computing offers to maintain a huge amount of data at a minimal cost as providers allow the migrated health organization to use the pay-as-you-go model. Outsourcing the information technology (IT) infrastructure (hardware and IT staffing) will reduce the overhead costs and allow health technical staff to focus on improving the patient's healthcare experience.

Cloud-based service providers support the upgrade and real-time updates with minimal human intervention of the services used by their clients, including health workers and patients. This benefits the healthcare sector to include faster access to medical information.

7.3 CLOUD COMPUTING-ASSISTED REAL-TIME HEALTH MONITORING AND TRACKING

7.3.1 HEALTHCARE APPLICATIONS WITH IOT AND FOG COMPUTING

The IoT and sensors have been used for healthcare systems. However, such systems still have many challenges with service availability, quality of real-time monitoring, provisioning, scaling, and centralization [3,4]. On the other hand, IoT offers smart devices connected to many nodes and connects them to a network that allows communication between nodes and devices. Therefore, integrating IoT and cloud computing will provide better platforms for healthcare applications to communicate with IoT devices and cloud services [4].

Healthcare IoT empowered by cloud services is about IoT-based applications for patients and consultants that enable the delivery of health services, such as real-time monitoring, healthcare IoT-based equipment tracking, and data sharing. Some recent research focuses on a real-time health monitoring system that integrates cloud, IoT, and 5G network [7], a real-time COVID-19 health monitoring system incorporating the use of IoT, cloud, and machine learning algorithm [24], and remote patient monitoring and classifying using cloud and IoT services [2]. Figure 7.3 illustrates the layers of IoT-enabled and cloud-based intelligent healthcare systems.

IoT and cloud computing integration allows the cloud to manage complex healthcare data and resources [25]. Cloud computing uses data centers to process, store, and deal with IoT streaming data from healthcare resources, devices, and stakeholders. However, this imposes more challenges such as delay latency and response time, privacy issues, and data protection [25]. Fog computing offers to shift from centralized computing to decentralized computing [4,25,26]. This allows fog computing to process the data analysis on the IoT devices (edges), supporting real-time processing, data privacy, and reducing time [4,25].

7.3.2 REAL-TIME HEALTH MONITORING AND TRACKING

Cloud computing provides IoT and fog computing foundations to collect and process health-related indicators and information [4,27]. Wearable sensors integrated into IoT nodes start to collect health indicators from the patients and transmit the collected data to fog or cloud computing (centralized or decentralized center) for storage and processing [4,27,28]. These data can be accessed or shared anytime and anywhere

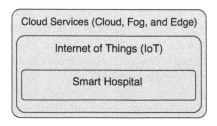

FIGURE 7.3   IoT-enabled and cloud-based intelligent healthcare systems.

through cloud services [29]. The way that cloud computing collects, shares, and preserves data is automatic, and in real time, all changes from any end will be tracked and monitored.

This facilitates setting up appropriate measurements in the patient monitoring IoT/cloud-based system to alarm the healthcare institutions about any potential health symptoms that could be life-threatening. In addition, this can automatically send a signal to the cloud data center or management system and change the case of the monitored patient from safe to unsafe [4,30]. Figure 7.4 illustrates monitoring and alerting systems in IoT, fog, and cloud-enabled healthcare systems. It shows that fog computing can help facilitate emergency circumstances alerts (i.e., abnormal vital indicators) directly from fog computing to the alerting system (i.e., ambulance system) without processing the alert inside the centralized cloud computing datacenter. This will help reduce the time of alerting the ambulance/specialist about a potential health risk, and this will enhance the quality of the healthcare service provided by the hospital/health center.

Recently published papers have presented work for real-time monitoring and health data tracking using IoT and related cloud computing technologies. For example, RESCUE [31] is an end-to-end framework for time-critical healthcare that integrates cloud technology with fog- and edge-based computing. This work presented experimental results that test the accuracy, delay, and power consumption of using the integration of IoT–edge–fog–cloud environments. Another aspect of newly published

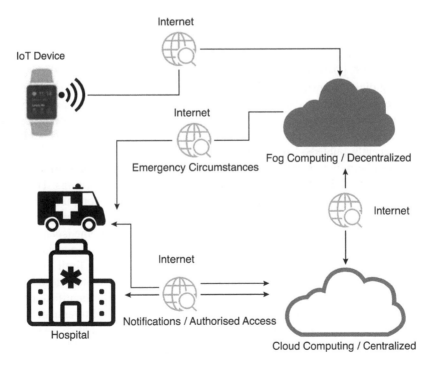

FIGURE 7.4   IoT, fog, and cloud-enabled healthcare paradigm.

papers focuses on using cloud computing capabilities to speed up the processing and monitoring of real-time healthcare data using some data science algorithms to increase the prediction rate. The authors of related studies [32,33] use effective data science techniques for IoT healthcare-monitoring systems that collect actual data and store it in cloud storage. They then use a forecasting algorithm connected to cloud data clustering that increases and enhances the prediction speed.

Incorporating fog and cloud computing into healthcare has not just contributed to decreasing healthcare service costs. This merging of technologies reduces the response time from request to request between IoT devices and data centers. As all devices connected to the healthcare system turn into a node to process data and manage tasks. Hence, this will decrease requests to the central cloud, which reduces the latency time [34]. This will increase the efficiency of the healthcare system as it reduces the processing overhead and number of requests between parts of the system.

7.4 THE NEED FOR CLOUD COMPUTING AND HEALTHCARE IN THE COVID-19 ERA

The impact of the COVID-19 pandemic forced all sectors to remote work [35], which put a challenge on the information and communication technology (ICT) platforms and solutions. This challenge has imposed multiple obstacles to finding suitable ways of working, teaching, and getting essential services. As a result, many sectors, including health and health education, are forced to use multiple platforms to facilitate their services [36].

Cloud computing offers many benefits that support the adoption of its services to the health sector: collaboration, data sharing, scalability and elasticity, security, availability, reliability mechanisms, and other attributes. This facilitates online services during COVID-19. In addition, the cloud provides an advanced infrastructure for enabling digital transformation by allowing and simplifying the work of health organizations to detect, track, and monitor newly infected COVID-19 patients [37]. In addition, cloud computing of various resources and services allows for building a healthcare system at scale and supports large-scale use [27].

Some recently published papers have studied the need for cloud computing in the COVID-19 era. For example, Shakor and Surameery [38] provide work to facilitate and secure COVID-19 health data by applying encryption algorithms. The work concludes that the security, flexibility, and availability of cloud computing make it suitable for storing COVID-19 sensitive data in the health sector. Another recent work [39] provides a cloud-based solution to monitor patients at home isolation. The proposed end-to-end framework for COVID-19 enables real-time monitoring, offers early detection for infected patients, and tracks patient contacts to limit the spread of the virus. In addition, the work [40] presented a novel IoT-fog-cloud-based healthcare system that monitors COVID-19 and can help in the early identification and prediction of COVID-19 virus infection. Other works contributed to enhancing the monitoring service of COVID-19 patients and trying to track any changes in the vital indicators of the COVID-19 patients to alert the healthcare staff [41–43].

This facilitates the monitoring and evaluation of COVID-19 virus infection in patients and allows for tracking, processing, and retrieving medical data to alert consultants or health workers of any abnormal case in vital indicators of COVID-19 patients. Furthermore, using artificial intelligence (AI) algorithms incorporated with the cloud-based healthcare system to predict and identify the early stage of infection, thus, will help to slow the spread of the virus.

7.5 CLOUD COMPUTING IN REAL-TIME HEALTHCARE CHALLENGES

Cloud computing enables many potentials and benefits to the health sector, especially when incorporated with IoT and fog computing. However, some challenges are imposed when using these empowering technologies. Large-scale scalability is a significant technical challenge. Healthcare cloud-based systems are required to deal with rapidly increasing data volumes (e.g., widespread 5G mobile video streaming for live monitoring) and the delivery through a considerable number of service points (e.g., millions to billions of IoT devices). This will pressurize cloud computing to deal with health workloads from different locations.

Security and privacy are sensitive and significant issues in cloud computing and healthcare. The advance in these technologies makes it a target for cyber-attacks. For example, IoT devices or fog computing nodes help attackers gain access to the whole structure of the systems [4]. Therefore, this needs collaboration from all parties related to the healthcare system, cloud providers, hospitals, and IoT vendors to enforce security mechanisms and policies. Furthermore, data is stored in cloud-based healthcare depending on the cloud vendor architecture. This exposes multiple issues such as high latency (i.e., the time delay between the request at one destination and getting the response from the other destination) and legal objections [34].

Big data is a huge and forthcoming challenge due to the heterogeneity of sources, formats, and data attributes from constant real-time monitoring [15]. This challenge imposes the use of intelligent ways of storing, processing, and retrieving diverse medical data. This needs big data analytics and machine learning algorithms to help deal with the amount, velocity, and heterogeneity of the collected medical data [44].

7.6 CONCLUSIONS

Through the advent of cloud computing and its services, health real-time monitoring and tracking have become more accessible. Cloud computing delivers accurate medical information faster and more securely through several ready-to-use services. E-healthcare systems are becoming an essential part of health services, especially in COVID-19, as patients need to be remotely monitored and advised. Thus, cloud computing efficiency is based on processing speed, working on real-time systems, and processing accuracy for data collection. Users and consultants can be alerted to any abnormal case in real time if any monitored indicators are alerted. Incorporating cloud computing capabilities with e-health systems will allow consultants and patients to be a part of a better healthcare system.

Nevertheless, some challenges are still imposed in using cloud computing incorporated with IoT and fog computing for healthcare, such as privacy, security, and scaling. First, this chapter discusses the computing services that facilitate and assist in real-time health monitoring and tracking, and then discusses cloud computing services and technologies that provide individuals and consultants with accurate data. Finally, the chapter discusses the challenges facing healthcare systems accompanied by cloud computing.

REFERENCES

[1] Joshi J, Kurian D, Bhasin S, et al. Health monitoring using wearable sensor and cloud computing. *2016 International Conference on Cybernetics, Robotics and Control (CRC)*. IEEE; 2016. pp. 104–108. DOI: 10.1109/CRC.2016.031.

[2] Iranpak S, Shahbahrami A, Shakeri H. Remote patient monitoring and classifying using the internet of things platform combined with cloud computing. *J. Big Data*. 2021;8. DOI: 10.1186/s40537-021-00507-w.

[3] Singh N, Raza M, Paranthaman VV, et al. Chapter 10- Internet of things and cloud computing. In: Godfrey A, Stuart SBT-DH, editors. *Digital Health Exploring Use and Integration of Wearables*. Academic Press; 2021. pp. 151–162. https://www.sciencedirect.com/science/article/pii/B9780128189146000132.

[4] Dang LM, Piran M, Han D, et al. A survey on internet of things and cloud computing for healthcare. *Electronics*. 2019;8:768. DOI: 10.3390/electronics8070768.

[5] Mordor Intelligence. Healthcare cloud computing market - Growth, trends, Covid-19 Impact, and forecasts (2021–2026) [Internet]. 2021. Available From: https://www.mordorintelligence.com/industry-reports/global-healthcare-cloud-computing-market-industry.

[6] Shahzad A, Lee YS, Lee M, et al. Real-time cloud-based health tracking and monitoring system in designed boundary for cardiology patients. *J. Sensors*. 2018. DOI: 10.1155/2018/3202787.

[7] Zhang Y, Chen G, Du H, et al. Real-time remote health monitoring system driven by 5G MEC-IoT. *Electronics*. 2020;9:1753. DOI: 10.3390/electronics9111753.

[8] IBM Cloud. Defining IaaS vs. PaaS vs. SaaS. [cited 2022 Apr 11]. Available From: https://www.ibm.com/uk-en/cloud/learn/iaas-paas-saas.

[9] Kaur PD, Chana I. Cloud based intelligent system for delivering health care as a service. *Comput. Methods Programs Biomed*. 2014;113:346–359. DOI: 10.1016/j.cmpb.2013.09.013.

[10] Jia C, Cai Y, Yu YT, et al. 5W+1H pattern: A perspective of systematic mapping studies and a case study on cloud software testing. *J. Syst. Softw*. 2016;116:206–219 [Intrenet]. Available From: http://linkinghub.elsevier.com/retrieve/pii/S0164121215000370.

[11] Armbrust M, Fox A, Griffith R, et al. A view of cloud computing. *Commun. ACM*. 2010;53:50–58.

[12] Chen M. NDNC-BAN: Supporting rich media healthcare services via named data networking in cloud-assisted wireless body area networks. *Inf. Sci. (Ny)*. 2014;284:142–156. DOI: 10.1016/j.ins.2014.06.023.

[13] Deng M, Petkovic M, Nalin M, et al. A home healthcare system in the cloud–addressing security and privacy challenges. *2011 IEEE 4th International Conference on Cloud Computing*. IEEE; 2011. pp. 549–556. DOI: 10.1109/CLOUD.2011.108.

[14] Cimler R, Matyska J, Sobeslav V. Cloud based solution for mobile healthcare application. *Proceedings of the 18th International Database Engineering & Applications Symposium*. 2014. pp. 298–301. DOI: 10.1145/2628194.2628217.

[15] Aceto G, Persico V, Pescapé A. Industry 4.0 and health: Internet of things, big data, and cloud computing for healthcare 4.0. *J. Ind. Inf. Integr*. 2020;18:100129. DOI: 10.1016/j.jii.2020.100129.

[16] Sultan N. Making use of cloud computing for healthcare provision: Opportunities and challenges. *Int. J. Inf. Manage.* 2014;34:177–184. DOI: 10.1016/j.ijinfomgt.2013.12.011.

[17] Li Z-R, Chang E-C, Huang K-H, et al. A secure electronic medical record sharing mechanism in the cloud computing platform. *2011 IEEE 15th International Symposium on Consumer Electronics (ISCE).* IEEE; 2011. pp. 98–103. DOI: 10.1109/ISCE.2011.5973792.

[18] Vaquero LM, Rodero-Merino L, Buyya R. Dynamically scaling applications in the cloud. *ACM SIGCOMM Comput. Commun. Rev.* 2011;41:45–52. DOI: 10.1145/1925861. 1925869.

[19] Al-Said Ahmad A, Andras P. Scalability analysis comparisons of cloud-based software services. *J. Cloud Comput.* 2019;8. DOI: 10.1186/s13677-019-0134-y.

[20] Erl T, Puttini R, Mahmood Z. *Cloud Computing: Concepts, Technology, & Architecture.* Pearson Education; 2013.

[21] Kumari P, Kaur P. A survey of fault tolerance in cloud computing. *J. King Saud Univ. - Comput. Inf. Sci.* [Internet]. 2021;33:1159–1176. Available From: http://www.sciencedirect.com/science/article/pii/S1319157818306438.

[22] Mesbahi M, Rahmani AM. Load balancing in cloud computing: A state of the art survey. *Int. J. Mod. Educ. Comput. Sci.* 2016;8:64. DOI: 10.5815/ijmecs.2016.03.08.

[23] Mesbahi MR, Rahmani AM, Hosseinzadeh M. Reliability and high availability in cloud computing environments: A reference roadmap. *Human-centric Comput. Inf. Sci.* 2018;8:1–31. DOI: 10.1186/s13673-018-0143-8.

[24] Dileep P, Thogaru M. Real time cloud computing based COVID-19 health monitoring system using IOT with integration of machine learning approach to create safety environment. *Ann. Rom. Soc. Cell Biol.* 2021; 25:2076–2086.

[25] Pareek K, Tiwari PK, Bhatnagar V. Fog computing in healthcare: A review. *IOP Conference Series: Materials Science and Engineering.* IOP Publishing; 2021. pp. 12025. DOI: 10.1109/ISCC.2018.8538671.

[26] Truong H-L, Dustdar S. Principles for engineering IoT cloud systems. *IEEE Cloud Comput.* 2015;2:68–76.

[27] Wang Q, Su M, Zhang M, et al. Integrating digital technologies and public health to fight covid-19 pandemic: Key technologies, applications, challenges and outlook of digital healthcare. *Int. J. Environ. Res. Public Health.* 2021;18:6053. DOI: 10.3390/ijerph18116053.

[28] Rolim CO, Koch FL, Westphall CB, et al. A cloud computing solution for patient's data collection in health care institutions. *2010 Second International Conference on eHealth, Telemedicine, and Social Medicine.* IEEE; 2010. p. 95–99. DOI: 10.1109/eTELEMED.2010.19.

[29] Joyia GJ, Liaqat RM, Farooq A, et al. Internet of medical things (IoMT): Applications, benefits and future challenges in healthcare domain. *J. Commun.* 2017;12:240–247. DOI: 10.12720/jcm.12.4.240-247.

[30] Verma P, Sood SK, Kalra S. Cloud-centric IoT based student healthcare monitoring framework. *J. Ambient Intell. Humaniz. Comput.* 2018;9:1293–1309. DOI: 10.1007/s12652-017-0520-6.

[31] Das J, Ghosh S, Mukherjee A, et al. RESCUE: Enabling green healthcare services using integrated IoT-edge-fog-cloud computing environments. *Softw. Pract. Exp.* 2022; DOI: 10.1002/spe.3078.

[32] M Abd El-Aziz R, Alanazi R, R Shahin O, et al. An effective data science technique for IoT-Assisted healthcare monitoring system with a rapid adoption of cloud computing. *Comput. Intell. Neurosci.* 2022;2022. DOI: 10.1155/2022/7425846.

[33] Lakshmanan K, Arumugam S. An efficient data science technique for IoT assisted healthcare monitoring system using cloud computing. *Concurr. Comput. Pract. Exp.* 2022;e6857. DOI: 10.1002/cpe.6857.

[34] Kamruzzaman MM, Yan B, Sarker MNI, et al. Blockchain and fog computing in IoT-driven healthcare services for smart cities. *J. Healthc. Eng.* 2022;2022. DOI: 10.1155/2022/9957888.

[35] Devarajan M, Subramaniyaswamy V, Vijayakumar V, et al. Fog-assisted personalized healthcare-support system for remote patients with diabetes. *J. Ambient Intell. Humaniz. Comput.* 2019;10:3747–3760. DOI: 10.1007/s12652-019-01291-5.

[36] Alhomdy S, Thabit F, Abdulrazzak FH, et al. The role of cloud computing technology: A savior to fight the lockdown in COVID 19 crisis, the benefits, characteristics and applications. *Int. J. Intell. Networks.* 2021;2:166–174. DOI: 10.1016/j.ijin.2021.08.001.

[37] Singh RP, Haleem A, Javaid M, et al. Cloud computing in solving problems of covid-19 pandemic. *J. Ind. Integr. Manag.* 2021;06:209–219. DOI: 10.1142/S2424862221500044.

[38] Shakor MY, Surameery NMS. Built-in encrypted health cloud environment for sharing covid-19 data. *2021 3rd International Conference on Computer Communication and the Internet (ICCCI).* IEEE; 2021. pp. 96–101. DOI: 10.1109/ICCCI51764.2021.9486774.

[39] El-Rashidy N, El-Sappagh S, Islam SM, et al. End-to-end deep learning framework for coronavirus (COVID-19) detection and monitoring. *Electronics.* 2020;9:1439. DOI: 10.3390/electronics9091439.

[40] Ahanger TA, Tariq U, Nusir M, et al. A novel IoT–fog–cloud-based healthcare system for monitoring and predicting COVID-19 outspread. *J. Supercomput.* 2022;78:1783–1806. DOI: 10.1007/s11227-021-03935-w.

[41] Nasser N, Emad-ul-Haq Q, Imran M, et al. A smart healthcare framework for detection and monitoring of COVID-19 using IoT and cloud computing. *Neural Comput. Appl.* 2021;1–15. DOI: 10.1007/s00521-021-06396-7.

[42] Ye Q, Zhou J, Wu H. Using information technology to manage the COVID-19 pandemic: Development of a technical framework based on practical experience in China. *JMIR Med. Informatics.* 2020;8:e19515. DOI: 10.2196/19515.

[43] Tang Z, Hu H, Xu C, et al. Exploring an efficient remote biomedical signal monitoring framework for personal health in the covid-19 pandemic. *Int. J. Environ. Res. Public Health.* 2021;18:9037. DOI: 10.3390/ijerph18179037.

[44] Raghupathi W, Raghupathi V. Big data analytics in healthcare: Promise and potential. *Heal. Inf. Sci. Syst.* 2014;2:1–10. DOI: 10.1186/2047-2501-2-3.

8 Supervision of Worldwide Healthcare through an IoT-Based System

Santosh Kumar Srivastava and Sunil Kumar Maakar
Galgotias University

Hare Ram Singh
GNIOT

Durgesh Srivastava
Chitkara University

Praveen Kantha
BRCM CET

CONTENTS

DOI: 10.1201/9781003326182-8

8.1 INTRODUCTION

In today's time, when there is the computer internet and its various technologies like artificial intelligence (AI) and machine learning, it would not be wrong to say that the Internet of things (IoT) is the technology revolution of today's era. Not long ago, our thinking used to say that everything in the universe was considered an object, but with the beginning of IoT [1], this technology has changed our thinking. Today, this technology forces us to believe that everything can be made smart, whether it is an inanimate object or a human. This technology allows them to communicate with each other, i.e., living and non-living things, through internet technologies [2]. Today, this technology builds such a bridge between humans and machines through the internet, removing all the time and distance barriers, making it physically true that even inanimate objects can become smart objects. With the beginning of the IoT, there has been such a big change in our thinking that now we can think of even those things we could not think of before, and this technology is proving itself by making those dreams come true, for example. Everything we see today, whether it is a home washing machine, a TV, a road light, or a car, starts doing our instructions only after being told by us, so our expectations are increasing more and more from this technology, and we believe that this technology has all the potential that we imagine. Today's research is always trying to find new experiments and discoveries to satisfy the expectations of others, but it would not be wrong to believe that this process is still infinite [3]. In the 1990s, the utility of the internet in the business and customer market had just started, the reason being that the speed of the internet was slow, due to which our limits were limited. It has led to more businesses online, although these devices are still primarily the internet for things that require more human interaction and monitoring through apps and the internet [1]. Research also says that the IoT, which does not include personal computers, tablets, PCs, and smartphones, will have 26 billion units installed by 2022, almost 30 times more than 0.9 billion in 2009 [1,2].

Motivation: The motivation behind this work came from the consistently rising demand for AI and IoT devices in our day-to-day life [4]. These cutting-edge technologies have the power to influence the working methodologies of humans and machines strongly. Unfortunately, life is too busy and fast [5]. My motivation for making this article is to help patients with the help of the current technological growth of IoT. If science helps humans, it is the most important and precious motivation.

Major contribution and objective: This article elaborates on the technological enhancement of artificial intelligence and IoT. Our contribution to the article is to touch every area of the IoT in the healthcare sector and illustrate the use of important sensors which can be helpful for the medical field.

In this article, we have illustrated the specifications and uses of the sensors. They provide power to the IoT technology, and when the IoT is done with the help of artificial intelligence, this combination becomes the future of the healthcare sector. Our objective is to introduce IoT technology into every area of the healthcare sector to provide better services for every human being. Our objective is to explore the sensors that can be helpful in the healthcare sector.

8.2 BACKGROUND

8.2.1 Expansion of the Healthcare System

Initial investigations are focused on changing the technology and getting the right treatment. Figure 8.1 expresses the timeline showing the first scan of the actual treatment system and the layout of the users and services [6–8].

This study suggests that individual healthcare providers should use systems healthcare systems that can be used anywhere and at any time. Create a complete treatment plan [9,10]. Your healthcare system needs to have a high-tech product to accomplish this task. Sensor technologies: Network and information processing technologies may be key for better medical systems. IoT aims to connect and integrate with any facility anywhere in any environment or network and service. Broad-spectrum health systems can be developed to promote IoT in health systems [11]. The expansion of the healthcare system is depicted in Figure 8.2.

8.2.2 Healthcare and IoT by Using IT Infrastructure

Without technological help, it is very difficult to even think of a top-notch healthcare system. Today, it is highly technical and involves sensor networks and data processing [12]. With the help of these, we can imagine a model of the healthcare structure, clearly marked in Figure 8.3. Under the health record system, this technology has also been included in this technology: software for data processing, digital image processing, and diagnosis, and an electronic healthcare system. A comparative study of various research has revealed that IoT is providing more potential in the field of medicine and the field of health; there is a lot of improvement in the quality of IoT in comparison to the old methods, access to care, and the most important thing is that this makes the cost relatively low. IoT ensures health care to such patients who live in far-flung places and cannot easily access health-related services. Research on IoT has revealed that mobile healthcare systems should be ensured [13,14]. Micro-wireless physiological sensor continues to provide meaningful data streams for

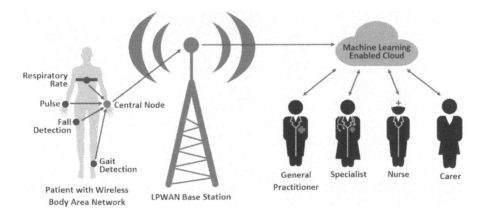

FIGURE 8.1 Overview of the proposed model.

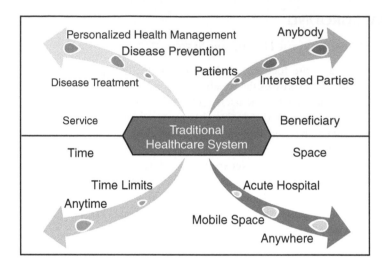

FIGURE 8.2 The expansion of healthcare systems.

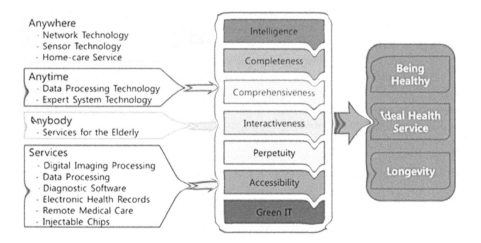

FIGURE 8.3 The paradigm of an ideal healthcare system.

better decision-making. This research by IoT has ensured that micro-wireless video logical sensors combined with smart mobile devices can be optimally used for continuous care monitoring and monitoring of patients in emergencies, taking care of them, treating them, and applying the alarm ring in an unavoidable situation. In this context, IoT uses sensor technology to collect all kinds of patient data for end sharing to the mobile healthcare system. Under this technology, the IoT platform for health care has been proposed as a suitable administration model for chronic diseases like obesity, hypertension, and diabetes. Under this research, the model presented for better integration and use of IoT in health care has four phases [13,15].

In the first phase, such sensors have been used so that the patient can be tracked and monitored anywhere. In the second phase, all the data from the sensors installed in his body can be processed. Data processing technology has been used in the third phase by providing proper information to every part of the body, immediately acting as an ideal health service. The service has been kept in mind in the final and fourth phases of research. A thorough study of the information received has been conducted, including digital image processing data processing diagnosis software [16,17].

The IoT is a device system combining applications, sensors, and network connectivity. It is a mixture whose function is to collect data in the best possible way with the help of all these sensors and make decisions from that information. When it comes to health-related services, the biggest feature of the IoT is that it continuously monitors remote patients through its various types of technology sensors in a better way and when needed. It keeps on giving information, like an alarm system. The biggest example of this is that where a patient has to be monitored round the clock as if he/she/they is in the intensive care unit (ICU) and even then the doctor is not able to sit near him/her/them all the time, and in such a situation, when his/her/their health suddenly starts deteriorating, then it is difficult to alert the doctor. It happens. In countries like India, whose medical system is still not that advanced and there is a huge shortage of doctors, in such a situation, technology like the IoT is helping us in our present times as a medical revolution [18].

Currently, the technology of IoT is being tested on many different types of patients as part of treating and monitoring patients with Parkinson's disease. Using this technology for regular monitoring of a person suffering from this disease, with the help of CCTV cameras around his/her/their house, the patient's walking pattern, any copy generated in his/her/their body, and all other methods of normal activity levels [19,20]. A high-quality sensor can be used to see and keep it on. Researchers emphasizing this technology also believe that with the help of AI and machine learning, the future of this technology can be very bright and generate multi-faceted plans in treatment [21].

8.3 A MODEL FOR IoT-BASED HEALTHCARE SYSTEMS IN THE FUTURE

A few framework planning requirements are revealed after a review of various existing IoT-based medical service frameworks [1]. The use of sensors to measure patients' well-being is the subject of these investigations. All agree that worn sensors, especially remote and remotely wearable ones, are crucial to their different frameworks. According to a few sources, natural or vision-based sensors should also be utilized around the home. However, this restricts the framework's use to a single physical site. All necessary sensors should be carried out as a small, easy-to-wear hub. Patients will be able to follow their health in a non-intrusive and pleasant manner wherever they go. Patients would be more willing to use health-monitoring devices if implanted sensors or cameras were not obligatory. Also, replacing or fixing remotely worn hubs would be forthright compared to fixed sensors or vision-based devices put in the house [1,22].

Every week, 168,000 new information focuses would be created if 1,000 people wore a single pulse sensor that interacted hourly with a distributed storage data set over an Low-Power Wide-Area Network (LPWAN). As more people wear sensors linked to the distributed storage system, and as new types of sensors become available, this number will rise. AI computations may be performed in the cloud's high-figuring environment using massive amounts of data that swiftly frame and fill distributed storage [1,23]. These equations might be used to sift through a large amount of data, identify previously undiscovered illness patterns, and provide diagnoses, treatment recommendations, and other services [24].

In light of these recent advances in the literature, we propose and support a four-section paradigm, as seen in Figure 8.1, to help create future IoT medical services frameworks, which will be described in further detail below. The sections that follow go further into each component of the projected paradigm. In key parts, the previously published material is presented and discussed. Finally, the benefits and drawbacks of momentum improvements are examined as potential research subjects for the future [25].

8.3.1 CENTRAL NODES AND WEARABLE SENSORS

Sensors that operate on physiological parameters are known as wearable sensor devices. The essential signals of heart rate, breathing rate, and internal temperature level are recommended sensors since they are the fundamental final needed for maintaining basic health. Pulse and blood oxygen sensors are two other sensors that might be used, as these borders are frequently crossed by the three essential signals [25–27]. For frameworks focusing on a certain condition, unique reason sensors such as blood-glucose, fall detection, and joint point sensors might be incorporated. The sensor hubs provide data to the focus hub. It analyses the information, may provide instructions, and then sends the data to an outside locality. A devoted, focused hub would be similar to a mobile phone in that battery life might be enhanced by taking only the features necessary for a medical IoT system [25].

8.3.2 COMMUNICATIONS WITHIN A SHORT DISTANCE

A short-range specialized technique is required for sensor connection to the focal hub. Many significant factors to reflect on once adopting a short-range exchange standard impact the human body, security, and dormancy [28]. The selected strategy should have no negative consequences on the human body since such belongings somewhat might cause people to develop further health difficulties. It should also have robust security safeguards to prevent unauthorized access to critical patient information. Finally, low dormancy is crucial for time-basic frameworks like one that checks fundamental well-being and requires a rescue vehicle if necessary [27]. In such cases, period intervals might mean the difference between life and death. In non-time-based requests, low dormancy is less important, yet it is still desirable [29–32].

8.3.3 LONG-DISTANCE COMMUNICATIONS

The information collected by the focal hub is only helpful if it can be put to good use. Therefore, this data should be provided to a data collection where it can be securely accessible by the right people (for example, overseers or specialists) [33]. When choosing suitable long-range communication rules for use in a medical care framework, security, blunder-correcting abilities, vigor against impedance, low inactivity, and high accessibility should be considered. Short-range interactions also need excellent security to ensure that critical patient data remains reserved and cannot be altered or duplicated. Low idleness is critical in time-sensitive applications such as crisis medical services, where delays in data transfer might harm patients. Excellent error-correcting skills and crucial energy in adversity are required [28,34].

It is important because it guarantees that the message sent is as old as the data acknowledged. It is critical in all medical settings, especially in crisis circumstances. Finally, good accessibility is required to guarantee that messages are delivered consistently, regardless of the patient's actual location. It is particularly critical for time-based applications, although many frameworks may benefit [35,36].

8.3.4 Protected Cloud Storage Architecture and Machine Learning

Clinical data collected from the patients should be properly kept for future use. Specialists are at an advantage by knowing a patient's medical antiquity, and AI will not be useful until large data sets are accessible. As a consequence, distributed storage is the best technique for data storage. Making medical service specialists accessible without jeopardizing security, on the other hand, is a key difficulty that experts creating medical services IoT frameworks should solve [37].

Furthermore, although AI has been mentioned in the collected works as an approach for enlightening medical care systems, it has not been properly investigated. Diagnostics and treatment plans: AI allows for detecting previously undiscovered patterns in clinical data, developing treatment plans and diagnostics, and transmitting explicit recommendations to medical practitioners for individual patients. Consequently, distributed storage architectures should be built to facilitate AI execution on large informative indexes [38–40].

8.4 HEALTHCARE SYSTEMS THAT CAN BE WORN

Consequently, the growth of precise sensors having a less structured factor is critical to the growth of such a framework. This article focuses on non-obtrusive and non-prominent sensors, avoiding implanted sensors. Consider the following five sensors: three for monitoring pulse, respiration rate, and internal heat level, and more for measuring circulatory strains and the oxygen levels in the blood, all of which are regularly recorded in a health clinic setting [41,42].

8.4.1 Pulse Sensors

The heartbeat may detect heart failure, aspiratory embolisms, and vasovagal syncope, among other emergency conditions. Therefore, beat sensors have been widely studied for clinical and wellness purposes [43].

The chest, wrist, ear cartilage, fingertip, and other sites may detect heartbeats.

Although ear cartilage and fingertip readings are accurate, they are not particularly wearable. While a chest-worn framework is wearable, wrist sensors are often selected for long-term wearability [44].

A few commercially marketed wellness-following chest ties and wristwatches with heartbeat estimation capacity are available: Garmin HRM-Tri, Polar H7, Fitbit Pure Pulse, and TomTom Spark Cardio. Regardless, each of these firms claims that its products are not intended for clinical use and should not be used to diagnose medical issues. Consequently, these devices' detecting frameworks are difficult to integrate into a simple health-monitoring framework [43].

Developing efficient methods for recognizing beats has taken a lot of time and effort. The sensor types created, employed, and broken down in ongoing research are tension, photoplethysmographic (PPG), ultrasonic, and radio frequency (RF) sensors [45–47].

An LED shines light into the conduit once a photodiode detects the amount that has not been consumed [37]. A PPG pulse sensor is depicted in Figure 8.4.

Figure 8.5 depicts blood as an energy source. Changes in light measurement may be recorded, allowing for calculating a heart rate while still in the air. This work employs PPG sensors to assess heart rate, beat rate inconstancy, and blood oxygen in a single compact wrist-worn sensor. Because movement impacts the accuracy of heartbeat readings from PPG sensors, an accelerometer is utilized to check for movement. The gadget changes to a low-power mode and stops recording beats when there is a lot of movement. It is not completely correct since the heartbeat is important when there is a lot of movement, such as when someone is seizing or has cardiovascular difficulties when exercising. Working on heartbeat sensor accuracy is better than ignoring signals while development levels are low when moving. The stakes are astronomically high [1,2].

Movement effects on PPG sensors are reduced by using two separate light-emitting diode (LED) sources and contrasting the amount of light received at the photodiode. Movement remnants are considerably minimized due to this approach, resulting in improved signal quality [1,48].

Pressure sensors simulate a medical care practitioner physically checking the outspread heartbeat by pressing down with their fingers. As illustrated in Figure 8.5, the

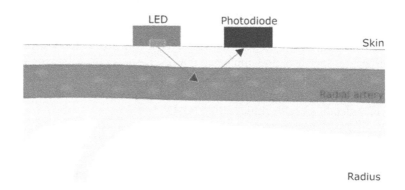

FIGURE 8.4   Photoplethysmographic pulse sensor.

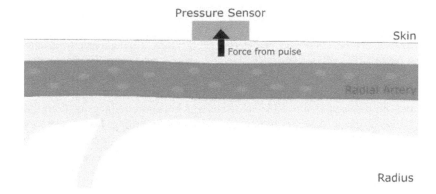

FIGURE 8.5   Pressure-based pulse sensor.

sensor is firmly pushed on the wrist, and strain is regularly monitored to provide a heartbeat waveform.

The creation and testing of a flexible and sensitive strain sensor for beat identification have shown promising results. On the other hand, expanding the affectability to more likely identifiable beats increases the amount of disturbance detected due to the wearer's growth. Furthermore, this sensor was only tested in very calm environments; therefore, additional study is required to see whether it performs well in motion.

Beat sensor modules with nine PPG sensors and one strain sensor are built by combining pressure sensors with PPG sensors. The heartbeat is measured from several locations on the wrist, resulting in clear heartbeat data and the ability to use these readings to diagnose specific conditions like diabetes [49,50].

8.4.2   Sensors for Respiratory Rate

The number of breaths and respiratory rate every minute is another crucial indication. Asthma attacks, anxiety-induced hyperventilation, apnea situations, cellular breakdown in the lungs, aviation route deterrents, tuberculosis, and other disorders may be detected by observing breath [51].

Because breathing is so important, several earlier studies have resulted in sensors that can detect respiratory rate. Many different types of respiration rate sensors were identified during research in earlier studies. The first is a thermistor-based nasal sensor, which is used. Exhaled air is hotter than the ambient temperature, which serves as the sensor's reference point. Overall, the sensor counts the number of breaths by sensing temperature rises and falls. However, other causes of temperature changes, such as when worn by a culinary expert working in a kitchen, may impair accuracy. Wearing it is also bothersome since it is obstructive and obtrusive.

An echocardiogram (ECG) signal may also be utilized to determine the breathing rate. ECG-derived respiration (EDR) is a method for identifying breath patterns and apnea occurrences using ECG [2]. Although it is again limited by wear capacity, this approach meticulously studies the respire conservative rate. ECG contacts are unpleasant and nearly always induce skin inflammation when worn continuously. Because ECG contacts are not reusable, they should be replaced regularly [1,2].

The respiratory rate may also be determined by using a mouthpiece to distinguish between breaths. The researchers wanted to see whether wheezing was a common side effect among asthmatics. The problem with utilizing a mouthpiece is that it will be utterly ineffective in the presence of external noise, making it unsuitable for long-term usage.

A fiber-optic sensor in a flexible substrate was built in one investigation; then, it was sensitive ample to detect pulsations prompted by breathing. It is shown to work in a solitary test, but it is uncertain if it would work in other situations. Moreover, this delicate material would be helpless to vibrations from several causes, including walking. Therefore, it is necessary to do more tests [52,53].

A strain-type sensor was created. Two capacitive plates, one on each side of the center, are equally separated. Considering an estimate of respiratory rate, the plates move wider apart during inner breath and expiration and then closer together during inward breath and exhalation. The accuracy of respiratory rate calculations was determined to be 95% when compared to a nasal sensor. It is more comfortable to wear than the nasal sensor it was compared. The idea of a tension sensor, on the other hand, may indicate that it is powerless to protest if it is affected by external stresses, such as walking against the wind [1].

A stretch sensor to determine breathing rate is a common practice. Stretch sensors are those whose features change due to exerting elastic force, such as when inhaling deeply.

The suggested sensor was made using a ferroelectric polymer transducer that produced a charge when tractable power was applied. The respiratory rate is considered while computing the progressions in this charge. Even though this sensor seemed to get a decent signal, its accuracy was not confirmed by a link to respiratory rate, as determined in numerous ways [54]. The respiration rate sensors employed change in opposition. The resistance rises as more power is applied to the sensor. The breathing rate may be determined using the voltage fluctuations induced by changing protections.

According to Atalay et al., movement antiquities were accessible when strolling and other developments were made. Furthermore, while sitting at a workstation, breathing was exact at 3.3 breaths per minute; nevertheless, the chance for mistakes rose when development was offered. Consequently, the sensor's limitation is that diverse developments might lead the sensor to receive malleable power, allowing the sensor to confuse development with relaxation [55–57].

Naturally, there are a variety of sensors that may be used to determine the respiratory rate. When picking a sensor type for a wireless body area network (WBAN), the most crucial element to consider is wearability. Stretch sensors, as a consequence, are highly recommended for future frameworks. In addition, the development of algorithms and ways to increase heartiness against movement should be the focus of future studies.

Instead of creating new sensors, current ones will be utilized [58–60].

8.4.3 BODY TEMPERATURE SENSORS

The third crucial signal is internal heat level, which may be used to identify hypothermia, heatstroke, fevers, and other illnesses. The internal heat level is a piece of good diagnostic equipment that should be remembered for a wearable medical service framework [61,62].

All contemporary projects requiring the evaluation of body temperature employ thermistor-type sensors. The typical Negative temperature coefficient (NTC) temperature sensors were employed, while Positive temperature coefficient (PTC) sensors were studied. The thermistors were utilized throughout the study to determine an appropriate temperature range for evaluating the human body with acceptable degrees of inaccuracy. As a consequence, future framework designers should unquestionably continue to employ these sensor types [1,2,48].

The closeness of the sensor to the human body limits the precision of temperature detection. Consequently, many studies have absorbed emerging sensors imprinted on light, flexible polymers with epoxy resin backing that may be applied straight to human skin. While this is a huge step forward, the study also suggests that temperature may be calculated with relative accuracy by embedding a temperature sensor in materials. Consequently, framework designers are advised to employ materials to hold temperature sensors until devices imprinted on adaptable polymers are more readily produced [63,64].

8.4.4 Body Temperature Sensors

Despite not being a fundamental sign in and of itself, blood pressure (BP) is commonly estimated by the three important indicators. Hypertension is a recognized risk factor for cardiovascular disease, particularly coronary artery disease. It is also one of Australia's most prevalent chronic conditions, affecting 32% of adults. Sixty-eight percent of those who were affected had uncontrolled or untreated hypertension. Consequently, integrating BP with a WBAN for medical therapy would provide a huge number of patients' vital information [20,62,65–67].

However, creating a wearable sensor for measuring circulatory strain on a frequent and unobtrusive basis remains a challenge in medical IoT. Several studies have tried to determine BP using pulse transit time (PTT), the amount of time it takes for a pulse to travel from the heart to another location, such as the ear cartilage or outspread course [63,64].

These studies show that using PTT to determine BP is presently ineffective. PTT is controlled by various parameters, including the firmness of the blood vessels and the thickness of the blood. In ideal settings, when gadgets had been adjusted for the person, and the individual generally remained throughout testing, the previously stated focuses used one estimate at the chest and another at the wrist generated satisfactory findings. However, it was discovered that estimates made between the ear and the wrist were erroneous. PTT was also estimated with acceptable accuracy between the palm and the fingertip, but the review could not translate it to pulse [1,33]. Given the high level of confidence shown in calculating PTT and the fact that the plan is the most wearable alternative for monitoring circulatory strain offered in this research, it deserves further investigation. According to one research, gadget recalibration would be required frequently since the human body develops with time.

Another problem with these frameworks is that they are obstructive, although not intrusive. In most circumstances, a chest-worn ECG is needed in addition to another device, and the two devices' connections may be linked. This difficulty was recognized in one research, which employed two easily worn PPG sensors—one on the ear cartilage and the other on the wrist—to assess beat appearance time (or time required to travel) between these two places and, as a consequence, circulatory strain [1]. The findings were promising, suggesting that credible estimations for healthy people in various settings could be made (like sitting and standing). However, the findings were not compared to those obtained using a typical sphygmomanometer attached to the sleeve. A relationship like this might jeopardize the correctness of the PPG-based architecture.

While no method for properly monitoring circulatory strain using a small wearable device has been created, this area deserves more research. It might be consummated by creating a device that uses at smallest two PPG sensors to detect PTT throughout the arm's length. Pulse is a critical feature of medical services, and the capacity to continually monitor it would significantly impact the sorts of medical services that may be delivered using a WBAN framework [1,2].

8.4.5 Pulse Oximetry Sensors

The quantity of oxygen in the blood is measured via pulse oximetry. The blood oxygen level, like the pulse, is not a crucial sign, but it can serve as a measure of respiratory capacity and may help diagnose illnesses like hypoxia (insufficient oxygen reaching the body's tissues). Overcoming oxime-attempt is an important component of a complete health-monitoring system [48].

Pulse oximeters collect PPG signals to evaluate blood oxygen levels. The skin generally synchronizes two LEDs; the first is red, and the other is infrared. Some of this light is engrossed by hemoglobin in the blood cells but not all of it. The quantity of light not consumed is estimated using photodiodes, and the difference between the two is utilized to determine the oxygen in the blood. Figure 8.6a and b demonstrates how LEDs may be directed toward an item or transported to a photodiode on the other side through a limb (typically a finger).

Pulse oximetry is a test that determines how much oxygen is in the blood. The blood oxygen level, like pulse, is not a vital sign, but it serves as a measure of respiratory capacity and may aid in the diagnosis of disorders like hypoxia (insufficient oxygen reaching the body's tissues). Overall, overcoming oxime attempts is a critical addition to a comprehensive health-monitoring system [1,2].

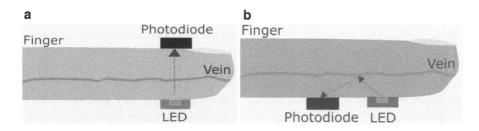

FIGURE 8.6 Absorbance-mode vs reflective-mode PPG sensors for pulse oximetry.

PPG signals are acquired by beat oximeters, which then measure blood oxygen. Two LEDs are normally synchronized via the skin, one red and one infrared. The blood's hemoglobin absorbs some of this light but not all of it. Therefore, getting photodiodes estimates the amount of light that is not absorbed, and the difference between the two is used to calculate blood oxygen. Figure 8.6 shows how LEDs may be directed toward an object or transferred through a limb (usually a finger) to a photodiode on the opposite side [1].

8.5 ANALYSIS AND DATA PROCESSING

Computational offloading and AI are two of the most important forms of information processing that may be altered by AI. Computational offloading refers to the use of the cloud to do complex data processing beyond the capability of low-cost wearables. By sending raw or partly processed sensor data to the cloud, the registration assets of several devices may be leveraged for handling. Using this sophisticated computing environment instead of a standalone mobile phone provides several benefits, including doing more complex computations, getting results considerably quicker, and extending cell phone battery life due to less internal processing [1].

Computational offloading would benefit confounded sensor hubs, such as those predicting ECG information, pulse, or accelerometers for fall detection. ECGs, for example, have a typical form, and various variations from this shape might indicate a variety of cardiac problems, including arrhythmia, heart irritation, and, shockingly, heart failure. Unfortunately, a small, poorly maintained sensor hub cannot decode ECG data quickly enough to use AI algorithms to identify the patient's health status. However, suppose the raw data were supplied to the cloud. In that case, high-powered processing might be used to ascertain the condition of the ECG before AI calculations compare it to the signature form, recognize any actual changes, and figure out what disease is causing them [1,2,48].

Furthermore, AI may be used in large datasets to extract useful information, such as recognizing previously unknown relationships between side effects.

By providing massive data sets and great computational power, distributed storage enables AI to execute fast and effectively. Because independent cell phones lack the storage capacity or processing resources needed to examine data using AI, data must be sent from the cloud. Sickness patterns, links between side effects, and the development of realistic therapeutic programs for particular patients are all examples of data that AI may collect.

Only a few scientists have recognized the importance of cognitive unloading in medical settings. Readings from WBAN sensors are relayed to a mobile phone, where some basic processing occurs. The data is then sent from the phone to the cloud, where it is treated with care using techniques such as highlight selection and categorization. The important information gathered might then be saved or shared with medical professionals. The main flaw is that it depends on a high-tech phone that, in the best-case scenario, would run out of power in a matter of days. Using a low-power communication standard, such as the newly discussed NarrowBand Internet of things(NB-IoT), unrefined data may be transferred straight to the cloud for thorough processing. Furthermore, the information gathered by favorable to cessing is not broken down any further; rather, it is delivered directly to an expert who physically observes the conclusion. It would be possible to do order computations that inform the expert when a peculiar shift in a patient's physiological indicators is detected.

Computational offloading for information processing assess ECG states and determines whether the shape is stable with congestive cardiovascular breakdown. Because this assessment would be much too difficult to do on a wearable device, it is a wonderful illustration of the usefulness of cloud-based information management advancements. After processing, the ECG data is retained in the patient's health record, enabling them to see and discuss their findings with their PCP. Furthermore, if the ECG shows a consistent cardiac cadence with congestive cardiovascular breakdown, a warning for crisis management personnel may be sent.

There has also been some study comparing AI computations. For example, for stroke prediction, deep neural networks (DNNs) are compared to gradient boosting decision tree (GBDT), logistic regression (LR), and support vector machine (SVM) computations. DNNs are very useful in this case.

The accuracy of the GBDT and LR calculations was 87.3%, while the execution of the GBDT and GBDT calculations was comparable at 86.8% and 86.6%, respectively. On the other hand, SVMs were the least accurate, with an accuracy of just 83.9%. It shows that DNNs are ideal for predicting assignments but must operate on distributed storage structures due to the intricacies of the computation [20].

Meanwhile, in multi-layer perception (MLP), SVMs for relapse (SVR), summarized relapse neural networks (GRNN), and k-nearest neighbor (kNN) relapse techniques were considered for determining an individual's psychological well-being list based on five key mental well-being boundaries. In contrast to previous work, the SVM-based computation worked well in this case, whereas the neural organization technique was poor. These two research papers demonstrate how there is no such thing as the optimal AI calculation for medical treatment; rather, there are computations that may be acceptable in one situation but completely inadequate in another. As a result, future framework builders should consider AI calculations that may be useful for their purpose and choose which calculation has the greatest features for the framework in question.

A few studies have specifically looked at computer offloading for IoT medical care. In any event, it has received a lot of attention for mobile phones, for example. The preceding evaluations provide detailed summaries of the research on this subject, proving that computer offloading to the cloud may rapidly increase energy productivity and handling capacities. In addition, these reviews provide an overview of the related topic of portable, distributed computing to the interested reader.

8.6 CONCLUSION AND FUTURE SCOPE

In this chapter, we aim to establish a paradigm for the future of IoT in medicine, and it can be done to study common and deep diseases in any human being. After this, our effort was also that we should ensure the model of all kinds of possibilities under which the work of recording all the types of senses capable of holding in the body has been done. After this, the discussion of how medical care can be used by long-distance and short-distance parliaments. Under this, it has been said that this technology can be used to measure some important factors like BP and the amount of oxygen present in the blood. In today's time, through cloud computing, data can be easily stored from anywhere. Keeping in mind that while transmitting its possibilities in IoT, it has been said that through cloud computing-based data storage, we can collect data from any place. It can ensure a thorough examination and study of the patient, and it is also a good option. This chapter also talked about data manipulation and cyber security, which is very important. Corrupting any database is a big obstacle to providing correct results, so further improvement in cyber security is necessary. By encrypting tax data, we can ensure its security. We have introduced and evaluated several wearable sensors during our analysis of this chapter, and we have ensured some very important topics for future researchers. Today, we cannot deny the possibility of developing AI through machine learning in a better way. In terms of IoT, encouraging the development of wearable medical care frameworks based on the forthcoming NB-IoT standard would be useful. However, despite its obvious benefits for this industry, no actual work has been done in a medical care context since this is a new norm. Therefore, in the future, we will test NB-IoT in medical service equipment to guarantee its compatibility before implementing it as the establishing communication standard for a medical care framework based on the concept provided in this research [68,69].

Although cloud-based data storage has received a lot of attention, data management is an area that needs further research. It is necessary to investigate the development of cloud-based computations capable of processing raw data from complex sensors and focusing vital data on a person's health. Another area of information management that might be beneficial in medical situations is AI. When used in the cloud's powerful registration environment, AI might convey diagnoses to patients, make new disclosures about sickness patterns, and aid in developing treatment methods. Despite these clear benefits, AI for medical applications has yet to be properly investigated, providing a tremendous research opportunity. It is an excellent opportunity for analysts who wish to make major progress in IoT-based medical services. For example, we would want to look at grouping and strategic relapse calculations to offer diagnoses based on basic and additional sign data in the future [70–72].

This work can be further extended to new levels as the adoption rate of AI is increasing rapidly, and IoT has already captured the market. Combining the two would lead to the development and implementation of much more sophisticated systems. These systems would restrict human interventions as most of the tasks would be effectively and efficiently performed by these smart systems only. For example, Google Assistant controlling different parameters and devices could be useful in health, agriculture, defense, security, etc. One can integrate multiple sensors and devices with the help of IoT platforms, and their controlling could be made easy using these AI-powered Virtual Personal Assistants (VPAs) like Google Assistant over the phone [73].

REFERENCES

[1] B. Stephanie Baker, Wei Xiang, (Senior Member, IEEE), and Ian Atkinson, "Internet of things for smart healthcare: Technologies, challenges, and opportunities," IEEE, vol. 5, 2017.

[2] CH. M. Shruthi, "Opportunities and challenges of integrating the internet of things (IoT) with infrastructure of healthcare units" *Int. Adv. Res. J. Sci., Eng. Technol.*, vol. 5, no. 10, pp. 58–63, 2018, ISSN (Online) 2393-8021 ISSN (Print) 2394-1588.

[3] E. Perrier, *Positive Disruption: Healthcare, Ageing and Participation in the Age of Technology.* Sydney, NSW, Australia: The McKell Institute, 2015.

[4] P. Gope and T. Hwang, "BSN-care: A secure IoT-based modern healthcare system using body sensor network," *IEEE Sensors J.*, vol. 16, no. 5, pp. 1368–1376, 2016.

[5] S.-H. Chang, R.-D. Chiang, S.-J. Wu, and W.-T. Chang, "A context-aware, interactive M-health system for diabetics," *IT Prof.*, vol. 18, no. 3, pp. 14–22, 2016.

[6] Y. J. Fan, Y. H. Yin, L. D. Xu, Y. Zeng, and F. Wu, "IoT-based smart rehabilitation system," *IEEE Trans. Ind. Informat.*, vol. 10, no. 2, pp. 1568–1577, 2014.

[7] S. Sarkar and S. Misra, "From micro to nano: The evolution of wireless sensor-based health care," *IEEE Pulse*, vol. 7, no. 1, pp. 21–25, 2016.

[8] Y. Yin, Y. Zeng, X. Chen, and Y. Fan, "The internet of things in healthcare: An overview," *J. Ind. Inf. Integr.*, vol. 1, pp. 3–13, 2016. [Online]. Available: http://www.sciencedirect.com/science/ article/pii/S2452414X16000066

[9] D. V. Dimitrov, "Medical internet of things and big data in healthcare," *Healthcare Inform. Res.*, vol. 22, no. 3, pp. 156–163, 2016. [Online]. Available: http://www.ncbi.nlm.nih.gov/pmc/articles/PMC4981575/

[10] Smart Parking. SmartEye, SmartRep, and RFID Technology— Westminster City Council—London, 2017. [Online]. Available: http://www.smartparking.com/keep-up-to-date/case-studies/3-500-vehicle-detection-sensors-and-epermit-technology-in-the-city-of-westminster-london

[11] P. K. Schwab, *The Fourth Industrial Revolution: What it Means, and How to Respond.* Cologny, Switzerland: World Economic Forum, 2016.

[12] Sensus. Smart Water—Smarter at Every Point, 2017. [Online]. Available: www.sensus.com/internet-of-things/smart-water

[13] H. El-Sayed and G. Thandavarayan, "Congestion detection and propagation in urban areas using histogram models," *IEEE Internet Things J.*, to be published.

[14] C. A. Tokognon, B. Gao, G. Tian, and Y. Yan, "Structural health monitoring framework based on internet of things: A survey," *IEEE Internet Things J.*, vol. 4, no. 3, pp. 619–635, 2017.

[15] L. Xu, D. Xu, H. Cai, C. Xie, J. Hu, and F. Bu, "Ubiquitous data accessing method in IoT-based information system for emergency medical services," *IEEE Trans Ind. Informat.*, vol. 10, no. 2, pp. 1578–1586, 2014.

[16] N. Zhu et al. "Bridging e-health and the internet of things: The SPHERE project," *IEEE Intell. Syst.*, vol. 30, no. 4, pp. 39–46, 2015.

[17] S. M. R. Islam, D. Kwak, H. Kabir, M. Hossain, and K.-S. Kwak, "The internet of things for health care: A comprehensive survey," *IEEE Access*, vol. 3, pp. 678–708, 2015.

[18] Garmin. HSM-Tri, 2017. [Online]. Available: https://buy.garmin.com/ en-AU/AU/p/136403

[19] FitBit. FitBitPurePulse, 2017. [Online]. Available: https://www.fitbit. com/au/purepulse

[20] D. Wang, D. Zhang, and G. Lu, "A novel multichannel wrist pulse system with different sensor arrays," *IEEE Trans. Instrum. Meas.*, vol. 64, no. 7, pp. 2020–2034, 2015.

[21] C. F. Pasluosta, H. Gassner, J. Winkler, J. Klucken, and B. M. Eskofier, "An emerging era in the management of Parkinson's disease: Wearable technologies and the internet of things," *IEEE J. Biomed. Health Inform.*, vol. 19, no. 6, pp. 1873–1881, 2015.

[22] K. Ozcan, S. Velipasalar, and P. K. Varshney, "Autonomous fall detection with wearable cameras by using relative entropy distance measure," *IEEE Trans. Human_Mach. Syst.*, vol. 47, no. 1, pp. 31–39, 2017.

[23] P. Pierleoni, A. Belli, L. Palma, M. Pellegrini, L. Pernini, and S. Valenti, "A high reliability wearable device for elderly fall detection," *IEEE Sensors J.*, vol. 15, no. 8, pp. 4544–4553, 2015.

[24] C. C. Y. Poon, B. P. L. Lo, M. R. Yuce, A. Alomainy, and Y. Hao, "Body sensor networks: In the era of big data and beyond," *IEEE Rev. Biomed. Eng.*, vol. 8, pp. 4–16, 2015.

[25] Security, Bluetooth Low Energy, 1st ed., *Bluetooth*, Kirkland, WA, USA, 2017, pp. 1–5. [Online]. Available: https://www.bluetooth.com/~/ media/_les/specication/bluetooth-low-energy-security.ashx

[26] M. Singh and N. Jain, "Performance and evaluation of smartphone based wireless blood pressure monitoring system using bluetooth," *IEEE Sensors J.*, vol. 16, no. 23, pp. 8322–8328, 2016.

[27] Daintree Networks. Zigbee Security, 2017. [Online]. Available: http://www.daintree. net/resources/zigbee-security/

[28] T. Cheng and W. Zhuang, "Bluetooth-enabled in-home patient monitoring system: Early detection of Alzheimer's disease," *IEEE Wireless Commun.*, vol. 17, no. 1, pp. 74–79, 2010.

[29] The University of New England. SMART Farm, 2017. [Online]. Available: http://www. une.edu.au/research/research-centres-institutes/smart-farm

[30] H.-C. Chang, Y.-L. Hsu, S.-C.Yang, J.-C. Lin, and Z.-H.Wu, "Awearable inertial measurement system with complementary filter for gait analysis of patients with stroke or Parkinson's disease," *IEEE Access*, vol. 4, pp. 8442–8453, 2016.

[31] H. F. Maqbool, M. A. B. Husman, M. I. Awad, A. Abouhossein, N. Iqbal, and A. A. Dehghani-Sanij, "A real-time gait event detection for lower limb prosthesis control and evaluation," *IEEE Trans. Neural Syst. Rehabil. Eng.*, vol. 25, no. 9, pp. 1500–1509, 2017.

[32] T. T. Pham et al., "Freezing of gait detection in Parkinson's disease: A subject-independent detector using anomaly scores," *IEEE Trans. Biomed. Eng.*, vol. 64, no. 11, pp. 2719–2728, 2017. [Online]. Available: http://ieeexplore.ieee.org/document/7845616/

[33] J. Gil et al., "A fully integrated low-power high-coexistence 2.4-GHz Zigbee transceiver for biomedical and healthcare applications," *IEEE Trans. Microw. Theory Techn.*, vol. 62, no. 9, pp. 1879–1889, 2014.

[34] Zigbee Alliance. Zigbee IP and 910IP, 2017. [Online]. Available: http://www.zigbee. org/zigbee-for-developers/network-speci_cations/ zigbeeip/

[35] K. M. Alam, M. Saini, and A. E. Saddik, "Toward social internet of vehicles: Concept, architecture, and applications," *IEEE Access*, vol. 3, pp. 343–357, 2015.

[36] I. Olaronke and O. Oluwaseun, "Big data in healthcare: Prospects, challenges and resolutions," in *2016 Future Technologies Conference (FTC)*, 2016, pp. 1152–1157.

[37] R. Miller, *LoRa Security: Building a Secure LoRa Solution*, 1st ed., Basingstoke, UK: MWR InfoSecurity, 2016. [Online]. Available: https://labs.mwrinfosecurity.com/assets/ BlogFiles/mwri-LoRa-securityguide-1.2-2016-03-22.pdf

[38] Polar. H7 Heart Rate Sensor, 2017. [Online]. Available: https://www. polar. com/au-en/products/accessories/H7_heart_rate_sensor

[39] S. Haxha and J. Jhoja, "Optical based noninvasive glucose monitoring sensor prototype," *IEEE Photon. J.*, vol. 8, no. 6, 2016, Art. no. 6805911.

[40] X. Xiao and Q. Li, "Anoninvasive measurement of blood glucose concentration by UWB microwave spectrum," *IEEE Antennas Wireless Propag. Lett.*, vol. 16, pp. 1040–1043, 2016.

[41] K. Ozcan and S.Velipasalar, "Wearable camera- and accelerometer-based fall detection on portable devices," *IEEE Embedded Syst. Lett.,* vol. 8, no. 1, pp. 6–9, 2016.

[42] P. Pierleoni et al., "A wearable fall detector for elderly people based on AHRS and barometric sensor," *IEEE Sensors J.,* vol. 16, no. 17, pp. 6733–6744, 2016.

[43] N. Mangalvedhe, R. Ratasuk, and A. Ghosh, "NB-IoT deployment study for low power wide area cellular IoT," in *2016 IEEE 27th Annual International Symposium on Personal, Indoor, and Mobile Radio Communications (PIMRC),* 2016,pp. 1–6.

[44] LoRaWAN: What is it? *A Technical Overview of LoRa and LoRaWAN,* 1st ed., LoRa Alliance, Beaverton, OR, USA, 2015. [Online]. Available: https://www.lora-alliance. org/lorawan-white-papers   and   https://docs.wixstatic.com/ugd/ecccla_ed71ealcd-969417493c74e4a13c55685.pdf

[45] K.-H. Chang, "Bluetooth: A viable solution for IoT? [Industry Perspectives]," *IEEE Wireless Commun.,* vol. 21, no. 6, pp. 6–7, 2014.

[46] Bluetooth. SIG introduces bluetooth low energy wireless technology, the next generation bluetooth wireless technology, 2009. [Online]. Available: https://www.bluetooth. com/news/pressreleases/2009/-12/17/sig-introduces-bluetooth-low-energy-wireless-technologythe-nextgeneration-of-bluetooth-wireless-technology

[47] R. Palattella et al., "Internet of Things in the 5G era: Enablers, architecture, and business models," *IEEE J. Sel. Areas Commun.,* vol. 34, no. 3, pp. 510–527, 2016.

[48] Australian Institute of Health and Welfare. Australia's Health. [Online]. Available: http://www.aihw.gov.au/WorkArea/DownloadAsset.aspx-?id=60129548150, 2014

[49] S. Tan, D. De, W.-Z. Song, J. Yang, and S. K. Das, "Survey of security advances in smart grid: A data-driven approach," *IEEE Commun. Surveys Tuts.,* vol. 19, no. 1, pp. 397–422, 2017.

[50] M. A. Cretikos, R. Bellomo, K. Hillman, J. Chen, S. Finfer, and Flabouris, "Respiratory rate: The neglected vital sign," *Med. J. Austral.,* vol. 188, no. 11, pp. 657–659, 2008.

[51] G. Cola, M. Avvenuti, A. Vecchio, G.-Z. Yang, and B. Lo, "An on-node processing approach for anomaly detection in gait," *IEEE Sensors J.,* vol. 15, no. 11, pp. 6640–6649, 2015.

[52] R. C. A. Alves, L. B. Gabriel, B. T. D. Oliveira, C. B. Margi, and C. L. D. Santos, "Assisting physical (hydro)therapy with wireless sensors networks," *IEEE Internet Things J.,* vol. 2, no. 2, pp. 113–120, 2015.

[53] G. Wolgast, C. Ehrenborg, A. Israelsson, J. Helander, E. Johansson, and H. Manefjord, "Wireless body area network for heart attack detection [education corner]," *IEEE Antennas Propag. Mag.,* vol. 58, no. 5, pp. 84–92, 2016.

[54] WAVIoT. Comparison of LPWAN technologies, 2016. [Online]. Available: http:// dgmatics.com/technology/waviot-lpwan-technologycomparison

[55] Digi. ZigBee wireless standard, 2017. [Online]. Available: https://www.digi.com/ resources/standards-and-technologies/rfmodems/zigbee-wireless-standard

[56] Digi. XBee/XBee-Pro RF modules (Datasheet), 2009. [Online]. Available: https://www. sparkfun.com/datasheets/Wireless/Zigbee/- XBee-Datasheet.pdf

[57] XBee-PRO 900HP/XBee-PRO XSC RF Modules, Digi, Shah Alam, Malaysia, 2014.

[58] T. Zillner, *ZigBee exploited,* 1st ed. Vienna, Austria: Cognosec, 2015. [Online]. Available: https://www.blackhat.com/docs/us-15/materials/us-15-Zillner-ZigBee-Exploited-The-Good-The-Bad-And-The-Uglywp.pdf

[59] M. Taub, S. B. Leeb, E. C. Lupton, R. T. Hinman, J. Ziesel, and S. Blackler, "The escort system: A safety monitor for people living with Alzheimer's disease," *IEEE Pervasive Comput.,* vol. 10, no. 2, pp. 68–77, 2011.

[60] Sigfox. Getting Started, 2017. [Online]. Available: http://makers.sigfox.com/getting-started/

[61] J. Zhou, Z. Cao, X. Dong, and A. V. Vasilakos, "Security and privacy for cloud-based IoT: Challenges," *IEEE Commun. Mag.,* vol. 55, no. 1, pp. 26–33, 2017.

[62] TomTom. TomTom Spark Cardio, 2017. [Online]. Available: https:// www.tomtom. com/en_au/sports/fitness-watches/gps-watch-cardio- spark/black-large/

[63] Shake It Up Australia Foundation. *Symptoms of Parkinson's*, 2017 [Online]. Available: https://shakeitup.org.au/understanding- parkinsons/symptoms-of-parkinsons/

[64] J. Ženko, M. Kos, and I. Kramberger, "Pulse rate variability and blood oxidation content identification using miniature wearable wrist device," in *2016 International Conference on Systems, Signals and Image Processing (IWSSIP)*, 2016, pp. 1–4.

[65] H. Lee, H. Ko, C. Jeong, and J. Lee, "Wearable photoplethysmographic sensor based on different LED light intensities," *IEEE Sensors J.*, vol. 17, no. 3, pp. 587–588, 2017.

[66] Y. Shu, C. Li, Z. Wang, W. Mi, Y. Li, and T.-L. Ren, "A pressure sensing system for heart rate monitoring with polymer-based pressure sensors and an anti-interference post processing circuit," *Sensors*, vol. 15, no. 2, pp. 3224–3235, 2015.

[67] D. Wang, D. Zhang, and G. Lu, "An optimal pulse system design by multichannel sensors fusion," *IEEE J. Biomed. Health Informat.*, vol. 20, no. 2, pp. 450–459, 2016.

[68] Burdekin Shire Council. Population of the Burdekin Shire, 2017. [Online]. Available: http://www.burdekin.qld.gov.au/council/business/-population-of-the-burdekin-shire/

[69] National Regional Pro_le: Burdekin (Statistical Area Level 2)_Environment/Energy, Austral. Bureau Statist., Canberra, Australia, 2013. https://dbr.abs.gov.au/

[70] VT Networks. Sigfox network overvie for technical professionals, 2016. [Online]. Available: http://vtnetworks.ie/wp-content/uploads/2016/12/Sigfox-Network-Overview. pdf

[71] Thinxtra. Empowering internet of things in Australia, New Zealand and Hong Kong, 2017. [Online]. Available: https://www.thinxtra.com/

[72] R. Ratasuk, B. Vejlgaard, N. Mangalvedhe, and A. Ghosh, "NB-IoT system for M2M communication," in *2016 IEEE Wireless Communications and Networking Conference*, 2016, pp. 1–5.

[73] Divya Agarwal, Santosh Kumar Srivastava, "Integration of 'Google Assistant' and 'AdafruitIO' via 'IFTTT' to implement an IoT based wireless multi-sensor network surveillance and multi-appliance control system," *Int. Res. J. Eng. Technol. (IRJET)*, vol. 7 no. 9, 2020.

9 Semantic Similarity Based on Association Measurement

Ahmad. K. Kayed
Sohar University

Abdelhakeem M. B. Abdelrahman
Sudan University of Science and Technology

CONTENTS

9.1 INTRODUCTION

Ontologies are a formal specification of a domain's shared conceptions and relationships between them [1]. Some ontologies, which are formal representations of knowledge, can build and share conceptual models within a domain to improve understanding, communication, and interoperability [2]. Ontology establishes a

DOI: 10.1201/9781003326182-9

shared understanding of a knowledge domain by identifying linkages between significant concepts and phrases used in that domain [3]. It is possible to create an ontology from scratch or reuse an existing one [4]. The currently provided ontology evaluation methods allow the user to examine the ontology's internal consistency. Because the entire set of tests or a specific test may be run at any moment, it facilitates ontology testing during both development and evolution [5]. In the medical field, a considerable number of clinical trials still rely on traditional data collection, such as paper-based methods [6].

Distributed knowledge-based systems, such as the semantic web and the evaluation of modeling languages, are two important applications of ontologies. These applications necessitate high-quality formal ontologies [7]. A formal ontology's quality requires a good conceptualization of a domain and specification that measure the concordance of functional and non-functional requirements. Ontology evaluation, on the other hand, can be categorized into three categories according to the type of evaluation: ranking, accuracy, and quality evaluation [8]. The ability to answer competency questions has been used to assess the quality of ontologies, which, unlike conceptual models, must fulfill both computational and representational constraints. Assessing ontology quality has become a critical topic in assisting ontology engineers in predicting ontology quality. Users will evaluate ontologies and choose a higher-quality ontology for a single domain from a larger pool of ontologies.

Ontology users can measure the quality of the ontology using quality metrics. Metrics are used to assess ontologies' structure and semantic quality [9]. We need a benchmark or standard definitions to assess the quality of ontologies. This study will look at creating a benchmark or standard definition in the health domain and how to measure it. Therefore, we aim to examine the features of common semantic ontologies and demonstrate the efficiency of proposed evaluation methodologies [10]. The use of the semantic web is dependent on two types of evaluation: first, ontology evaluation of semantic web content, which is required to prevent using incorrect, redundant, and inconsistent ontologies. The second is the assessment of the technologies that use semantic web content (semantic web technology evaluation) [11].

In this work, we used RDFs and OWL as interchange languages for evaluating the ontology content. We used a comparison study to evaluate the obtained results and the results of human experts based on the correlation coefficient to verify the validity of the proposed method.

9.2   BIOMEDICAL ONTOLOGIES

The main ideas of biomedical domain ontologies are presented in this section. The goal of biomedical terminology is to collect the names of items and classes used in the biomedical domain that is relevant to biomedicine. Biomedical ontologies can show how biomedical data is organized and managed as web functionality. The study of biomedical ontology encompasses a wide range of items and processes (including biological product names, regulated vocabularies, and knowledge structures) (i.e., acquiring ontological relations, integrating heterogeneous databases, and using ontologies for biological knowledge).

In modern information science, ontology is defined as a systematic description of all terms in a particular field, explaining their characteristics and the relationships that link them. OWL, the web's ontology language, analyzes ontologies, identifies their attributes, and communicates concepts. Stanford University has developed a free, open-source platform called Protégé to analyze and classify medical data which can be used to design intelligent systems for indexing and summarizing data in the medical field. Modern machine learning algorithms help develop models that can predict and elicit specific ontology vocabulary. Various methods are used to evaluate the accuracy of the extracted or predicted data.

9.2.1 Unified Medical Language System (UMLS)

UMLS is an example of terminology that incorporates over 100 different vocabularies and contains many clinical phrases [12,13]. The UMLS is a collection of files and software that "brings together many health and biomedical vocabularies and standards to facilitate computer system interoperability." E-Health records, dictionaries, classification techniques, and natural language translators are among the applications that UMLS improves or develops [14]. It is made up of three main sources of information in the semantic network: semantic types, semantic relations, and lexicon [15]. In contrast, the Metathesaurus provides concepts and their codes using multiple vocabularies (such as ICD-10-CM, ICD-10-AM, Medical Subject Headings, SNOMED-CT, etc.) [16].

9.2.1.1 Medical Subject Headings (MeSH)

Medical Subject Headings (**MeSH**) is a primary source of vocabulary used in UMLS [17]. MeSH includes 15 high-level clusters. Each class is separated into subclasses defined with a unique letter, such as letter A for anatomy, letter B for organisms, letter C for disease type, etc.

9.2.1.2 SNOMED-CT

SNOMED-CT stands for systemized nomenclature of medicine clinical term [17], comprehensive clinical terminology included in UMLS in May 2004. The recent version of SNOMED-CT contains about 360,000 concepts, 975,000 synonyms, and 1.45 million relationships categorized into 18 rankings.

9.2.2 ICD

ICD [4] stands for International Classification of Diseases, an essential international medical terminological system issued in 1893. The World Health Organization (WHO) has maintained it since its sixth revision in 1948. Then, the current version of the ICD is (ICD-10), published in 1992. It is the leading index for disease identification and classification [18].

The ICD attempts to give an international classification of death causes to provide globally uniform and hence comparable mortality statistics. Other global classification systems such as the International Classification of Functioning, Disabilities, and Health (ICF) and the International Classification of Health Inventions (ICHI) are part of the WHO family.

The ICD-10 includes 22 main subcategories of diseases, including the blood and blood-forming organs (D50–D89), nervous system diseases (G00–G99), metabolic diseases (E00–E90), and, mental and behavioral disorders (F00–F99), etc.

9.2.3 THE SEMANTIC WEB

This section will discuss the main concepts related to semantic web ontologies and their main structure.

9.2.3.1 Ontologies

Ontology is a Greek terminology that means onto (begin) + logos (word). It was introduced in the 19th century by German philosophers [19]. However, ontology is the backbone of knowledge representation in the semantic web context and a vital component of building the semantic web [20]. It is implemented as a computer-based system to promote applications such as natural language processing, data annotation, information retrieval, and decision support [21]. Nguyen [22] describe ontology as a definition of concepts and their relationships in a shared domain to represent all kind of *IS-A* (*is-a-kind-of, is-a-part-of*) hierarchical relationship in the biomedical domain framework of UMLS.

9.2.3.2 Structure of Ontologies

The World Wide Web has standardized the web ontology language (OWL) as a conceptual modeling language [10]. OWL-Lite, OWL-DL, and OWL-Full are the three sublanguages. The semantics of OWL-DL and OWL-Lite are computational characteristics and support automated reasoning. In addition, the OWL-Full is used to support compatibility with the resource description framework (RDF) schema. OWL ontology consists of axioms that establish logical constraints on individual classes and their relationships in a domain of interest, as shown in Figure 9.1. The sets of axioms deliver a complete description of logic based on formal semantics to infer implicit knowledge using explicit representation knowledge.

9.3 PROPOSED SEMANTIC SIMILARITY MEASUREMENT

Because of the large quantity, size, and complexity of biological ontologies; therefore, selecting the most relevant ontologies for a particular domain is considered a difficult task. To improve the quality of ontologies in the biomedical area, methodologies

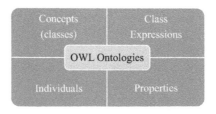

FIGURE 9.1 OWL ontologies.

or standard definitions are required to verify the quality of knowledge sources. According to Aouicha and Hisham Al-Mubaid [12,13], there is no well-defined method or standard definition in the health sector for evaluating the quality of ontology using semantic similarity measures.

The major challenge is determining the type of method used to classify medical terms based on the type of resources that exist and follow (ICD-10) and choosing the most appropriate evaluation for assessing ontology in the health field. This work aims to develop techniques and criteria for ontology evaluation in the biomedical sector.

9.3.1 RESEARCH QUESTIONS

Based on the problem definition and study objectives:
The fundamental question addressed in this study is:

How can we construct a method or standard description for solving an ontology evaluation technique problem?

Then, the following sub-questions are required:

1. How can we use the given method to use one of the available similarity measures to verify the quality of an ontology?
2. How can we extract datasets from domain knowledge sources like ICD-10 and utilize them to assess the quality of ontologies?

9.3.2 RESEARCH HYPOTHESIS

The following are the assumptions we used to create the standard definition or methodology:

1. The UMLS framework contains many ontologies in the biomedical area.
2. The UMLS framework has various knowledge resources in the biological area.
3. There is no methodology or standard definition in the biomedical area within the UMLS framework.

9.4 ONTOLOGY EVALUATION

The purposes of evaluating software depend on each specific case, which is summarized as follows [23–25]:

- To describe the software and establish baselines for comparisons.
- To evaluate the software quality requirements for determining the level of the software product quality and determine its weaknesses.
- To enhance the software quality compared with the standard baselines.
- To compare different software products or versions of the same product.
- To ensure that the software quality meets the required level of standard quality.

Multiple levels of evaluation were conducted [26,27].

1. Direct evaluation level of the ontology structure and its content.
2. Application-based evaluation level to examine an application's results using ontology.
3. Analysis-based evaluation level to assess ontology in scientific data analysis.

This work follows the "direct evaluation level" via conceptualization and ontology domain identification.

Several evaluation methods are deployed, such as the triangulation method (lexical/conceptual and semantic relations), Protégé method (hierarchy/taxonomy, syntactic, and architectural), and expert review method (lexical/conceptual, semantic relations, and context/application). As this is foundational domain ontological work, there is no global standard for comparison. Similarly, the domain source data has not been normalized to ensure that it can make a standardized comparison. As a result, the methodology used in this research falls within the categories of application and human evaluation [28].

Three basic assumptions underpin ontology content evaluation:

• The evaluation of the ontology contents should perform throughout the life cycle of the ontology.
• Throughout the current ontology-building phase, ontology development tools should facilitate content evaluation.
• A knowledge representation (KR) model represents the vocabulary of a particular language for the application of an ontology that will significantly influence the evaluation of the content of that ontology. More accurate construction of vocabulary representation of the language helps build an ontology with correct and easily identifiable classifications.

9.5   SEMANTIC SIMILARITY MEASURES

Most semantic similarity algorithms are used in information retrieval (IR), information extraction (IE), and other intelligent knowledge-based systems. Similarity measurements, such as plagiarism detection and similarity metrics, are crucial tools in IR for deciding the correct match between query terms and the retrieved content.

The degree of "exactness" of terms determined by comparing the description of the information and its attributes [29] is called the semantic similarity of documents. Several approaches have been presented to compute semantic similarity. However, we will discuss the following two main approaches:

9.5.1   Semantic Similarity Measure Classification

Figure 9.2 illustrates the semantic similarity classification for a single ontology and cross ontologies. The shortest path-length algorithm is used to find the semantic ontology similarity between two concepts that used the ontology (is-a or part of) [12]. Many approaches have been implemented using ontology as a primary information

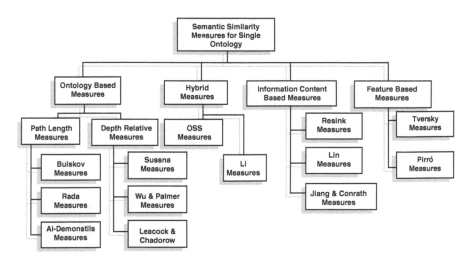

FIGURE 9.2   Semantic similarity classification of single ontology.

source. However, most semantic similarity techniques, such as general English ontology, are based on the structure similarity measures method adapted to the biomedical field within the UMLS framework.

The current experiment utilized the hierarchical taxonomy to examine the similarity value between two classes (concepts). The similarity between the two conceptions of the biomedical domain is computed using the SemDist (Al-Mubaid) measure method [13]. The SemDist calculation showed higher correlations with expert scores than with physician scores. Therefore, the best measurement is to utilize the proposed benchmark dataset.

The proposed approach can be used in the biomedical domain (ICD-10 Ontology). The "Certain Infectious and Parasitic Diseases (A00- B99)" coding system is used in this work because it consists of the most extensively used vocabulary resources. It concludes with a description of the Infectious Disease Ontology (IDO) suite of interoperable ontology modules covering the entire contagious disease domain.

9.5.2   Semantic Similarity Measures for Cross-Ontology

The concept similarity in the cross-ontology is measured in two different ontologies, in which the common nodes connect the secondary ontology with the primary ontology. If the two nodes (secondary and primary) refer to the same concept, then the two ontologies are equivalent. Figure 9.3 shows the classification of semantic similarity measures for cross-ontology.

9.5.3   Ontology-Based Semantic Similarity

Ontology-based semantic similarity measures the similarity between two main concepts, widely used in IR or IE [30]. Sometimes, we seek relatedness semantic similarity to define the relationship between two concepts, such as "customer"

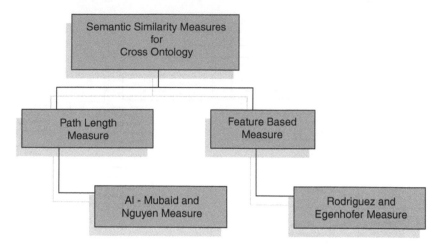

FIGURE 9.3 Semantic similarity classification of cross-ontology.

and "shopping" are related, but there is not much similarity in the current form, but "customer" and "shopper" are similar to some degree. Therefore, a relatedness degree is more general than similarity.

Furthermore, semantic distance is the semantic similarity with less distance between two concepts. The transformation function in Equation (9.1) ensures that the conversion from semantic distance to semantic similarity does not change the correlation significance rate.

$$\text{Sim (C1, C2)} = \text{MaxDist - Dist (C1, C2)} \dots \tag{9.1}$$

where Dist (C1, C2) is the distance between the concepts semantic (C1, C2), MaxDist is the maximum distance of two concepts (C1, C2), and Sim is the transformation function of semantic similarity of the two concepts.

Figure 9.4 shows the steps used to calculate the similarity between pairs of concepts implemented in the proposed methodology. It starts with a reading class list and then sets all the classes in one cluster. After that, we begin with one collection and compare the first concepts with all other concepts. The result will be split into the most dissimilar classes (concepts) and compared until all concepts are fitted into their clusters. The SemDist measure architecture divides the hierarchical clustering, which has information on objects and their measured features.

In this experiment, we utilized the biomedical domain type (ICD-10 Ontology) as the primary data source, containing 738 pairs of concepts. Then we compute the similarity value between them using the SemDist algorithm proposed by *Hisham Al-Mubaid* [13]. The calculation is done based on the following two equations (9.2 and 9.3).

$$\text{Sim (C1, C2)} = \log_2([\text{Path Length(C1, C2) -1}]\alpha \times [\text{CSpec(C1,C2)}]^\beta + k) \dots \tag{9.2}$$

$$\text{CSpec(C1,C2)} = \text{D} - \text{depth (LCS(C1,C2))} \dots \tag{9.3}$$

where α and β are the contributing factors of two features (Path and CSpec) that should be a positive value >0. Also, the depth (LCS(C1, C2)) is the depth of the two

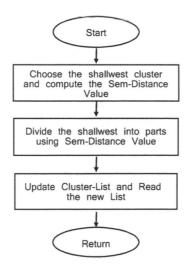

FIGURE 9.4   Flowchart of computing concept similarity.

concepts (C1, C2) based on the node counting. Path Length (C1, C2) is the shortest path length between the two concepts. D is the maximum depth of the taxonomy to reach. K is a constant value greater or equal to one (k≥1). The value of the CSpec feature is calculated as in Equation (9.3).

Path-length measure calculates the semantic distance between two concepts on the ontology using the shortest path length [31] defined in Equation (9.4).

$$\text{Shortest Path}(C1, C2) = 2 * \text{Maxdepth} - \text{len}(C1, C2) \ldots \qquad (9.4)$$

Example 9.1

Consider the following two concepts (C1, C2):
   C1: "Hypertensive renal disease with renal failure" with a code of (I12.0)
   C2: "Hypertensive renal disease with renal failure" with a code of (I12.0).
Compute the similarity value between C1 and C2 using the shortest path-length method.
   The node counting is equal to Max_Depth of the Taxonomy = 5.
   The length between the two concepts is len(C1, C2) = 0.
   Then,
   Shortest Path(C1, C2) = 2 * Max_depth - len(C1, C2)
So, Sim (C1, C2) = 2*5 – 0 = 10, as shown in Table 9.1.

Example 9.2:

Consider the ontology tree shown in Figure 9.5.
   The following concepts were defined in this ontology as follows:

- [A00_0] is the "Cholera due to Vibrio cholerae 01, biovar"
- [A00_1] is the "Cholera due to Vibrio cholerae 01, biovareltor"

TABLE 9.1

Similarity Value for Two Concepts Using Path-Length-Based Measures

Id	Concept 1	Concept 2	LCA(c1 c2)	Length	Similarity
4	Hypertensive renal disease with renal failure (I12.0)	Hypertensive renal disease with renal failure (I12.0)	Hypertensive renal disease with renal failure (I12.0)	0	100%
11	Congestive heart failure (I50.0)	Left ventricular failure (I50.1)	Heart failure (I50.0)	2	80%
30	Pure hypercholesterolemia (E78.0)	Lymph nodes of the head, face, and neck (C77.0)	ICD10_chapter	8	20%

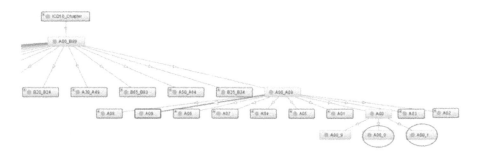

FIGURE 9.5 A fragment example in ICD10 ontology of the A00 class.

- [A00_9] is the "Cholera, unspecified"
- [A01_0] is the "Typhoid fever"
- [A08_5] is the "Other specified intestinal infections"
- [A00] is the "Cholera"
- [A00_A09] is the "Intestinal infectious diseases"

Also, we need to compute the similarity between the following two concepts:

- "Cholera due to Vibrio cholerae 01, biovar cholera [A00_0]" and
- "Cholera due to Vibrio cholerae 01, biovareltor [A00_1]"

The shortest path length is 3 by deploying the node counting between the first concept "Cholera due to Vibrio cholerae 01, biovar [A00.0]" and the second "Cholera, unspecified [A00.9]".

The depth of the least common subsume (LCS) is calculated as follows:

$$\text{LCS (A00.0, A00.0)} = \text{A00.0, and}$$
$$\text{CSpec (A00.0, A00.0)} = D - \text{depth (LCS (A00.0))}$$

Hence, it is equal to $5 - 5 = 0$

TABLE 9.2

The Similarity Score between Two Concepts Using SemDist (Cluster One)

ID	Concept 1	Concept 2	LCS (c1,c2)	Path Len. (c1,c2)	CsPec (c1,c2)	SemDist (c1,c2)
1	A00_0	A00_0	A00_0	1	0	0
2	A00_0	A00_1	A00	3	1	1.6
3	A00_0	A00_9	A00	3	1	1.6
4	A00_0	A01_0	A00_A09	5	2	3.2

Therefore, the similarity value is calculated as follows:

$$\text{SemDist (A00.0, A00.0)} = \log2([1-1]1 \times [0]1 + 1) = \log2(1) = 0$$

However, the similarity is often highest when the two concepts occur at the lower level of the hierarchy. Therefore, the concepts are more interconnected and share more similar information when you get a lower similarity score (between the two concepts), as shown in Table 9.2.

The SemDist measure architecture divides the hierarchical clustering into classes according to their score, which has objects' information and measured features. Then, we will choose the concepts with a lower semantic similarity value from all pairs (more similar and more share information) and put them all together to create the last cluster (cluster 20), as shown in Table 9.3.

Also, the Wu and Palmer measure method [16] is used to calculate the similarity of concepts by taking the depths of concept nodes only, which is computed as in Equation (9.5).

$$\text{Sim (c1, c2)} = 2 * \text{depth(LCS(C1, C2))} / (\text{depth(C1)} + \text{depth(C2)})... \quad (9.5)$$

The similarity score is usually a positive value because the depth of the LCS is positive. The root depth value is 1, and the similarity score of the same classes is 1. Therefore, the score value is between {0 and1].

The similarity score is defined as in Equation (9.6)

$$\text{Sim (C1, C2)} = 2N / (N1+N2+2N)... \quad (9.6)$$

where N is the depth of the LCS (c1, c2), equal to the lowest score of the parent node of C1 and C2.

Example 9.3:

From the ICD-10 "V1.0" taxonomy, consider the following concepts (classes):
C1: "Hypertensive renal disease with renal failure".
C2: "hypertensive renal disease with renal failure".
C3: "Pure hypercholesterolemia".
C4: "Lymph nodes of head".
C5: "face and neck".
Compute the similarity score between classes c1 and c2.

TABLE 9.3
Clustered the Concepts with Similar and Share Information

ID	Concept 1 (Class)	ICD-10 Code	Concept2 (Class)	ICD-10 Code	SemDist
1	Cholera due to Vibrio cholerae 01, biovar cholera	A00.0	Cholera due to Vibrio cholerae 01, biovar cholera	A00.0	0
2	Cholera due to Vibrio cholerae 01, biovar cholera	A00.0	Cholera due to Vibrio cholerae 01, biovareltor	A00.1	1.6
3	Cholera due to Vibrio cholerae 01, biovar cholera	A00.0	Cholera, unspecified	A00.9	1.6
4	Tuberculosis of lung, confined by sputum microscopy with or without culture	A15.0	Tuberculosis of lung, confined by sputum microscopy with or without culture	A15.0	0
5	Tuberculosis of lung, confined by sputum microscopy with or without culture	A15.0	Tuberculosis of the lung, confirmed by culture only	A15.1	1.6
131	..... Streptococcus, group A, as the cause of diseases classified to other chapters	... B95.0	Unspecified staphylococcus as the cause of diseases classified to other chapters	B95.8	

Similarly, (C1, C2) = 2N / (N1+N2+2N), the value of N is 2.
Sim (C1, C2) = 2*5 / (0+0+(2*5)) = 1 = 100%
Similarly, the similarity of (C3, C4, C5) is equal to 2*1 /(4+4+(2*1)) = 0.2 = 20%
Table 9.4 presents the calculated similarity score of the selected concepts from the ICD-10 taxonomy using Wu and Palmer methods (path length-based measures) [32].

9.6   RESULTS AND DISCUSSION

The chapter implements different experiments using ICD10 ontologies as an information source for computing the semantic similarity measurement and evaluation methods. All the similarity measures were calculated using the node counting of concept for path lengths and depths. The computed correlations compared with human scores using the dataset are presented in Table 9.5.

Table 9.6 presents the used datasets that consist of 30 pairs of medical concepts. The experiments found 24 terms in ICD10 out of 30 selected concepts. In contrast, six teams that did not found in ICD10 ontology. Figure 9.6 illustrates the obtained results by deploying different methods for computing the similarity score. The experimental results showed that the proposed method (SimDist) measurement correlated highly with human similarity scores.

TABLE 9.4

The Calculated Similarity Score of the Selected Concepts Using Wu & Palmer

Id	Concept 1	Concept 2	LCA(c1 c2)	Wu & Palmer	Similarity
4	Hypertensive renal disease with renal failure (I12.0)	Hypertensive renal disease with renal failure (I12.0)	Hypertensive renal disease with renal failure	1.00	100%
11	Congestive heart failure (I50.0)	Left ventricular failure (I50.1)	Heart failure	0.80	80%
30	Pure hypercholesterolemia (E78.0)	Lymph nodes of head, face, and neck (C77.0)	ICD10_chapter	0.20	20%

TABLE 9.5

The Correlations Results Compared with Human Scores of Selected Datasets

Measure	Phys. (Rank)	Expert (Rank)	Both (Rank)
SimDist	0.6007 (3)	**0.6641 (1)**	**0.6548 (1)**
Lin	0.6045 (2)	0.6563 (2)	0.6526 (2)
Path Length	**0.6118 (1)**	0.6505 (5)	0.6436 (4)
Wu Palmer	0.5865 (4)	0.6508 (4)	0.6451 (3)
L&C	0.5801 (5)	0.6558 (3)	0.6401 (5)
Resink	0.5576 (6)	0.6207 (6)	0.6096 (6)

9.7 CONCLUSION

Building automatic systems capable of identifying the ontology of concepts, especially medical, is a complex issue and requires accumulated experience. The accuracy of evaluating these systems depends on the type of data used and the methods for classifying and assessing them. Therefore, this chapter deals with finding a strategy for organizing and indexing medical data characterized by accuracy and speed.

The results produced in this chapter for examining the SemDist (C1, C2) similarity score are interesting, with a high matching similarity score of two medical concepts compared to the expert's assessment. In addition, many experiments using ICD10 ontologies as an information source for computing semantic similarity measurement and evaluation methodologies have been conducted.

For path lengths and depths, all similarity metrics were determined using the node counting technique. We intend to create a web-based system for all of these semantic similarity measures in the future work of this research and make it available to scholars via the internet.

TABLE 9.6

The used Medical Concepts Datasets

Id	Concept1	Concept 2	Phys	Expert
4	Renal failure (I12.0)	Kidney failure (I12.0)	4.0000	4.0000
5	Heart (I51.5)	Myocardium (I51.5)	3.3333	3.0000
1	Stroke (I64)	Infarct (I64)	3.0000	2.7778
7	Abortion O03	Miscarriage O03	3.0000	3.3333
9	Delusion (F06.2)	Schizophrenia (F06.2)	3.0000	2.2222
11	Congestive heart failure (150.0)	Pulmonary edema (150.1)	3.0000	1.4444
8	Metastasis (C77.0)	Adenocarcinoma (C08.9)	2.6667	1.7778
17	Calcification (M61)	Stenosis (H04.5)	2.6667	2.0000
10	Diarrhea	Stomach cramps	2.3333	1.3333
19	Mitral stenosis (I05.0)	Atrial fibrillation (148)	2.3333	1.3333
20	Chronic obstructive pulmonary disease (J44.9)	Lung infiltrates (J82)	2.0000	1.8889
2	Rheumatoid arthritis (M05.3)	Lupus (L93)	2.0000	1.1111
3	Brain tumor (G94.8)	Intracranial hemorrhage (I 69.2)	2.0000	1.3333
15	Carpal tunnel Syndrome (G56.0)	Osteoarthritis (M19.9)	2.0000	1.1111
18	Diabetes mellitus (E10-E14)	Hypertension (I10-I15)	2.0000	1.0000
27	Acne	Syringe	2.0000	1.0000
12	Antibiotic (Z88.1)	Allergy (Z88.1)	1.6667	1.2222
13	Cortisone	Total knee replacement	1.6667	1.0000
14	Pulmonary embolus	Myocardial infarction	1.6667	1.2222
16	Pulmonary Fibrosis (E84.0)	Lung Cancer (C34.1)	1.6667	1.4444
6	Cholangiocarcinoma	Colonoscopy	1.3333	1.0000
29	Lymphoid hyperplasia (K38.0)	Laryngeal Cancer (C32.0)	1.3333	1.0000
21	Multiple Sclerosis (F06.8)	Psychosis (F06.8)	1.0000	1,0000
22	Appendicitis (K35)	Osteoporosis (M80)	1.0000	1,0000
23	Rectal polyp (K62,1)	Aorta (I70.0)	1.0000	1,0000
24	Xerostomia (K11.7)	Alcoholic cirrhosis (K70.3)	1.0000	1.0000
25	Peptic ulcer disease (K21.0)	Myopia (H52.1)	1.0000	1.0000
26	Depression (F2.0.4)	Cellulitis (H60.1)	1.0000	1,0000
28	Varicose vein	Entire knee meniscus	1.0000	1.0000
30	HyperliFidenna (E78.0)	Metastasis (C77.0)	1.0000	1,0000

To develop future work for the classification of medical data, we have to do the following:

1. Finding a standard global classification of medical data that includes all the concepts and their features is tedious for the amount of extensive data. Therefore, we have to resort to effectively classifying data based on parts of speech.
2. Develop automated methods that rely on deep learning to link concepts with their features and retrieve them accurately and quickly.

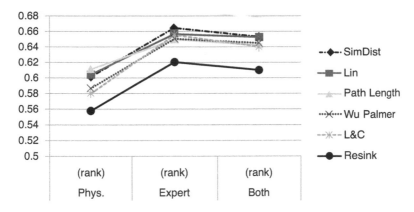

FIGURE 9.6   The correlation score compared with human scores.

3. Implement algorithms based on bidirectional memory in designing linguistic dictionaries that can be integrated from information systems to retrieve concepts and their features.

REFERENCES

[1] Waloszek W. Towards use of ontoclean for ontology contextualization. *Procedia Computer Science*. 2021;192: 786–795.

[2] Khadir AC, Aliane H, Guessoum A. Ontology learning: Grand tour and challenges. *Computer Science Review*. 2021;39: 100339.

[3] Pérez-Pérez M, Ferreira T, Lourenço A, Igrejas G, Fdez-Riverola F. Boosting biomedical document classification through the use of domain entity recognizers and semantic ontologies for document representation: The case of gluten bibliome. *Neurocomputing*. 2022 May 1;484:223–37.

[4] Shannon GJ, Rayapati N, Corns SM, Wunsch II DC. Comparative study using inverse ontology cogency and alternatives for concept recognition in the annotated national library of medicine database. *Neural Networks*. 2021;139: 86–104.

[5] Tran V-A et al. OnWARD: Ontology-driven web-based framework for multi-center clinical studies. *Journal of Biomedical Informatics*. 2011; 44(2011): S48–S53.

[6] Harispe S et al. A framework for unifying ontology-based semantic similarity measures: A study in the biomedical domain. *Journal of Biomedical Informatics*. 2014 Apr 1;48:38–53.

[7] Kulandai Josephine J, Thenmozhi, JD. Ontology based EMR for decision making in health care using SNOMED CT. In *2012 International Conference on Recent Trends in Information Technology*, Chennai, Tamil Nadu, India, 2012 Apr 19 (pp. 514–519). IEEE.

[8] Ayeldeen H, et al. Evaluation of semantic similarity across MeSH ontology: A Cairo University thesis - Mining case study. In *2013 12th Mexican International Conference on Artificial Intelligence*, Mexico 2013 Nov 24 (pp. 139–144). IEEE.

[9] Sathya D, Uthayan KR. Proposal for semantic metric to assess the quality of ontologies. *Proceedings of 2011 International Conference on Signal Processing, Communication, Computing and Networking Technologies (ICSCCN 2011)*. Thuckalay, India, 2011, pp. 754–756.

[10] David S, *Defining a Benchmark Suite for Evaluating the Import of OWL Lite Ontologies*. Master thesis, July, 2006.

[11] Yoshiura VT, Yamada DB, Pellison FC, de Lima IB, Damian IP, Rijo RP, de Azevedo Marques JM, Alves D. Towards a health observatory conceptual model based on the semantic web. *Procedia Computer Science.* 2018;138:131–136.

[12] Aouicha MB, Taieb MA. Computing semantic similarity between biomedical concepts using new information content approach. *Journal of Biomedical Informatics.* 2016;59:258–275.

[13] Al-Mubaid H, Nguyen HA. A cluster-based approach for semantic similarity in the biomedical domain. In: *2006 International Conference of the IEEE Engineering in Medicine and Biology Society.* New York, NY 2006 (pp. 2713–2717). IEEE.

[14] Reitz KM, Hall DE, Shinall Jr MC, Shireman PK, Silverstein JC. Using the unified medical language system to expand the operative stress score–first use case. *Journal of Surgical Research.* 2021;268:552–561.

[15] Alonso I, Contreras D. Evaluation of semantic similarity metrics applied to the automatic retrieval of medical documents: An UMLS approach. *Expert Systems with Applications.* 2016;44:386–399.

[16] Mayhew M, DeBar LL, Deyo RA, Kerns RD, Goulet JL, Brandt CA, Von Korff M. Development and assessment of a crosswalk between ICD-9-CM and ICD-10-CM to identify patients with common pain conditions. *The Journal of Pain.* 2019;20(12):1429–1445.

[17] Sánchez D, Batet M, Martínez S, Domingo-Ferrer J. Semantic variance: An intuitive measure for ontology accuracy evaluation. *Engineering Applications of Artificial Intelligence.* 2015;39:89–99.

[18] Silachan K, Tantatsanawong P. Domain ontology health informatics service from text medical data classification. In *2011 Annual SRII Global Conference*, San Jose, California USA, 2011 (pp. 357–362). IEEE.

[19] Grove MJ. *Development of an Ontology for Rehabilitation: Traumatic Brain Injury.* University of Minnesota, Ph.D. dissertation. September 2013. https://hdl.handle.net/11299/159711

[20] Henry S, McQuilkin A, McInnes BT. Association measures for estimating semantic similarity and relatedness between biomedical concepts. *Artificial Intelligence in Medicine.* 2019;93:1–10.

[21] Bright TJ, Furuya EY, Kuperman GJ, Cimino JJ, Bakken S. Development and evaluation of an ontology for guiding appropriate antibiotic prescribing. *Journal of Biomedical Informatics.* 2012;45(1):120–128.

[22] Nguyen HA, Al-Mubaid H. New semantic similarity techniques of concepts applied in the biomedical domain and WordNet (Doctoral dissertation, University of Houston-Clear Lake).

[23] Achtert E, Kriegel HP, Zimek A. ELKI: a software system for evaluation of subspace clustering algorithms. In *International Conference on Scientific and Statistical Database Management.* 2008 (pp. 580–585). Springer, Berlin, Heidelberg.

[24] Abdelrahman AM. A Methodology for Evaluating Ontologies in the Biomedical Domain (Doctoral dissertation, Sudan University of Science & Technology).

[25] Wohlin C, Runeson P, Höst M, Ohlsson MC, Regnell B, Wesslén A. *Experimentation in Software Engineering.* Springer-Verlag Berlin Heidelberg, 2012.

[26] Hoehndorf R, Dumontier M, Gkoutos GV. Evaluation of research in biomedical ontologies. *Briefings in Bioinformatics.* 2013;14(6):696–712.

[27] Kaur P, Pannu HS, Malhi AK. Comparative analysis on cross-modal information retrieval: a review. *Computer Science Review.* 2021;39: 100336.

[28] Brank J, Grobelnik M, Mladenic D. A survey of ontology evaluation techniques. In *Proceedings of the Conference on Data Mining and Data Warehouses (SiKDD 2005)*, 2005 (pp. 166–170). Citeseer Ljubljana, Slovenia.

[29] Yankova-Doseva M. *TERMS: Text Extraction from Redundant and Multiple Sources* (Doctoral dissertation, University of Sheffield). 2010.

[30] Harispe S, Sánchez D, Ranwez S, Janaqi S, Montmain J. A framework for unifying ontology-based semantic similarity measures: A study in the biomedical domain. *Journal of Biomedical Informatics*. 2014;48:38–53.

[31] Rada R, Mili H, Bicknell E, Blettner M. Development and application of a metric on semantic nets. *IEEE Transactions on Systems, Man, and Cybernetics*. 1989;19(1):17–30.

[32] Wu Z, Palmer M. Verb semantics and lexical selection. arXiv preprint cmp-lg/9406033. 1994.

10 IoT: Emerging Approach for Pharmaceutical and Healthcare Systems

Sudhanshu Mishra and Smriti Ojha
Madan Mohan Malviya University of Technology

Akhalesh Kumar
Maharishi University of Information Technology

CONTENTS

DOI: 10.1201/9781003326182-10

10.1 INTRODUCTION

The Internet of things (IoT) integrates various smart tools with the internet, permitting data to be delivered and received across the network. Various sensors are all examples of how the IoT concept has evolved. Smart organizations providing healthcare benefits with the aid of IoT concepts and other technology are at the heart of it. Smart gadgets can capture and communicate data in everyday life to complete the task at hand. IoT applications benefit day-to-day living including various devices (Liu et al. 2015; Nasajpour et al. 2020; Tariq et al. 2020), planning for smart cities and areas, entertainment devices, housing, diagnosis with therapy, and disease management (Nasajpour et al., 2020). The advanced technologies improve fruitfulness and wholesomeness (Rahman et al. 2020; Javaid et al. 2020).

The IoT links all computational data to devices; these smart devices further send data over the internet, reducing the chances of error (Singh et al. 2018). This technology is flowering in terms of improved treatment and faster diagnosis of diseases that too without physical visits and monitoring during the COVID-19 pandemic (Bai et al. 2020).

In the healthcare profession, it is critical to have the right equipment to run a successful surgery. IoT has a strong ability to perform successful surgical procedures and evaluate operational outcomes (Haleem and Javaid 2019; Klonoff 2017). Medical devices and artificial intelligence (AI)-linked algorithms are to be connected to smart devices to communicate essential health data to a physician effectively and flawlessly (Rath and Pattanayak 2019). These smart devices also collect and calculate information on oxygen levels, blood pressure, body weight, and sugar levels, among other things (Javaid and Khan 2021). These technological advances can digitally calculate, collect, analyze, and provide cloud storage of data. All clinical records and patient data are kept safe using digital storage, and this information may be easily transferred in emergencies, allowing clinicians to work more efficiently (Otoom et al. 2020).

Software is critical to maintaining effective management and monitoring of patient data. All records are kept in strict confidence to provide the best possible care in the future. AI improves the performance of doctors and surgeons and helps to improve treatment accuracy, efficiency, and consistency (Tran et al. 2020). This technology can help patients feel better by reducing discomfort and quickly identifying bone abnormalities so that appropriate treatment can be given (Yang et al. 2020).

The IoT has increased a person's sovereignty and enhanced their potential to contact and correlated with the outside world. Futuristic approaches, and algorithms, have made IoT become a significant contributor to worldwide communication. Through this platform, a variety of items and programs are connected to the internet, including wireless sensors, home appliances, and electrical devices (Peng et al. 2017; Lin et al. 2017). Perhaps the most significant and personal influence will be on medicine. By 2020, health-related IoT technology will account for 40% of all IoT-related technology, accounting for a $117 billion market (Khan, Han, and Karthik 2018).

The present chapter summarizes various IoT-related platforms which have created a new door to innovations in the field of the healthcare system and disease management. IoT is an emerging and advanced information technology that enables proactive solutions, drugs, and machinery management, especially in the health-related area, via digitalization and management of patients' health-related data.

10.2   ELECTRONIC HEALTH RECORDS

An electronic health record (EHR) is a digital record of patient and population health and medical history; this data is collected systemically and is stored in a digital format. These digital records can be used, generated, and shared in a variety of healthcare settings and clinical cases. This EHR is used to

- Improve standard, customization, welfare, and potency and avoid medical variations.
- Educate patients and families to reduce medical errors.
- Improve care coordination and reduce delays in healthcare strategies.
- Maintain confidentiality of patient's medical data.
- Enhance research potential and business perspective.
- Provide quick and coordinated access to data with enhanced precision and efficiency.

10.3   INTERNET APPROACHES IN THE PHARMACEUTICAL SECTOR

Pharma corporations knew a long time ago that simply selling traditional medicines would not be enough to generate growth or even maintain competitiveness. Moving "beyond the pill" is a fundamental shift that typically results from two comprehensions: (i) Medicines alone are usually insufficient to provide patients with the best possible therapeutic outcomes and (ii) as the pharmaceutical industry business is moving toward "beyond-the-pill," which is a new source of business platforms as well as revenue. This has sparked a surge in interest in ways to use new technology and business processes to improve drug and product manufacturing for enhanced patient care.

Patients, clinicians, and other medical professionals will be able to receive or provide therapy with embedded sensor techniques, as well as build individualized care services and processes, thanks to Pharma IoT (Product 2.0). These sensors are useful for dementia, Parkinson's, and multiple sclerosis patients, which help to manage medicines and their timely administration to improve patient health outcomes and their quality of life.

Various medical device items, like oxygen saturation, magnetic fields, and insulin monitors, can also be attached to the specific sensors, and these technologies are used to collect data for further interpretation and individualized treatment. These digitally recorded systemic data provide a potential platform for research and patient individualization. These outcomes are helpful for individual medical care or enhanced health benefits (Dzubur et al. 2015).

The shift is not without its difficulties: pharma enterprises must also consider the upcoming record safety protocols and regulations, as well as patients' authority over their healthcare data. Patients will be able to transfer their medical information stored in a digital mode across numerous physicians, clinicians, or healthcare professionals, for example, resulting in the establishment of new health service platforms and related business models, such as data brokers.

10.4 MEDICAL IMAGING

The remarkable advances in sophisticated imaging technologies have resulted in significant improvements in a physician's capacity to identify a wide range of ailments. However, because the usage of and expenditures for imaging services have risen faster than other physician-ordered procedures, without accompanying proof of their overall benefit, government and commercial insurers have taken efforts to curb their expansion (Dimitrov 2016). In the healthcare setting, rapid digitalization is taking place. Many large corporations are creating systems that will allow a hospital's myriad of equipment to work in an integrated way. For example, in Philips' Healthsuite, medical tenets used health devices to process, analyze, and forward data, which could be obtained by healthcare professionals such as physicians (via mobile devices or desktop computers), among others, and play a large part in advising treatment-related judgments ("Medtech and the Internet of Medical Things How Connected Medical Devices Are Transforming Health Care" 2018).

Another use of IoT is real-time data and networked data created and gathered by health-related equipment and devices in the various therapeutic management of patients ("Philips EICU Program |Philips Healthcare | ICU Telemedicine Solution" 2022) through various medical instrumentations and related machines providing and generating histological and pathological images as digital data that may assist in speedier therapeutic judgments to manage disease (Michalakis and Caridakis 2017).

The phrase "digital pathology" refers to actionable information created by AI algorithms on photographs of sick tissues such as wounds, tumors, or other pathological conditions. Another example of MedTech firms incorporating ability is GE and Roche Diagnostics, which have worked on AI platforms to provide disease perspectives and pathogenesis to oncologists (Pantanowitz et al. 2018). These AI-assisted technologies are being used worldwide as an aid for health cures and management of recent situations like COVID-19, including community monitoring, finding out infected persons, disease-related treatments, symptomatic evaluations of therapy, etc. (Ting et al. 2020).

10.5 ARTIFICIAL INTELLIGENCE (AI)

A "smart healthcare organization" is a notion that arose as an aftereffect of fast digitalization throughout the pharmaceutical sector via the application of AI-assisted platforms, primarily the IoT, and the provision of tailored assistance ("Medtech and the Internet of Medical Things How Connected Medical Devices Are Transforming Health Care" 2018).

The use of AI technologies in the healthcare industry has a good standing experience of advancement. In turn, certain lengthy issues and obstacles in the medical profession have spurred various scientists to explore their in-depth exploration of

AI. AI technology become increasingly frequently used in the medical profession as new technologies have been developed. Furthermore, the deep collaboration of AI and IoT technologies together qualifies the steady enhancement of medical diagnostic and treatment capacities to give more effective services to the public. The bottom structure of IoT includes cloud computing, big data resources, and machine learning as well as deep learning in drug development, combined with concepts of distinct algorithms such as activity identification, behavior, and conduct identification, peculiarity recognition, and decision-making provisions (Dey et al. 2019).

The application of AI is dependent on authentic data sources, integration of pertinent knocking technologies, and valedictory health-related shreds of evidence with clinical applications, to pictorial segmentation, automated measurements, and, eventually, automated diagnosis. AI may cut costs and increase value during the picture-gathering, interpretation, and decision-making processes (Ruusuvuori et al. 2022). Figure 10.1 illustrates the advantages of choosing AI for healthcare.

Without a question, AI is a hotly debated issue in image research related to diagnosis and treatment today. The number of AI articles in diagnostic imaging alone has surged from 100–150 to 1000–1100 in the past decade. AI has been used by researchers to recognize complex behavior in neuroimaging and provide quantitative assessments of radiographic qualities. In radiation oncology, AI has been used in many imaging modalities utilized at various phases of therapy specifically, tumor identification and therapy evaluation (Sadoughi, Behmanesh, and Sayfouri 2020).

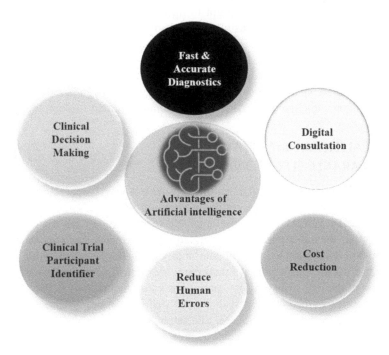

FIGURE 10.1   Advantages of choosing AI for healthcare.

10.6　CREATING AN IoT PLATFORM FOR DISORDER EVALUATION, DIAGNOSIS, PREVENTION, AND THERAPY

Technology has transformed the way people exchange and access information. Since the emergence of contemporary online services, social networks, and ubiquitous access via devices, information extraction is now easier than ever. Patients' awareness, competency, and involvement in health decision-making techniques can all benefit from access to online healthcare information. Although the internet has not frequently been used in certain clinical sub-areas, the significant increase in health-related internet research most likely will lead to the inclusion of more medical sub-fields in the next years. General healthcare clinicians should understand that patients are accessing the internet as a source of medical and health information and should be equipped to change recommendations for web-based health resources and aid patients in monitoring the efficiency of medical material accessible online. There are some inherent issues with online health information as well (Tang 2020). Online health information is difficult to monitor, making quality management difficult, and individuals' health data literacy varies greatly (Yang et al. 2020).

The fast improvement and adoption of technology and IoT-based technologies have opened up new avenues for technical breakthroughs in numerous parts of life. The primary purpose of IoT technologies is to simplify procedures in many domains, to increase system efficiency (technology or specialized activities), and, lastly, to improve life quality. The dynamic growth of IoT technologies is providing various positive benefits, but this rapid development must be properly monitored and analyzed from an environmental standpoint to minimize the existence of detrimental repercussions and promote the sensible exploitation of a finite resource base (Kelly et al. 2020). Various medical investigation disciplines have employed IoT as a data source, but its potential in public health monitoring has not even been properly investigated and leveraged consistently (Sahu et al. 2021). The IoT is a platform of wireless, interconnected, and linked electronic technology that can gather, distribute, and store information without requiring human-to-human or human-to-computer contact.

10.7　HEALTHCARE IoT RELATED TO WEARABLE ELECTRONICS

IoT is a novel idea that allows for healthcare monitoring via wearable technology. Wearable devices have received significant attention from academicians, researchers, and clinical segments over the previous few years, and they have lately become highly popular. Wearable gazettes are defined as "electronics that may be attached to human skin with suitable mode to continually analyze operations while disrupting or restricting the user's normal functioning." In today's society, working people, spend most of the day struggling for many jobs while ignoring their health and fitness. Even a simple meeting with a doctor at a clinic can necessitate a battery of tests for evaluation, prescriptions, and, ultimately, treatment, all of which can take a significant amount of time. As a consequence, many individuals only visit a clinic rarely or at a critical stage. As a result, many individuals are looking for an alternative, such as electronic smart devices or gadgets to monitor the user's health and also provide timely insights on numerous health metrics to both the patient and clinician (Haghi, Thurow, and Stoll 2017). Wearable technologies have several benefits in the health sector; however, authorized clinical gadgets are reluctant to materialize. In stroke patients' hand rehabilitation treatment, wearable gadgets, such as data gloves (to capture finger action), insoles, hats, and smartwatches, are often placed straight on the participant's body, within clothes, or in flexible constructions. They may converse with one another by using the living body as a communication channel. This increased data transfer speed is used in digital healthcare to improve medical centers, public health, and, eventually, community welfare. Human behavior identification is a critical component in the development of human-interaction applications in fitness and strength and wellness (Gao et al. 2016).

The increasing need for enhancing the quality of life, availability of drug products, and affordability for therapy will necessitate continual accurate and thorough monitoring and treatment via wearable technology for wellness coaching (Xu et al. 2014). This smart technology has extensive promise in the coming years to reduce the cost of therapy and diagnosis. Computing in healthcare research can lead to clinical development in how healthcare is given in the coming years (Griebel et al. 2015).

10.8 WIRELESS COMMUNICATION OR MOBILE COMPUTING IN HEALTHCARE SYSTEM

The IoT has changed many sectors affecting human living, but its impact on the healthcare industry has been particularly significant due to its cutting-edge nature. When mobile computing technologies are employed to support the IoT, the IoT takes on a greater significance. Mobile computing, which provides considerable support in the form of mobile health, extends the capabilities of IoT in a healthcare setting (Kuo 2011).

Clinics, with indoor patients (IPD) and outdoor patients (OPD) services, emergency wards, surgical theaters, intensive care units (ICUs), and laboratories are all examples of the dispersed healthcare sector (Kuo 2011). Mobile devices meet this criterion by offering several communication choices, including phone and video calling, text, e-mail, and multimedia messaging, as well as video conferencing (Kudtarkar et al. 2010). Glucose level analysis, blood pressure determination, body temperature management, oxygen saturation level recordings and management, electrocardiogram (ECG) analysis, wheelchair management, and rehabilitation are only a few of the IoT applications (Vijayan et al. 2021).

10.9 IMPACT OF MOBILE COMPUTING

10.9.1 COLLABORATIVE EFFECTS ON THE DEVELOPMENT OF MOBILE COMPUTING SYSTEMS

In the organization, mobile computing has a good impact on healthcare management resulting (Xu et al. 2014) in faster system developments and increased innovation, but it may have an impact on quality. The study included 18 initiatives aimed at detecting flaws in systems after mobile computing collaboration. The study reveals that the collaboration was well-liked but progressed slowly. Some initiatives with goal C have a small likelihood of fewer developments and slower projects. More than 6% of bugs and potential dangers were detected as a result of the study (Mell and Grance 2011).

10.9.2 MOBILE COMPUTING POWER AND BIG DATA TECHNOLOGIES

Spatiotemporal big data (PSTBD) is a smart grid technology that is based on mobile computing and has seen a significant increase in usage in enterprises that use big data technologies (Ahuja, Mani, and Zambrano 2012). The comparison of the variations in features, platform, and architecture in both conventional and PSTBD technologies. The PSTBD offers a lot of efficiencies, but it also has a lot of obstacles in terms of implementation.

10.9.3 MOBILE COMPUTING-BASED SECURITY MONITORING

In the information technology industry, security is critical because it protects data from breaches and attacks. Mobile computing uses the ability to operate sensing devices to construct a cluster to create a machine learning-trained model. The advanced model developed by scientists serves as an asynchronous parallel model that corrects any technology imperfections that have occurred. The model effect by reducing the amount of the barrier improved the performance of the systems (Al-Zaiti, Shusterman, and Carey 2013).

10.9.4 COMPUTING AND HEALTHCARE

With mobile computing, medical professionals may easily access patient information on demand. Information sharing will save time and money. Staff will have access to electronic health records via mobile health devices. Patients can also use mobile (Fong and Chung 2013). Computing to keep track of their information and receive updates from their doctors m It will make it easier for them to access information such as charts, reports, payments, and appointment scheduling.

10.10 APPLICATIONS OF MOBILE COMPUTING IN HEALTHCARE

The mobile computing application is discussed under two major categories that are physiological functions monitoring-based applications and patient communication and support-based application.

10.10.1 PHYSIOLOGICAL FUNCTION MONITORING-BASED APPLICATIONS

These apps allow for remote analysis, computation, and management of many health-related parameters. This leads to more up-to-date and accurate diagnosis, which improves the health of patients (Takeuchi et al. 2013). They allow for continuous surveillance of patients as they go about their everyday routines (Xia, Asif, and Zhao 2013). Among these applications are:

- **Heart Function Monitoring**

    It first appeared in 1947. This gadget allowed for continuous heart function monitoring outside of a clinical setting. The monitor consists of pair of electrodes linked to the patient's chest and is usually worn by the patients. The patient usually wears this gadget for 24 hours before returning it to their doctor for a study of the results. The readings can now be wirelessly communicated by newer devices (Takeuchi et al. 2013). Long-term cardiac monitoring, according to studies, can detect a wider spectrum of issues than short-term monitoring.
- **Blood Glucose Monitoring**

    Diabetes can lead to heart disease, pregnancy difficulties, and limb and other associated complications if it is not effectively managed. A diabetic patient must regularly manage his or her blood sugar level to avoid such consequences. Diabetics and doctors may find that wireless and ubiquitous devices can help them better manage their disease (Shih et al. 2012). Digital data can also be forwarded to a personal physician at the user's choosing. Tracking a patient's health status can assist physicians in recommending a prescription modification (Clemmensen et al. 2005).

10.10.2 PATIENT COMMUNICATION AND SUPPORT-BASED APPLICATION

Mobile and the internet give a broad perspective for data transmission between patients and clinicians or practitioners, in addition to providing remote monitoring. These apps not only allow clinicians to contact patients at any time and from any location, but also give health-related information at a time and location with control (Gao, Thiebes, and Sunyaev 2018). As a result, health-related costs are reduced.

- **Maintenance of Patient Records**

    Smartphone features are available in several systems, including eClinicalWorks, LifeRecord, and MacPracticeMD. Public health records (PHRs) will also gain traction as consumers become more involved in tracking their health records (Lebeda, Zalatoris, and Scheerer 2018). For smartphones, there are a few PHRs to choose from. Polka, for example, is compatible with iPhone. This saves, identifies, and computes the consumer's personal health information, as well as provides health reminders. There are various additional emergency apps available in addition to this one (Wang et al. 2013).
- **Health Education**

    Reaching out to young people to educate them about health is a challenge for most health educators. Cell phones have the potential to be an effective tool for reaching out to the general public. Various programs that send text messages to mobile phones can be a safe option (Fujita et al. 2013). The San Francisco Department of Public Health, for example, established SexInfo in 2006. SexInfo is a free text-messaging service that answers sex-related inquiries for teenagers. It also includes phone numbers and addresses for local clinics (Gu et al. 2020).

- **Appointment Reminders**

  Using text messages or an interactive application to send out regular reminders about patient visits can improve managerial effectiveness and improves the usefulness of healthcare providers. This could save money on disease management in the long run.

- **Health Alerts**

  Text messaging can aid in the surveillance of disease outbreaks as well as the delivery of timely alerts about health concerns or epidemics. Other possible applications include sending out warnings about harmful pollution levels or alerting people about impending tsunamis or infection zone like it is being used by every person during the COVID-19 pandemic.

10.11   HEALTHY CONVERSATION MODES FOR HEALTHCARE PROFESSIONALS AND SERVICE SEEKERS

Healthy communication between the healthcare professional and the patient is critical in conveying essential information to the patient or updating the doctor on the patient's health status so that the doctor can respond quickly. While these technologies can assist physicians in providing more prompt diagnoses and treatments, they also make healthcare more comfortable and enjoyable for individuals.

10.12   ADVANTAGES AND DISADVANTAGES OF MOBILE COMPUTING IN HEALTHCARE

- **Advantages**
  1. Always with you" is one of the major benefits. For the medical industry, quick data processing is a unique and extremely significant advantage. Because it does not necessitate a large infrastructure on either side, the interaction ability of patients is given context.
  2. Applications, in general, are simple and require no or little technical knowledge for user groups.
  3. Application development for mobile solutions can be realized within modest budgets.

- **Disadvantages**
  1. It might also be understood as a greater emphasis on technical aspects, leading to stressful conditions for both patients and medical personnel. The data input must be protected and stored. It is possible that the infrastructure will not meet the same specific features and criteria.
  2. There is still a lot of confusion about radiation, and it must be understood clearly. The entire team should follow a given set of industry standards, which is now not the case.

10.13 VARIOUS AREAS OF MOBILE COMPUTING IN THE HEALTHCARE INDUSTRY

From the standpoint of an information technology (IT) organization, it is understood that the reduced cost of therapy by the integration of cell phones and wireless communication as a component of whole processes is substantially larger than in most other industries. The bulk is not assigned to a certain mainframe, but rather moves about the building complex on a regular basis. As a result, IT processes could only be used in a substandard manner until recently.

10.14 CONCLUSION

The adoption of cutting-edge technology will result in a considerable improvement in healthcare practice, and doctors will be forced to use them. IoT is a rapidly developing segment with enormous roles in healthcare and disease management. It allows cost-effective compilation, investigation, and scrutiny of critical data, and testing results. Therapeutic innovations, checklists, inventory, and distribution panels will get benefit in terms of delivery of the correct therapeutic agent at the required time and location. Intelligent devices for the IoT would be self-contained, disruptive, and innovative. Data are digitally controlled and saved systematically on the cloud, linked software will be available, allowing for more effective disease detection and follow-up. This breakthrough information system innovation will support smarter healthcare services in the Medical 4.0 setting. These smart devices are very much helpful to provide quick analytical information which is utilized to improve patients' health conditions and disease management. The challenges are now only going to become more complex as the marketplace for healthcare IoT expands. Thus, to be productive in utilizing IoT, adequate identification and authorization will be necessary.

REFERENCES

Ahuja, Sanjay P., Sindhu Mani, and Jesus Zambrano. 2012. "A Survey of the State of Cloud Computing in Healthcare." *Network and Communication Technologies* 1 (2). doi:10.5539/NCT.V1N2P12.

Al-Zaiti, Salah S., Vladimir Shusterman, and Mary G. Carey. 2013. "Novel Technical Solutions for Wireless ECG Transmission & Analysis in the Age of the Internet Cloud." *Journal of Electrocardiology* 46 (6): 540–545. doi:10.1016/J.JELECTROCARD.2013.07.002.

Bai, Li, Dawei Yang, Xun Wang, Lin Tong, Xiaodan Zhu, Nanshan Zhong, Chunxue Bai, et al. 2020. "Chinese Experts' Consensus on the Internet of Things-Aided Diagnosis and Treatment of Coronavirus Disease 2019 (COVID-19)." *Clinical EHealth* 3: 7. doi:10.1016/J.CEH.2020.03.001.

Clemmensen, Peter, Maria Sejersten, Martin Sillesen, David Hampton, Galen S. Wagner, and Søren Loumann-Nielsen. 2005. "Diversion of ST-Elevation Myocardial Infarction Patients for Primary Angioplasty Based on Wireless Prehospital 12-Lead Electrocardiographic Transmission Directly to the Cardiologist's Handheld Computer: A Progress Report." *Journal of Electrocardiology* 38 (4 SUPPL.): 194–198. doi:10.1016/j.jelectrocard.2005.06.035.

Deloitte Centre for Health Solutions' Report. Medtech and the Internet of Medical Things: How connected medical devices are transforming health care. 2018. https://www2.deloitte.com/content/dam/Deloitte/global/Documents/Life-Sciences-Health-Care/gx-lshc-medtech-iomt-brochure.pdf

Dey, Damini, Piotr J. Slomka, Paul Leeson, Dorin Comaniciu, Sirish Shrestha, Partho P. Sengupta, and Thomas H. Marwick. 2019. "Artificial Intelligence in Cardiovascular Imaging: JACC State-of-the-Art Review." *Journal of the American College of Cardiology* 73 (11): 1317–1335. doi:10.1016/J.JACC.2018.12.054.

Dimitrov, Dimiter v. 2016. "Medical Internet of Things and Big Data in Healthcare." *Healthcare Informatics Research* 22 (3): 156. doi:10.4258/HIR.2016.22.3.156.

Dzubur, Eldin, Marilyn Li, Keito Kawabata, Yifei Sun, Rob McConnell, Stephen Intille, and Genevieve Fridlund Dunton. 2015. "Design of a Smartphone Application to Monitor Stress, Asthma, and Asthma Inhaler Use." *Annals of Allergy, Asthma & Immunology : Official Publication of the American College of Allergy, Asthma, & Immunology* 114 (4): 341. doi:10.1016/J.ANAI.2014.12.017.

Fong, Ee May, and Wan Young Chung. 2013. "Mobile Cloud-Computing-Based Healthcare Service by Noncontact ECG Monitoring." *Sensors (Switzerland)* 13 (12): 16451–16473. doi:10.3390/s131216451.

Fujita, Hideo, Yuji Uchimura, Kayo Waki, Koji Omae, Ichiro Takeuchi, and Kazuhiko Ohe. 2013. "Development and Clinical Study of Mobile 12-Lead Electrocardiography Based on Cloud Computing for Cardiac Emergency." *Studies in Health Technology and Informatics* 192 (1–2): 1077. doi:10.3233/978-1-61499-289-9-1077.

Gao, Fangjian, Scott Thiebes, and Ali Sunyaev. 2018. "Rethinking the Meaning of Cloud Computing for Health Care: A Taxonomic Perspective and Future Research Directions." *Journal of Medical Internet Research* 20 (7). doi:10.2196/10041.

Gao, Wei, Sam Emaminejad, Hnin Yin Yin Nyein, Samyuktha Challa, Kevin Chen, Austin Peck, Hossain M. Fahad, et al. 2016. "Fully Integrated Wearable Sensor Arrays for Multiplexed in Situ Perspiration Analysis." *Nature* 529 (7587): 509–514. doi:10.1038/NATURE16521.

Griebel, Lena, Hans Ulrich Prokosch, Felix Köpcke, Dennis Toddenroth, Jan Christoph, Ines Leb, Igor Engel, and Martin Sedlmayr. 2015. "A Scoping Review of Cloud Computing in Healthcare." *BMC Medical Informatics and Decision Making* 15 (1). doi:10.1186/S12911-015-0145-7.

Gu, Dongxiao, Xuejie Yang, Shuyuan Deng, Changyong Liang, Xiaoyu Wang, Jiao Wu, and Jingjing Guo. 2020. "Tracking Knowledge Evolution in Cloud Health Care Research: Knowledge Map and Common Word Analysis." *Journal of Medical Internet Research* 22 (2). doi:10.2196/15142.

Haghi, Mostafa, Kerstin Thurow, and Regina Stoll. 2017. "Wearable Devices in Medical Internet of Things: Scientific Research and Commercially Available Devices." *Healthcare Informatics Research* 23 (1): 4. doi:10.4258/HIR.2017.23.1.4.

Haleem, Abid, and Mohd Javaid. 2019. "3D Scanning Applications in Medical Field: A Literature-Based Review." *Clinical Epidemiology and Global Health* 7 (2): 199–210. doi:10.1016/J.CEGH.2018.05.006.

Javaid, Mohd, Abid Haleem, Raju Vaishya, Shashi Bahl, Rajiv Suman, and Abhishek Vaish. 2020. "Industry 4.0 Technologies and Their Applications in Fighting COVID-19 Pandemic." *Diabetes & Metabolic Syndrome* 14 (4): 419. doi:10.1016/J.DSX.2020.04.032.

Javaid, Mohd, and Ibrahim Haleem Khan. 2021. "Internet of Things (IoT) Enabled Healthcare Helps to Take the Challenges of COVID-19 Pandemic." *Journal of Oral Biology and Craniofacial Research* 11 (2): 209. doi:10.1016/J.JOBCR.2021.01.015.

Kelly, Jaimon T., Katrina L. Campbell, Enying Gong, and Paul Scuffham. 2020. "The Internet of Things: Impact and Implications for Health Care Delivery." *Journal of Medical Internet Research* 22 (11). doi:10.2196/20135.

Khan, Murad, Kijun Han, and S. Karthik. 2018. "Designing Smart Control Systems Based on Internet of Things and Big Data Analytics." *Wireless Personal Communications* 99 (4): 1683–1697. doi:10.1007/S11277-018-5336-Y.

Klonoff, David C. 2017. "Fog Computing and Edge Computing Architectures for Processing Data From Diabetes Devices Connected to the Medical Internet of Things." *Journal of Diabetes Science and Technology* 11 (4): 647–652. doi:10.1177/1932296817717007.

Kudtarkar, Parul, Todd F. DeLuca, Vincent A. Fusaro, Peter J. Tonellato, and Dennis P. Wall. 2010. "Cost-Effective Cloud Computing: A Case Study Using the Comparative Genomics Tool, Roundup." *Evolutionary Bioinformatics Online* 6 (6): 197. doi:10.4137/EBO.S6259.

Kuo, Alex Mu Hsing. 2011. "Opportunities and Challenges of Cloud Computing to Improve Health Care Services." *Journal of Medical Internet Research* 13 (3). doi:10.2196/JMIR.1867.

Lebeda, Frank J., Jeffrey J. Zalatoris, and Julia B. Scheerer. 2018. "Government Cloud Computing Policies: Potential Opportunities for Advancing Military Biomedical Research." *Military Medicine* 183 (11–12) E438–E447. doi:10.1093/milmed/usx114.

Lin, Jie, Wei Yu, Nan Zhang, Xinyu Yang, Hanlin Zhang, and Wei Zhao. 2017. "A Survey on Internet of Things: Architecture, Enabling Technologies, Security and Privacy, and Applications." *IEEE Internet of Things Journal* 4 (5): 1125–1142. doi:10.1109/JIOT.2017.2683200.

Liu, Yu, Beibei Dong, Benzhen Guo, Jingjing Yang, and Wei Peng. 2015. "Combination of Cloud Computing and Internet of Things (IOT) in Medical Monitoring Systems." *International Journal of Hybrid Information Technology* 8 (12): 367–376. doi:10.14257/IJHIT.2015.8.12.28.

Mell, P M, and T Grance. 2011. *"The NIST Definition of Cloud Computing."* Gaithersburg, MD. doi:10.6028/NIST.SP.800-145.

Michalakis, Konstantinos, and George Caridakis. 2017. "IoT Contextual Factors on Healthcare." *Advances in Experimental Medicine and Biology* 989: 189–200. doi:10.1007/978-3-319-57348-9_16.

Nasajpour, Mohammad, Seyedamin Pouriyeh, Reza M. Parizi, Mohsen Dorodchi, Maria Valero, and Hamid R. Arabnia. 2020. "Internet of Things for Current COVID-19 and Future Pandemics: An Exploratory Study." *Journal of Healthcare Informatics Research* 4 (4): 325–364. doi:10.1007/S41666-020-00080-6.

Otoom, Mwaffaq, Nesreen Otoum, Mohammad A. Alzubaidi, Yousef Etoom, and Rudaina Banihani. 2020. "An IoT-Based Framework for Early Identification and Monitoring of COVID-19 Cases." *Biomedical Signal Processing and Control* 62 (September): 102149. doi:10.1016/J.BSPC.2020.102149.

Pantanowitz, Liron, Ashish Sharma, Alexis B. Carter, Tahsin Kurc, Alan Sussman, and Joel Saltz. 2018. "Twenty Years of Digital Pathology: An Overview of the Road Travelled, What Is on the Horizon, and the Emergence of Vendor-Neutral Archives." *Journal of Pathology Informatics* 9 (1). doi:10.4103/JPI.JPI_69_18.

Peng, Haipeng, Ye Tian, Jurgen Kurths, Lixiang Li, Yixian Yang, and Daoshun Wang. 2017. "Secure and Energy-Efficient Data Transmission System Based on Chaotic Compressive Sensing in Body-to-Body Networks." *IEEE Transactions on Biomedical Circuits and Systems* 11 (3): 558–573. doi:10.1109/TBCAS.2017.2665659.

"Philips EICU Program |Philips Healthcare | ICU Telemedicine Solution." 2022. Accessed April 14. https://www.usa.philips.com/healthcare/resources/landing/teleicu.

Rahman, Md Siddikur, Noah C. Peeri, Nistha Shrestha, Rafdzah Zaki, Ubydul Haque, and Siti Hafizah Ab Hamid. 2020. "Defending against the Novel Coronavirus (COVID-19) Outbreak: How Can the Internet of Things (IoT) Help to Save the World?" *Health Policy and Technology* 9 (2): 136–138. doi:10.1016/J.HLPT.2020.04.005.

Rath, Mamata, and Binod Pattanayak. 2019. "Technological Improvement in Modern Health Care Applications Using Internet of Things (IoT) and Proposal of Novel Health Care Approach." *International Journal of Human Rights in Healthcare* 12 (2): 148–162. doi:10.1108/IJHRH-01-2018-0007/FULL/XML.

Ruusuvuori, Pekka, Masi Valkonen, Kimmo Kartasalo, Mira Valkonen, Tapio Visakorpi, Matti Nykter, and Leena Latonen. 2022. "Spatial Analysis of Histology in 3D: Quantification and Visualization of Organ and Tumor Level Tissue Environment." *Heliyon* 8 (1). doi:10.1016/J.HELIYON.2022.E08762.

Sadoughi, Farahnaz, Ali Behmanesh, and Nasrin Sayfouri. 2020. "Internet of Things in Medicine: A Systematic Mapping Study." *Journal of Biomedical Informatics* 103 (March): 103383. doi:10.1016/J.JBI.2020.103383.

Sahu, Kirti Sundar, Shannon E. Majowicz, Joel A. Dubin, and Plinio Pelegrini Morita. 2021. "NextGen Public Health Surveillance and the Internet of Things (IoT)." *Frontiers in Public Health* 9 (December): 1976. doi:10.3389/FPUBH.2021.756675/BIBTEX.

Shih, F. J., Y. W. Fan, C. M. Chiu, F. Ji Shih, and S. S. Wang. 2012. "The Dilemma of 'to Be or Not to Be': Developing Electronically e-Health & Cloud Computing Documents for Overseas Transplant Patients from Taiwan Organ Transplant Health Professionals' Perspective." *Transplantation Proceedings* 44 (4): 835–838. doi:10.1016/J. TRANSPROCEED.2012.02.001.

Singh, Sonia, Ankita Bansal, Rajinder Sandhu, and Jagpreet Sidhu. 2018. "Fog Computing and IoT Based Healthcare Support Service for Dengue Fever." *International Journal of Pervasive Computing and Communications* 14 (2): 197–207. doi:10.1108/IJPCC-D-18-00012.

Takeuchi, Ichiro, Hideo Fujita, Kazuhiko Ohe, Ryuta Imaki, Nobuhiro Sato, Kazui Soma, Shinichi Niwano, and Tohru Izumi. 2013. "Initial Experience of Mobile Cloud ECG System Contributing to the Shortening of Door to Balloon Time in an Acute Myocardial Infarction Patient." *International Heart Journal* 54 (1): 45–47. doi:10.1536/ihj.54.45.

Tang, Xiaoli. 2020. "The Role of Artificial Intelligence in Medical Imaging Research." *BJR Open* 2 (1): 20190031. doi:10.1259/BJRO.20190031.

Tariq, Muhammad Imran, Natash Ali Mian, Abid Sohail, Tahir Alyas, and Rehan Ahmad. 2020. "Evaluation of the Challenges in the Internet of Medical Things with Multicriteria Decision Making (AHP and TOPSIS) to Overcome Its Obstruction under Fuzzy Environment." *Mobile Information Systems* 2020. doi:10.1155/2020/8815651.

Ting, Daniel Shu Wei, Lawrence Carin, Victor Dzau, and Tien Y. Wong. 2020. "Digital Technology and COVID-19." *Nature Medicine* 26 (4): 459–461. doi:10.1038/S41591-020-0824-5.

Tran, Bach Xuan, Giang Hai Ha, Giang Thu Vu, Chi Linh Hoang, Son Hoang Nguyen, Cuong Tat Nguyen, Carl A. Latkin, Wilson Ws Tam, Cyrus S.H. Ho, and Roger C.M. Ho. 2020. "How Have Excessive Electronics Devices and Internet Uses Been Concerned? Implications for Global Research Agenda from a Bibliometric Analysis." *Journal of Behavioral Addictions* 9 (2): 469–482. doi:10.1556/2006.2020.00031.

Vijayan, Vini, James Connolly, Joan Condell, Nigel McKelvey, and Philip Gardiner. 2021. "Review of Wearable Devices and Data Collection Considerations for Connected Health." *Sensors* 21 (16): 5589. doi:10.3390/S21165589.

Wang, Xiaoliang, Qiong Gui, Bingwei Liu, Zhanpeng Jin, and Yu Chen. 2013. "Enabling Smart Personalized Healthcare: A Hybrid Mobile-Cloud Approach for ECG Telemonitoring." *IEEE Journal of Biomedical and Health Informatics* 18 (3): 739–745. doi:10.1109/JBHI.2013.2286157.

Xia, Henian, Irfan Asif, and Xiaopeng Zhao. 2013. "Cloud-ECG for Real Time ECG Monitoring and Analysis." *Computer Methods and Programs in Biomedicine* 110 (3): 253–259. doi:10.1016/j.cmpb.2012.11.008.

Xu, Sheng, Yihui Zhang, Lin Jia, Kyle E. Mathewson, Kyung In Jang, Jeonghyun Kim, Haoran Fu, et al. 2014. "Soft Microfluidic Assemblies of Sensors, Circuits, and Radios for the Skin." *Science (New York, N.Y.)* 344 (6179): 70–74. doi:10.1126/SCIENCE.1250169.

Yang, Xuejie, Xiaoyu Wang, Xingguo Li, Dongxiao Gu, Changyong Liang, Kang Li, Gongrang Zhang, and Jinhong Zhong. 2020a. "Exploring Emerging IoT Technologies in Smart Health Research: A Knowledge Graph Analysis." *BMC Medical Informatics and Decision Making* 20 (1). doi:10.1186/s12911-020-01278-9.

11 Blockchain Technology Effects on Healthcare Systems Using the IoT

Maryam Gharib Aljabri and Jabar H. Yousif
Sohar University

CONTENTS

11.1 INTRODUCTION

In recent years, blockchain has developed a reputation for being a tool that can address existing open information issues. The spending on the blockchain solution globally [1] is increased to reach 4.5 billion in 2020, and it is forecasted to reach 19 billion, as shown in Figure 11.1. The use of blockchain technology can increase transparency, security and privacy, traceability, and efficiency in the healthcare system [2]. Blockchain is a type of ledger and database that is a public ledger. Rather than storing data in individual blocks, blockchain chains them together with digital signatures over a distributed network. New data is added to blocks as it comes in. In order to achieve overall system reliability, ledger consistency, and user security, distributed consensus and asymmetric cryptography algorithms have been implemented. Furthermore, blockchain technology has many essential characteristics, including persistence, anonymity, auditability, and decentralization. As a result, it can significantly reduce costs and increase efficiency [3].

The advancement of information and communication technology led to the development of internet-connected devices such as smartphones, home appliances, wearable devices, and the Internet of things (IoT). In addition, an IoT system enables communication between a human and a device, a device, and a human, and a human and a human. With the help of electronic devices, IoT systems redefine the world in which everything is interconnected, and data is shared both within and between humans in a smart way [4].

DOI: 10.1201/9781003326182-11

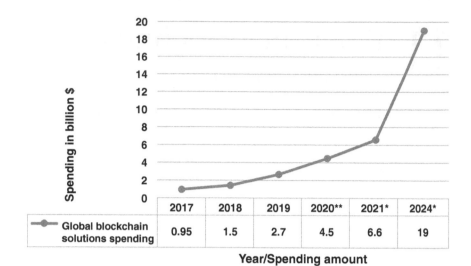

FIGURE 11.1   Global blockchain solution spending.

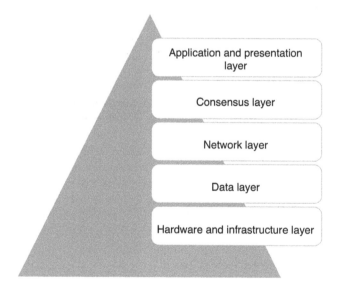

FIGURE 11.2   IoT layers' architectures.

The network environment consists of a platform for processing the data collected by these devices, creating meaningful data, and providing various services.

The IoT layers are categorized into five layers according to their architecture: application and presentation layer, consensus layer, network layer, data layer, and hardware and infrastructure layer, as shown in Figure 11.2.

The IoT platform, in particular, provides a means for managing data generated from devices and delivering it to application services. Blockchain technology can be classified as public, private, hybrid, or consortium. In the public blockchain, anyone can access and sign on to a blockchain platform and become an authorized node with non-restrictive and permissionless. A blockchain network that works in a restricted context, such as a closed network, or is controlled by a single entity is called a private blockchain. Organizations that desire the best of both worlds will sometimes employ hybrid blockchain, which blends private and public blockchain aspects. A consortium blockchain is considered as a private blockchain with restricted access to a specific group, removing the possibility of a single party controlling the network [4].

E-health has become one of the most popular research topics with the advent of the IoT. Patient privacy seems to be a challenge, given the sensitive nature of patient information. Furthermore, Patients in many societies worldwide face a significant increase in medical patients, and access to primary doctors has become more challenging. Researchers estimate that more than 75 billion devices will be able to communicate with the internet by 2025 as a result of the IoT [5]. IoT is one of the main applications for healthcare, and it can help doctors treat more patients and provide more comfort and convenience to them [5]. The security of blockchain systems is based on the concept of proof of work, which requires nodes to prove that enough work has been done by themselves to validate a transaction [6].

This chapter provides a thorough examination of the implications of blockchain technology in the healthcare sector. It is based on PRISMA recommendations for evaluating metadata analysis of selected studies to find, retrieve, and evaluate relevant articles across various databases. Several studies have recommended blockchain technology in the healthcare sector, based on the review, with promising outcomes and solutions to crucial concerns.

11.2 PROBLEM STATEMENT

IoT helps improve the quality of care and reduce costs by effectively allocating medical resources in healthcare. However, IoT devices can be attacked by a variety of different intruders. In fact, the majority of personal medical information accidents occur during the sharing or transmitting of information. Therefore, this chapter discusses how analyzing blockchains and the IoT impact the healthcare sector based on a literature review.

The following concepts will be discussed and answered:

1. The meaning of the IoT and blockchain in healthcare
2. Discover how blockchain and IoT are deployed in healthcare
3. The impact of blockchain and the IoT on healthcare

11.3 RESEARCH METHODS

The work is a systemic review of previous studies in the blockchain and IoT in healthcare domains using PRISMA guidelines for examining metadata analyses of selected studies to identify, extract, and analyze relevant publications across specific databases. A topically used literature review of 211 papers discusses the use of blockchain and IoT in healthcare domains. Furthermore, we determined and examined the research

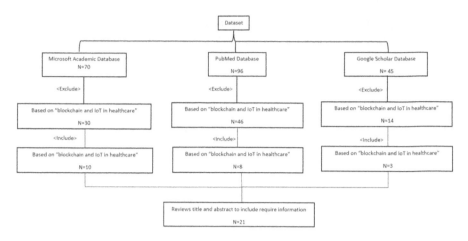

FIGURE 11.3 Database search diagram.

objectives, questions, and selection criteria for this study. Finally, we will explore the current advances in blockchain for securing IoT systems in 12 academic papers.

The Microsoft Academy, PubMed, and Google Scholar searches were conducted to gather papers that discuss blockchain and IoT in healthcare. It follows the guidelines for Preferred Reporting Items for Systematic Reviews and Meta-Analyses. A search was made over the past 5 years (from 2017 to 2021). Papers that were not relevant to the research's keywords were removed from the results.

Microsoft Academic was used as the first search engine to look for information about blockchain and IoT in healthcare, as shown in Figure 11.3. The following keywords were entered:

- Blockchain and IoT in healthcare; the result was 70.
- Allintitile: Blockchain and IoT in healthcare; the result was 30.
- Allintitile: (Blockchain) and (IoT) in healthcare; the result was 10.

A second search engine, PubMed, was used to look up information about IoT and blockchain in healthcare as shown in Figure 11.3. Using PubMed, the following keywords were entered:

- Blockchain and IoT in healthcare; the result was 96.
- Allintitile: Blockchain and IoT in healthcare; the result was 46.
- Allintitile: (Blockchain) and (IoT) in healthcare; the result was 8.

A third search engine, Google Scholar, was used to look up information about IoT and blockchain in healthcare as shown in Figure 11.3. The following keywords were entered:

- Blockchain and IoT in healthcare; the result was 45.
- Allintitile: Blockchain and IoT in healthcare; the result was 14.
- Allintitile: (Blockchain) and (IoT) in healthcare; the result was 3.

11.4   RESULTS AND DISCUSSION

A summary of each of the 21 selected research papers relevant to our systematic literature review is presented in the following tables.

Tables 11.1 and 11.2 explain the importance of blockchain and IoT in healthcare as an answer to the first research question.

In Table 11.1, the author explains what blockchain means. Blockchain is a distributed ledger or distributed presentation of data that can record store and provide access to digital transactions without the need for centralized authority, as demonstrated [11–13]. Additionally, as shown in [16–18], the blockchain is used as a peer-to-peer ledger for recording Bitcoin cryptocurrency transactions.

As shown in [3,4,6,20–22], the IoT consists of many internet-connected devices, including smartphones, home appliances, and wearable devices, operating in a network environment for the purpose of processing and creating various services based on the collected data.

Additionally, the IoT system described in [15] uses unique identifiers to allow real-world entities to communicate among themselves. Furthermore, as illustrated

TABLE 11.1
The Meaning of Blockchain

Reference	Blockchain Meaning
[7,8]	Blockchain technology creates a decentralized environment where data and transactions are never controlled by third parties.
[9,10]	Blockchain technology is a technique that affects our society by reducing the role of one of its most important economic and regulatory factors, the middleman.
[11–13]	Blockchain is a distributed ledger or a distributed presentation of data that can record, store, and enable access to digital transactions without requiring centralized authority.
[14,15]	A blockchain is an ongoing ledger of transactions that are organized into blocks and cryptography is used to secure each block.
[16–18]	Blockchain is used to record transactions pertaining to the Bitcoin cryptocurrency as a peer-to-peer ledger.

TABLE 11.2
Meaning of the IoT

Reference	IoT Meaning
[3,4,6,20–22]	The IoT refers to the number of internet-connected devices, including smartphones, home appliances, and wearable devices, operating in a network environment for processing data collected by these devices and creating various services based on this data.
[15]	An IoT system uses unique identifiers to allow real-world entities to communicate across a network.
[19]	The IoT refers to physical devices that are connected to computing platforms via the internet.

TABLE 11.3

Analysis of the Impact of Blockchain and the IoT on Healthcare

Reference	Problem	Solution	Impact
[2]	Integrity, security, and privacy of data	The development of a telemedical laboratory using the IoT in a federated cloud hospital environment	Improved data security, privacy, and integrity in the event of a pandemic
[3]	Lock of review in the field of blockchain and IoT in the healthcare sector	IoT, machine learning, and blockchain are examined for their applications in healthcare	A number of challenges associated with integrating blockchain into the IoT are outlined in the healthcare sector
[4]	Enhance the reliability of such Personal information management	Utilized the blockchain-based technology IoT to develop smart health-based monitoring systems	It significantly increased reliability and security
[5]	Healthcare data and privacy security	A blockchain-based IoT platform is proposed to address privacy and security concerns in E-health	Allows patients to control and own the health data collected from IoT wearable devices. By storing access control policies in a blockchain ledger, patients can specify which medical staff members are permitted to access patients' data, enabling ownership and full control
[6]	Security privacy and	IoT system architecture is designed to address most security and privacy concerns while taking into consideration the limited resources available	Combining the advantages of public-key cryptography, private-key cryptography, blockchain, and other lightweight cryptography primitives has resulted in the development of a complex, yet lightweight, hybrid approach to securing and protecting patient-centric electronic medical records
[15]	IoT blockchain integration contributing to	Analyze the role of blockchain in agriculture and healthcare systems	A blockchain-based IoT platform plays an increasingly crucial role in agriculture and healthcare,
	food supply chain management in agriculture and healthcare	based on the literature review	As it helps manage food supply chains, drug supply chains, product traceability, smart contracts, monitoring of products, and intelligent prediction of outcomes
[21]	Transparency and secrecy	A blockchain-based framework is proposed for securely and transparently sharing patient records, access to documentation, and shipment processes between doctors and patients	Monitoring intermediate activities, patient records, or medicine shipments from IoT objects connected to components moving between locations or providers

in [19], the IoT refers to physical devices that are connected to computing platforms via the internet.

The second research question discovers how blockchain and IoT are being applied to healthcare. In [21], researchers demonstrated a blockchain-based healthcare solution, also known as the IoT, which collected and integrated patient data using smart devices. The use of blockchains and IoT in E-health was studied to address privacy and security concerns, ensure the security of patient information, provide access to documentation, streamline the delivery processes between doctors and patients, and examine their application in healthcare [5].

In the last research question, the IoT and blockchain impact on healthcare is examined in Table 11.3. Researchers have demonstrated the common benefits of the IoT and blockchain in healthcare by improving security, privacy, and integration [2–4]. In addition, they found that the IoT and blockchain enhanced security and reliability in healthcare [4]. Researchers showed in [5] that blockchain and IoT in healthcare will allow patients to own and control the health data collected by IoT wearable devices. Patients can specify which members of the medical staff are permitted to access their patient data by storing their access control policies in blockchain ledgers, enabling full ownership and control.

11.5 CONCLUSION

This chapter examined the effects of blockchain technology on healthcare systems using the IoT. First, we introduced the meaning of blockchain and the IoT and favored its use in improving healthcare quality. Three questions were answered in this study. The second question concerns the application of the concept of blockchain and the IoT to healthcare. The survey showed the effective solutions provided by researchers to provide healthcare based on the concept of blockchain and the IoT by collecting scattered patient data and unifying it in one place using smart devices. By providing access to documents and simplifying handovers between physicians and patients, the study was able to address privacy concerns, ensure the security of patient information, and examine their healthcare applications in an easy and fast way.

The third question was also answered by examining the impact of IoT and blockchain on healthcare, as shown in Table 11.3. The researchers demonstrated the combined benefits of IoT and blockchain in healthcare applications by improving security, privacy, and data integration, enhancing healthcare systems' reliability. It also explains that the application of blockchain and the IoT in healthcare will allow patients to own and control their data at home with wearable IoT devices. Patients can also specify which medical staff members can access their patient data by storing their access control policies through blockchain features, which allow for complete ownership and control.

REFERENCES

[1] Statista, Worldwide blockchain solutions spending, 2021. Online resource [Accessed 25.12.2021]https://www.statista.com/statistics/800426/worldwide-blockchain-solutions https://www.statista.com/statistics/800426/worldwide-blockchain-solutions-spending/ spending/

[2] A. Celesti, A. Ruggeri, M. Fazio, A. Galletta, M. Villari, and A. Romano, "Blockchainbased healthcare workflow for tele-medical laboratory in federated hospital IoT clouds," *Sensors (Switzerland)*, vol. 20, no. 9, 2020, doi: 10.3390/s20092590.

[3] M. Imran, U. Zaman, Imran, J. Imtiaz, M. Fayaz, and J. Gwak, "Comprehensive survey of iot, machine learning, and blockchain for health care applications: A topical assessment for pandemic preparedness, challenges, and solutions," *Electron.*, vol. 10, no. 20, pp. 1–36, 2021, doi: 10.3390/electronics10202501.

[4] S. Jeong, J. H. Shen, and B. Ahn, "A study on smart healthcare monitoring using IoT based on blockchain," *Wirel. Commun. Mob. Comput.*, vol. 2021, 2021, doi: 10.1155/2021/9932091.

[5] S. Meisami and B. A. Mohammad, "Using blockchain to achieve decentralized privacy in IoT healthcare." arXiv preprint arXiv:2109.14812, 2021.

[6] A. D. Dwivedi, G. Srivastava, S. Dhar, and R. Singh, "A decentralized privacy-preserving healthcare blockchain for IoT," *Sensors (Switzerland)*, vol. 19, no. 2, pp. 1–17, 2019, doi: 10.3390/s19020326.

[7] M. J. M. Chowdhury, A. Colman, M. A. Kabir, J. Han, and P. Sarda, "Blockchain versus database: A critical analysis," *2018 17th IEEE International Conference On Trust, Security And Privacy In Computing And Communications/ 12th IEEE International Conference On Big Data Science And Engineering (TrustCom/BigDataSE)*, pp. 1348–1353, 2018, doi: 10.1109/TrustCom/BigDataSE.2018.00186.

[8] W. J. Gordon and C. Catalini, "Blockchain technology for healthcare: Facilitating the transition to patient-driven interoperability," *Comput. Struct. Biotechnol. J.*, vol. 16, pp. 224–230, 2018, doi: 10.1016/j.csbj.2018.06.003.

[9] A. Wright and P. De Filippi, "Decentralized blockchain technology and the rise of lex cryptographia," *SSRN Electron. J.*, 2015, doi: 10.2139/ssrn.2580664.

[10] P. Zhang, J. White, D. C. Schmidt, and G. Lenz, "Applying software patterns to address interoperability in blockchain-based healthcare apps," 2017, [Online]. Available: http://arxiv.org/abs/1706.03700.

[11] Z. Aliyev and I. Safarov, "Logos, mythos and ethos of blockchain: An integrated framework for anti-corruptiion," OECD Glob. Anti-Corruption Integr. Forum, 2019.

[12] B. Pillai, K. Biswas, and V. Muthukkumarasamy, "Cross-chain interoperability among blockchain-based systems using transactions," *Knowl. Eng. Rev.* 2021, 2020, doi: 10.1017/S0269888920000314.

[13] S. Mehta, K. Grant, and A. Ackery, "Future of blockchain in healthcare: Potential to improve the accessibility, security and interoperability of electronic health records," *BMJ Heal. Care Informatics*, vol. 27, no. 3, 2020, doi: 10.1136/bmjhci-2020-100217.

[14] K. Mentzer, M. Frydenberg, and D. J. Yates, "Teaching applications and implications of blockchain via project-based learning: A case study," *Inf. Syst. Educ. J.*, vol. 18, no. 6, p. 18, 2020, [Online]. Available: https://isedj.org/;http://iscap.infohttps://isedj.org/;http://iscap.info.

[15] P. Singh and N. Singh, "Blockchain based framework for educational certificates verification," *Int. J. Appl. Evol. Comput.*, vol. 11, no. 4, pp. 13–27, 2020, doi: 10.4018/ijaec.2020100102.

[16] P. Bhaskar, C. K. Tiwari, and A. Joshi, "Blockchain in education management: Present and future applications," *Interact. Technol. Smart Educ.*, 2020, doi: 10.1108/ITSE-072020-0102.

[17] S. H. Theses and S. Grone, "DigitalCommons @ EMU facilitating cross-chain cryptocurrency exchanges: An inquiry into blockchain technology and interoperability with an emphasis on cryptocurrency arbitrage," 2020.

[18] Joshi, P. and Gokhale, P., "Electronic health record using blockchain and off chain storage: A systematic review," *Inf. Technol. Ind.*, vol. 9, no. 1, pp. 247–253, 2021, doi: 10.17762/itii.v9i1.125.

[19] F. A. Abadi, J. Ellul, and G. Azzopardi, "The blockchain of things, beyond bitcoin: A systematic review," *Proc. - 2018 IEEE International Conference on Internet of Things (iThings) and IEEE Green Computing and Communications (GreenCom) and IEEE Cyber, Physical and Social Computing (CPSCom) and IEEE Smart Data (SmartData),* pp. 1666–1672, 2018, doi: 10.1109/Cybermatics_2018.2018.00278.

[20] A. O. Almagrabi, R. Ali, D. Alghazzawi, A. AlBarakati, and T. Khurshaid, "Blockchainas-a-utility for next-generation healthcare internet of things," *Comput. Mater. Contin.,* vol. 68, no. 1, pp. 359–376, 2021, doi: 10.32604/cmc.2021.014753.

[21] G. Rathee, A. Sharma, H. Saini, R. Kumar, and R. Iqbal, "A hybrid framework for multimedia data processing in IoT-healthcare using blockchain technology," *Multimed. Tools Appl.,* vol. 79, no. 15–16, pp. 9711–9733, 2020, doi: 10.1007/s11042-019-07835-3.

[22] I. Yaqoob, K. Salah, R. Jayaraman, and Y. Al-Hammadi, "Blockchain for healthcare data management: Opportunities, challenges, and future recommendations," *Neural Comput. Appl.,* no. January, 2021, doi: 10.1007/s00521-020-05519-w.

12 Deep Learning Approach for Classification of Alzheimer's Disease

Abbas H. Hassin Alasadi and Faten Salim Hanoon
University of Basrah

CONTENTS

DOI: 10.1201/9781003326182-12

12.1   INTRODUCTION

Alzheimer's disease (AD) is a progressive neurological disease, which worsens over time. Additionally, it is regarded as the most common cause of dementia [1]. The term AD was coined in 1901 when Dr. Alois Alzheimer discovered a disease in a patient named Auguste Deter, who died of the disease in 1906 [2] (see Figure 12.1). The disease that would bear his name was first described in the scientific literature in 1910. The symptoms of AD are a decrease in memory, an impairment of cognitive abilities, a lack of logical thinking and judgment, and difficulty in expression and comprehension. Symptoms result from damage or destruction of brain cells that impair thinking, learning, and memory. As the disease progresses gradually, nerve cells in other parts of the brain are damaged, resulting in a total loss of brain function. As life expectancy increases, the number of people suffering from AD is expected to rise dramatically in the future.

According to the World Alzheimer's Report [3] statistics, an estimated 50 million people had AD in 2015. By 2050, this number is expected to increase to 131.5 million people worldwide.

FIGURE 12.1   Dr. Alois Alzheimer (left) and Auguste Deter (right). Deter was Dr. Alois Alzheimer's patient and the world's first patient diagnosed with AD [2].

12.2   DEEP LEARNING

Deep learning (DL) is a branch of machine learning and a subfield under the umbrella term "Artificial Intelligence" that involves building large neural network models capable of making accurate data-driven decisions [4]. The relationship between artificial intelligence, machine learning, and DL is shown in Figure 12.2. Dechter developed the concept of DL in 1986 [5]. In recent years, two key technological trends have driven the growth of DL. First, a huge amount of data is freely available. According to IDC, the global datasphere will reach 175 zettabytes by 2025 [6]. DL is particularly suited for complex data cases, and there are huge datasets to work with.

Second, one of the major factors for the widespread adoption of DL has been the innovation and advancement in the computational capabilities of parallel computing hardware, which has made it easy to parallelize the computations required for deep learning on these devices. DL has the following advantages over machine learning: The most important aspect of DL is that DL algorithms can automatically extract features from raw data, which helps to improve accuracy on a variety of problems [4]. In contrast, processing raw data and extracting features in traditional machine learning is limited and requires extensive expertise. It is considered a labor-intensive task that requires and consumes a significant amount of time and project budget. DL has a high learning capacity and also performs better based on the learning outcomes [7]. The depth of the model is the other aspect that distinguishes DL from other machine learning techniques. DL neural networks have multiple layers and a wide breadth of applications, so DL can solve highly complex problems [8]. Data dependency is a

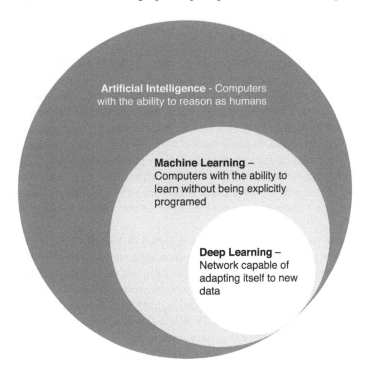

FIGURE 12.2   The relationship between artificial intelligence, machine learning, and DL [4].

feature of DL. Relevant experiments have shown that the larger the amount of data available, the better the performance of DL.

Some tasks, such as image recognition, face recognition, and natural language processing, even outperformed human performance [9]. DL has excellent portability [10]. Due to the superior performance of DL, numerous frameworks such as MATLAB, TensorFlow, and Pytorch are now available for DL deployment. These frameworks are compatible with a variety of platforms, including Windows, Linux, and Mac OS. DL is now used by most online businesses and high-end consumer technologies. For example, Facebook uses DL to analyze text in online conversations. Google and Microsoft also use DL for machine translation and image search.

In addition, DL systems now run on all modern smartphones. It is used as a standard technology for speech recognition and face recognition on digital cameras. DL is also considered to be at the heart of self-driving cars. It is used for localization and mapping, motion planning and control, environmental awareness, and driver state tracking. In healthcare, DL is used to analyze medical imaging scans (X-rays, CT, and magnetic resonance imaging (MRI)) to make diagnoses. Convolutional neural networks (CNNs) have gained prominence in a variety of fields, including image processing and analysis, computer vision tasks, and medical imaging applications such as cerebral microbleed detection [11], automatic myocardial infarction detection [12], brain tumor segmentation [13], and COVID-19 detection [14]. In this chapter, CNN architecture is used in order to solve the four-stage classification problem of AD.

12.3   DL BUILDING BLOCK

Artificial neural networks (ANNs), also known as feedforward neural networks (FNNs) or multilayer perceptrons (MLPs), are the fundamental building blocks of numerous DL models that have achieved considerable success in processing high-dimensional imaging datasets [4]. ANNs simulate the neural network systems of the human brain. The human brain, which functions as the nerve system's command center, is composed of billions of neurons linked by approximately (1,014) synapses. Each neuron has three parts: a cell body, dendrites, and an axon, and is regarded as the brain's computing unit. The neuron takes input signals from its dendrites, processes them, and then transmits output signals via its axon. The biological neuron structure of the human brain is depicted in Figure 12.3a.

According to the mathematical model depicted in Figure 12.3b, signals (Si) that depend on the strength of synapses (Wi) interact multiplicatively (SiWi) with the dendrites of other neurons. This model can be used to demonstrate how synapse strengths (weights) can learn and control one neuron's influence on other neurons. Figure 12.3 illustrates the path taken by all signals from dendrites to the body cell, which accumulates all incoming signals. When the sum surpasses a specific threshold, neurons fire and send a signal spike via the axon.

In 1958, Rosenblatt created the perceptron [16], the world's first learning neural computer, to imitate human learning. The perceptron is an abstract model of a single

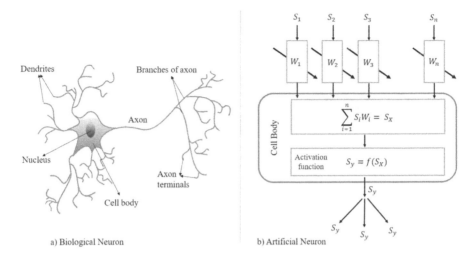

a) Biological Neuron   b) Artificial Neuron

FIGURE 12.3   (a) Biological neuron and (b) mathematical model for an artificial neuron [15].

neuron that has one output and several inputs. The output of the perceptron is the sum of all the weighted inputs xi plus the bias b as expressed in Equation (12.1).

$$f(x) = \varphi(b + \sum_{i=1}^{n} x_i .w_i) \ldots \tag{12.1}$$

The Heavyside step function is denoted by the symbol (φ), described by Equation (12.2).

$$\varphi(x) = \begin{cases} 1 & if \ x \geq 0 \\ 0 & else \end{cases} \quad \ldots \tag{12.2}$$

This network was used to perform binary classification. If the summation result is greater than or equal to zero, the network votes for the first class, and if the summation result is less than zero, the network votes for the opposite class.

Neural networks have been developed to improve the limited representational capabilities of the perceptron. They are made up of a series of arranged layers, each of which comprises a collection of perceptrons known as units or neurons. The input layer is the first layer, the output layer is the last, while layers that lie between the input and output layers are referred to as hidden layers. The nodes in one layer are connected to those in the next and previous layers. These connections are weighted edges, called weights. One of the most commonly used architectures is the multilayer perceptron, which has multiple hidden layers.

DL uses an architecture known as "deep neural networks. " Deep neural networks are a type of neural network that contains numerous hidden layers of neurons. For a neural network to be considered deep, at least two hidden layers are required [4]. However, most DL networks contain many more than two hidden layers

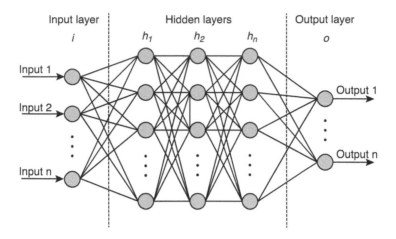

FIGURE 12.4   ANN with multi-hidden layers [18].

(see Figure 12.4). The key point is that the depth of a network is defined by the number of hidden layers plus the output layer. However, deeper networks empirically outperform external networks with one hidden layer and have lower generalization errors. Nielson [17] attributes the superior performance of deeper networks to learning a complex hierarchy of concepts. In image classification, after the network has obtained all the required information from the input layer, each hidden layer detects a different set of features in an image, ranging from less detailed to more detailed. For example, the first hidden layer detects edges and lines, the second layer detects shapes, and the third layer detects specific image elements, such as a face or a wheel. The predictions of the network are made in the output layer. The predicted image classes are compared to the labels that were manually inserted by humans. If they are wrong, the network uses a technique called backpropagation (which will be discussed later) to adjust its learning process in order to provide more accurate estimates in subsequent iterations. After a sufficient amount of training, a network can make classifications automatically without the need for human intervention.

12.4   CONVOLUTIONAL NEURAL NETWORK (CNN)

A CNN is a special ANN that applies image processing directly to pixels without requiring any prior processing [19]. Yann LeCun proposed it for effective image recognition [4]. It is a part of DL technologies. CNNs are used in various applications, including image classification, segmentation, and pattern recognition [20,21]. Due to its autonomous nature, it has become an important tool for machine vision and artificial intelligence. A convolutional layer consists of units and an atypical neural network but with a different order and connection of units. The main differences between them and neural networks are the following:

1. The units are not arranged in one dimension but three dimensions. The colored image is responsible for the three-dimensional arrangement. A colored image typically has three channels (red, green, and blue), each of

which is represented by a two-dimensional matrix. As a result, ConvNet's input is a three-dimensional matrix. The output of a convolutional layer is a three-dimensional matrix with two-dimensional feature maps multiplied by the number of filters in that layer. Each filter generates one feature map.

2. Weight sharing: The use of the same weights for various output units is called weight sharing, which results in ConvNet having one property, feature invariance to translation. This means that the feature is present on the entire input.

3. Local connectivity: Local connectivity is a term that relates to the concept of each neuron being connected to a portion of the input image, as contrasted to a neural network in which all neurons are connected to the full input image. This contributes to the reduction of the total number of parameters in the system and increases the computation efficiency.

12.4.1 BASIC BUILDING BLOCKS OF CNNs

In this section, the basic layers of the CNN will be explained in detail.

12.4.1.1 Convolutional Layer

The convolutional layer is the building block of the CNN algorithm. It is responsible for extracting the essential and useful features from the input images using a set of trainable filters that form a feature map [22]. Convolution is a mathematical technique in which a filter is applied to an n-dimensional field (image). The filter also consists of a set of numbers called weights or parameters. The values are multiplied by the original pixel values of the image as the filter slides over or convolves the input image [23]. In other words, it multiplies element by element. All of these multiplications are summed. When the filter slides over the entire image, the result is a filtered image (called the feature map). In one layer, many filters are applied to the initial image, and each filter represents a set of weights that were learned during the training process. Equation (12.3) expresses the convolution operation.

$$m_j^f \rightarrow (s,\ t) = \sum_z \sum_{x,y} r_z(x,y) \cdot e_j^f \cdot (w,\ h) \ldots \quad (12.3)$$

where $r_z(x,y)$ represents an element of the input image tensor R_z, x is the xth coordinate under consideration of an image, y is the yth coordinate under consideration of an image, z is the index of the channel, e_j^f (w, h) is the index of the fth convolutional filter f_j of the jth layer, J is the total number of layers, j is the layer number, F is the total number of filters of the jth layer, f_j is the filter number of the jth layer, w is the wth row under consideration, h is the hth column under consideration, S is the total number of rows of the feature matrix, T is the total number of columns of the feature matrix, s is the sth row under consideration, t is the tth column under consideration, and m_j^f (s, t) is an element of the feature map shown in the notion:

$$M_j^f = \left[m_j^f\ (1,1), \ldots, m_j^f\ (s,t), \ldots m_j^f\ (S,T) \right]$$

where M_j^f is the input feature matrix for the jth layer and the fth neuron.

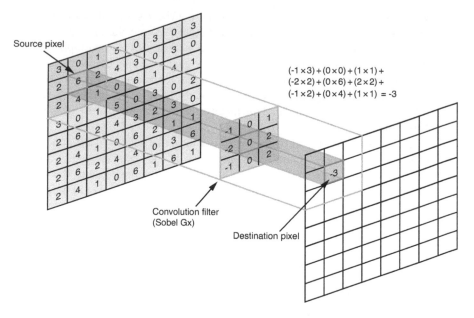

FIGURE 12.5   Visualization of the convolution process [24].

As shown in Figure 12.5, the filter matrix whose size is (3×3) was used with the matrix in a region in the input image whose size is (3×3) to perform a dot product multiplication. Then, the resulting matrix elements are added, and the sum yields a single numerical value (target pixel) on the feature map. This process is repeated by moving the matrix of the filter over the input matrix to complete the feature map by multiplying the dot product by each remaining combination of 3×3 sized areas. A set of filters are applied to an input image and the resultant feature maps are combined to provide the final output of a single convolutional layer.

Convolutional layers have two other key concepts: strides and padding [24]. A stride is the number of pixels that a kernel or filter moves across the input matrix. The default value for strides is 1, but occasionally a stride greater than 1 is used to minimize feature maps. At the same time, padding is used when the filter does not fit the input matrix. Padding is classified into two types: valid padding, which discards the input matrix's edge pixels, and null or equal padding, which adds zeros to the edges to make the filter fit the input matrix. In addition, two hyperparameters are important for convolution operations: the first is the kernel size, which is usually 3×3 but can sometimes be 5×5 or 7×7, and the second is the number of kernels, which determines the depth of the output feature maps [25].

12.4.1.2   Pooling Layer

The pooling layer (also called the down-sampling layer) is responsible for reducing the spatial size of the convolved feature [26]. Dimensionality reduction reduces the computational power required to process the data. As a result, it reduces the number of parameters and the risk of over-fitting the data. It also helps in extracting the most

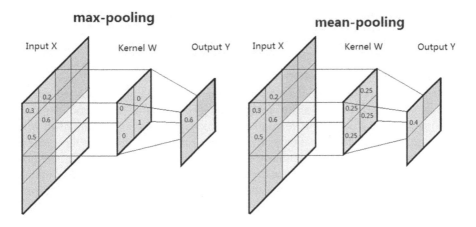

FIGURE 12.6   Pooling operation (max pooling, average pooling) [24].

important and useful features. The fact that there are no learnable parameters in any of the pooling layers should be noted. Pooling operations, like convolution operations, use hyperparameters like filter size, stride, and padding [25]. Equation (12.4) illustrates the pooling operation, where P_j^f represents the feature map after pooling the jth layer for the fth Input feature map M_j^f, g_p (.) determines the type of pooling operation.

$$P_j^f = g_p(M_j^f)\ldots \tag{12.4}$$

Max pooling is the most widely used pooling method, where patches are taken from the input feature maps, the highest value is output, and the rest is discarded (see Figure 12.6). In practice, max pooling is often used with a filter size of 2×2 and a stride of 2. Average pooling is the other type of pooling operation. Average pooling returns the average value of the pixels of the image covered by the kernel. Usually, this operation is performed only once before the fully connected layers.

12.4.1.3   Activation Layer

Typically, after each convolutional layer, an activation layer is applied. It gives non-linear characteristics to a system that has recently completed a linear calculation in a convolutional layer. The activation function serves as a decision-making mechanism and facilitates the learning of complex patterns. Utilizing the appropriate activation function helps accelerate the learning process. The activation function for a convolved feature map is defined by Equation (12.5).

$$K_j^f = g_a\left(M_j^f\right)\ldots \tag{12.5}$$

According to the formula of Equation (12.5), a convolution's output $\left(M_j^f\right)$ is given to an activation function g_a (.), which adds nonlinearity and returns a transformed output K_j^f for the jth layer. A variety of activation functions are used in the literature to inculcate nonlinear combinations of features, such as sigmoid, tanh, maxout, SWISH, rectified linear unit (ReLU), and versions of ReLU, such as leaky ReLU, ELU, and PReLU. ReLU and its variants, on the other hand, are recommended because they help overcome the vanishing gradient problem [27].

12.4.1.4 Batch Normalization Layer

These layers are typically placed after activation layers, yielding normalized activation maps by subtracting the mean and dividing it by the standard deviation for each training batch. The network is forced to periodically change its activations to zero mean and unit standard deviation as the training batch passes through these layers by including batch normalization layers. This acts as a regularizer for the network, accelerates training, and reduces the network's reliance on careful parameter initialization [28]. Equation (12.6) illustrates batch normalization for a transformed feature map F_l^k.

$$ N_j^f = \frac{M_j^f - \mu_B}{\sqrt{\sigma_B^2 + \varepsilon}} \quad \dots \tag{12.6} $$

where M_j^f is the input feature map, and μ_B and σ_B^2 represent the mean and variance of a feature map for a mini batch, respectively. N_j^f is the normalized feature map.

12.4.1.5 Dropout Layer

The dropout layer is typically used to control over-fitting to prevent it from occurring [29,30]. During the forward pass, it discards a random activation parameter set by setting it to zero to ensure that the neural network will not affect the training samples overmatching, thereby alleviating over-fitting issues.

12.4.1.6 Fully Connected Layer

The fully connected layer is typically found at the network's end and is utilized for classification purposes. It is a global operation, unlike pooling and convolution. It receives inputs from the feature extraction layers and analyses the outputs of all the previous layers at a global level. As a result, a nonlinear combination of selected features is created, which is used to classify the data.

The network uses a fully connected layer to map higher level activation mappings to the output layer classification and construct an n-dimensional vector, where n denotes the number of classifications in the output layer [31]. This n-dimensional vector represents the probability of the recognized image in N classifications. Figure 12.7 illustrates the fundamental building blocks of a typical CNN.

12.4.2 Training CNN

A CNN is trained by finding kernels in convolutional layers and weights in fully connected layers that reduce the differences between output predictions and predefined ground-truth labels in the training dataset. A backpropagation algorithm is a popular approach to neural network training that relies heavily on the loss function, and gradient descent optimization algorithm. A loss function computes the performance of a model under certain kernels and weights using forward propagation on a training

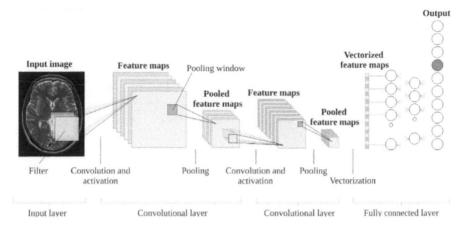

FIGURE 12.7   The fundamental building blocks of a typical CNN [28].

dataset. Learning parameters such as kernels and weights are updated according to the loss value using a backpropagation algorithm and gradient descent.

Fully training a new CNN from scratch is not without challenges. First, a CNN requires large amounts of labeled data for the training process, which can be difficult to obtain, especially in medical imaging. In addition, training a CNN requires the use of many computational and storage resources. Otherwise, without these resources, the training process would take a very long time. Tuning hyperparameters is time-consuming and complicated and may lead to over-fitting or under-fitting, resulting in poor model performance. Researchers have developed a promising alternative method, called transfer learning, to overcome these obstacles.

Transfer learning involves improving a new task by transferring knowledge from a previously learned task [32].

12.4.3   Basic CNN Architecture

In this section, the basic CNN architectures are explained.

12.4.3.1   LeNet-5

The LeNet-5 is the first CNN architecture proposed by LeCun et al. [33] in 1998 for classifying handwritten digits. The LeNet-5 consists of five trainable layers, of which three are convolutional, and two are fully connected. The first two convolutional layers are each followed by a max-pooling layer and two fully connected layers follow the last convolutional layer. The final layer of these fully connected layers serves as a classifier that can classify ten digits. The architecture of LeNet-5 is shown in Figure 12.8.

12.4.3.2   AlexNet

Krizhevsky et al. [34] created the first large CNN model called AlexNet in 2012, which is based on LeNet and is employed to classify ImageNet data. It has eight

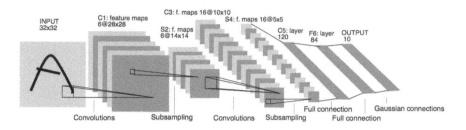

FIGURE 12.8　The architecture of LeNet-5 [36].

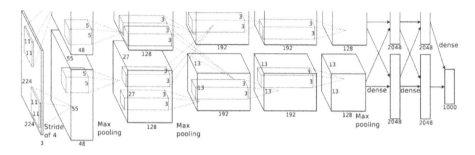

FIGURE 12.9　The architecture of AlexNet [36].

layers for learning, the first five of which are convolutional and the last three of which are fully connected [35]. Because it was developed for ImageNet data, the final output layer classifies the input images with 1,000 units into one of the ImageNet dataset's 1,000 classes. The architecture of AlexNet is shown in Figure 12.9.

12.4.3.3　ZFNet

Zeiler and Fergus presented ZFNet [37] at ECCV-2014. It has a similar design to AlexNet, with the exception that the first convolutional layer uses 7×7 filters with Stride 2. When it comes to the first convolutional layer of AlexNet, Krizhevky et al. employed an 11×11 filter with Stride 4. As a result, ZFNet exceeds AlexNet in terms of efficiency, earning it the title of ILSVRC-2013 winner. Figure 12.10 depicts the ZFNet architecture.

12.4.3.4　VGG

VGG is one of the most widely used CNN architectures, introduced in 2014 by Simonyan and Zisserman. VGGNet's popularity arises from its simple architecture and the use of small-scale filters for convolutional processes [36]. This network illustrates that, when used, a stack of filters of size 3×3 in convolution operation has the same effective effect as a stack of large-sized filters. For example, two layers of filter with a size of 3×3 have the same effect as a filter with a size of 5×5 in convolution operation. Three layers of filters with a size of 3×3 have the same effect as filters with a size of 7×7. The important thing is that when filters of small size are used, the

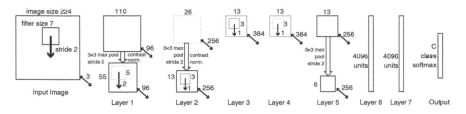

FIGURE 12.10 The architecture of ZFNet [36].

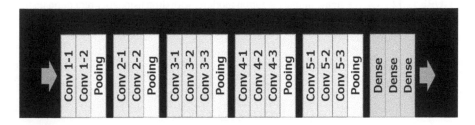

FIGURE 12.11 The architecture of VGG [36].

number of parameters in the network is reduced. The architecture of VGG is shown in Figure 12.11.

12.4.3.5 GoogLeNet

GoogLeNet was proposed by Szegedy et al. in 2014. In contrast to the traditional CNN models previously addressed, GoogLeNet [36] employs network branches rather than a single-line sequential architecture. The GoogLeNet has 22 learnable layers and is built using the Inception Module, which represents the fundamental building block for this network. This module's processing occurs in parallel across the network. Each module is composed of convolution layers with filters of the following sizes: 1×1, 3×3, and 5×5, which operate in a parallel way, resulting in combined feature maps with extremely high dimensions. To address the issue of the generated feature maps having high dimensions, they used the inception module to reduce the dimensions (as illustrated in Figure 12.12).

12.4.3.6 ResNet

Backpropagation over a deep CNN (a CNN with a large number of layers, e.g., 1,000) requires the computation of loss gradients (errors) concerning the corresponding weights in the neurons of each layer that update these weights. This task uses the derivative operation, which causes the gradients to become smaller and smaller. For this reason, the neurons in the earlier layer receive minimal gradients (sometimes the gradients become almost zero), which causes the weights in the previous layer to receive only minor updates, and learning for these layers becomes slow and inefficient. This is known as the "vanishing gradient problem" [36].

The residual neural network, known as ResNet, was proposed in 2016 by He et al. [38] to solve this problem. ResNet ranked first in the 2015 ILSVRC classification

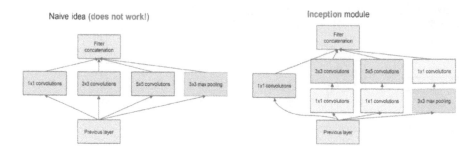

FIGURE 12.12   On the right, simple inception module, with dimensionality reduction on the left inception module [36].

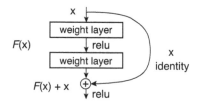

FIGURE 12.13   Structure of residual block [36].

competition with an error rate of 3.57. ResNet inventively uses shortcuts known as "skip connections," i.e., direct connections between two non-consecutive layers [39,40]. Adding the input x to the output after a few convolutional layers avoids the vanishing gradient problem. Residual blocks are designed to fit a residual mapping $F(x)$ rather than the desired underlying mapping $H(x)$ to assist in the optimization of deeper models, and entire ResNet architectures are built by stacking residual blocks. Figure 12.13 illustrates the concept of a residual block. If the input is x, the output of the convolutional layer is $F(x)$, which is added to x as a mapping input, and the resulting output $H(x) = F(x) + x$ is passed to the next layer. This is much simpler than fitting an identity map through a collection of nonlinear layers, and the network does not need to include additional parameters and computations. At the same time, the training speed and effectiveness of the model can be significantly increased as the number of layers increases. This residual block structure can effectively solve the gradient disappearance problem in deep networks [38]. There are two types of residual blocks in ResNet. While the first type is suitable for training shallow networks, the second type (bottleneck) is recommended for more than 50 layers. Moreover, both types have a similar time complexity.

12.5   PROPOSED FRAMEWORK

Accuracy in medical diagnosis is more important than anything else, even more important than speed of diagnosis. After all, the wrong diagnosis of an ordinary person as a patient causes severe consequences and psychological pressure, as well as diagnosing a patient, as normal, leads to the development of the disease because the wrong diagnosis, in this case, will delay treatment. Therefore, building an automated medical diagnostic system must be of a high level of accuracy.

This section presents the general architecture of the proposed framework. The proposed framework consists of the following stages: data collection, data preparation, model selection, and training stage to build the model that helps in diagnosis, validation, and evaluation. Each stage is independent of the other and is responsible for implementing a specific function. At the same time, these stages can communicate with each other since the result of one stage will be the input to the following stage. Figure 12.14 describes the proposed framework.

12.5.1 DATA COLLECTION STAGE

Data collection is the first step in the machine learning pipeline for training the selected model. The accuracy of machine learning systems' predictions is only good when the data used to train them is good. Therefore, the first stage in the framework of the proposed work in this chapter is to collect data and obtain it from data sources related to this work in order to solve the research problem, test the hypothesis, and evaluate the results.

In this chapter, the Alzheimer's brain MRI dataset was obtained from the open access of the Kaggle website. The dataset contains 6,400 images with a size of 176×208 pixels. It has four classes (NonDemented, MildDemented, ModerateDemented, VeryMildDemented) with a non-uniform distribution of the images per class.

12.5.2 DATA PREPARATION STAGE

This stage contains four steps for preparing the selected data:

12.5.2.1 Convert to RGB

In this step, the images are converted to RGB because the network used in our work is pre-trained on color images.

12.5.2.2 Resize

In this step, the size of images is changed to different sizes according to the selected experiment, for example, (50×50), (75×75), and (125×125). This step decreases the time for training the neural network by lowering the number of pixels in an image because more pixels in an image lead to an increase in the model's complexity. Another reason is that try the training of the network with different sizes of images.

12.5.2.3 Augmentation

Because of the non-uniform distribution of images in each class, new training examples are generated using one of the data augmentation techniques only on the training set to improve deep neural network generalization capabilities and prevent over-fitting. Horizontal flipping is the augmentation technique used in this step. This technique works by shifting all of the pixels in an image in the horizontal direction, or in other words, by reversing the entire rows and columns of image pixels horizontally.

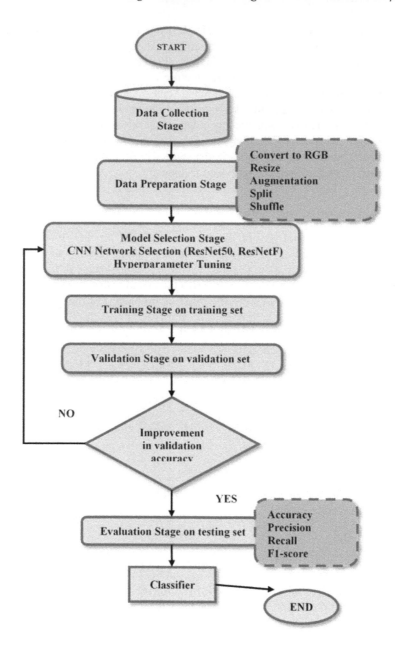

FIGURE 12.14 Flowchart of the proposed framework for early diagnosis of AD.

12.5.2.4   Splitting

The dataset is separated into two independent sets; the training set and the testing set. The training set is then partitioned into a validation set and a new training set. The proposed model is trained using the new training set. In contrast, the validation set periodically evaluates the model's performance during the training phase to avoid over-fitting problems. The testing set is later used to evaluate how well the model generalizes to unseen data.

12.5.2.5   Shuffling

Shuffling is the last step in data preparation. This step shuffles the training data after each epoch to pass different inputs to the neurons in each epoch. This procedure prevents the model from learning the order of training samples and thus prevents bias. This step eventually helps the training to converge quickly so that the network can provide better generalizations.

By way of the validation set and testing set, no shuffling process was performed. During the validation phase and testing phase, there is no updating process for the model's parameters. During the validation and testing phases only, accuracy and loss are calculated. Their calculation method is not sensitive to the order of samples, so shuffling does not affect the testing and validation data.

12.5.3   Model Selection Stage

In this stage, the structure of a model is chosen. The algorithm and hyperparameters for the training stage are preliminarily determined.

12.5.3.1   Algorithm Selection

In this chapter, two CNNs are studied to build a model for the early diagnosis of AD. The structure of each network and its components are explained in detail.

12.5.3.1.1   ResNet-50 Architecture

ResNet-50 is a residual DL network that deals with vanishing gradients in deep CNNs. During backpropagation, jump connections are used to jump across three layers.

The residual block in ResNet-50 always consists of 1×1, 3×3, and 1×1 convolutional layers stacked on top of each other. Figure 12.15 illustrates the concept of a residual block in ResNet-50.

The architecture of resnet50 consists of the following components:

1. A convolutional layer contains 64 different kernels. Each kernel has a size of 7×7 and a step size of two, followed by a max-pooling layer of the same size as the kernel step.
2. The first residual block contains a convolutional layer that has 64 kernels and each kernel is in the size of 1×1. Another convolutional layer follows this layer with 3×3 and 64 kernels. The final layer is also a convolutional layer that has 256 kernels and each kernel has a size of 1×1. This block is repeated three times, giving this step nine layers.
3. The second residual block contains a convolutional layer which has 128 kernels and each kernel is in the size of 1×1. Another convolutional layer

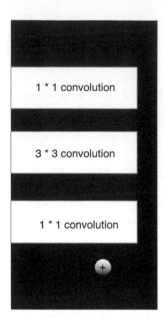

FIGURE 12.15   Structure of bottleneck block in ResNet-50.

follows this layer with 3×3 and 128 kernels. The final layer is also a convolutional layer which has 512 kernels and each kernel has a size of 1×1. This block is repeated four times, giving this step 12 layers.

4. The third residual block contains a convolutional layer which has 256 kernels and each kernel is in the size of 1×1. Another convolutional layer follows this layer with 3×3 and 256 kernels. The final layer is also a convolutional layer which has 1024 kernels and each kernel has a size of 1×1. This block is repeated six times, giving this step 18 layers.

5. The fourth residual block contains a convolutional layer which has 512 kernels and each kernel is in the size of 1×1. Another convolutional layer follows this layer with 3×3 and 512 kernels. The final layer is also a convolutional layer which has 2048 kernels and each kernel has a size of 1×1. This block is repeated six times, giving this step nine layers.

6. This is followed by an average pooling layer, followed by a fully connected layer with 1,000 nodes, replacing this with four nodes according to the number of disease stages. The final layer is a softmax function, resulting in one layer.

In each residual block, after the convolutional layer come the batch normalization layer and then the activation function layer that uses ReLU, except for the last convolutional layer, which is only followed by batch normalization.

12.5.3.1.2   ResNetF Architecture

ResNetF is a modified residual neural network that is proposed based on ResNet50. The modification of RESNET50 is made as follows:

1. A convolution layer that has 64 different kernels. The size of each kernel is 7×7 and each has a step size of 2, followed by a max-pooling layer with the same step size as the kernel.
2. The number of convolution layers is increased by repeating the first residual block three times, the second residual block six times, the third residual block seven times, and the fourth residual block three times. The expanding number of convolution layers leads to the extraction of richer and more diverse features from the different layers. Because the more deeply embedded the network is, the more abstract the features that are extracted. Thus, the network's ability to extract features improves, and its effectiveness in diagnosing AD is increased. As a result, 58 convolution layers are structured in the proposed network.
3. Each residual block has a different number of kernels and comprises three convolution layers with different kernel sizes. Following the first and second layers are the batch normalization and activation function layers. As for the final layer, it is followed only by the batch normalization layer. Figure 12.16 illustrates layers of the residual block.
4. The average pooling layer is used after the last residual block. Then, to ensure that over-fitting is effectively avoided when this network is used, a dropout layer is added before the fully connected layer. The dropout ratio is set to 50%. In the end of the network, a fully connected layer was added that contains four nodes, based on the number of disease stages, and it concludes with a softmax function. See Figure 12.17.
5. In ResNet50, the ReLU is commonly used as an activation function. Basically, on CNN, ReLU takes the negative parts of its input and drops them to zero, and retains the positive parts. However, these negative inputs may contain useful feature information that could aid in the development of high-level discriminative features [41]. If a neuron's output is 0, its gradient

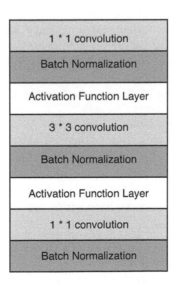

FIGURE 12.16   Layers of the residual block.

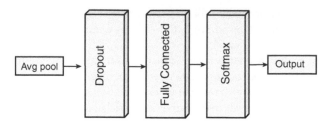

FIGURE 12.17   Last layers in ResNetF architecture.

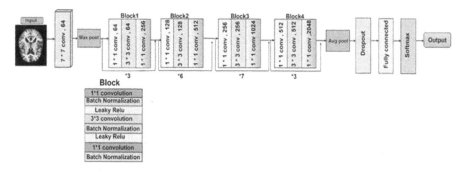

FIGURE 12.18   Modified residual neural network (ResNetF) structure.

will never update its weight, resulting in the neuron never being activated. When the network contains a high number of inactive neurons, the convergence of the model becomes extremely difficult. This may prevent the network from learning and result in underperformance. Accordingly, this is referred to as the dying ReLU problem [42].

6. For this reason, ReLU is replaced with leaky ReLU (LReLU) in order to prevent any potential loss of input information. LReLU has added an alpha parameter to the semi-axis of ReLU, resulting in a slight gradient but not zero. Nodes that were previously inactive with ReLU will now be weight-adjusted. Figure 12.18 shows the ResNetF network.

12.5.3.2   Hyperparameter Tuning

Hyperparameters are parameters whose values are used to control and regulate the learning process. The adjustment of hyperparameters has a significant impact on the accuracy of the trained model. Therefore, an optimal set of hyperparameters must be selected for the learning algorithm before it is trained. This process is called hyperparameter tuning. Experiments have been conducted to tune the hyperparameters, which are shown in Table 12.1.

12.5.4   TRAINING STAGE

In this stage, five experiments have been conducted to train the ResNetF architecture from scratch and perform transfer learning with the ResNet-50 architecture using the

TABLE 12.1
A Set of Experiments to Tune the Hyperparameters

Hyperparameter	EXP1	EXP2	EXP3	EXP4	EXP5
Size of image	(50×50)	(50×50)	(75×75)	(125×125)	(125×125)
Size training sample	65%	70%	70%	80%	80%
Size validation sample	35%	30%	30%	20%	20%
No. of training samples	3,328	3,584	3,584	4,096	4,096
No. of validation samples	1,793	1,537	1,537	1,025	1,025
Batch size	10	20	20	40	40
Length training batches	333	180	180	103	103
Length valid batches	180	77	77	26	26
No. of epochs	30	50	50	100	100
Learning rate	0.05	0.03	0.03	0.0003	0.00001

hyperparameters. In particular, two architectures are used in the experiments during the training phase. First, a pre-trained network (ResNet-50) is used to initialize the weights. Transfer learning was performed using a technique called off-the-shelf (OTS) transfer learning. In this approach, the last dense layer of the original network was replaced by a new dense layer corresponding to the number of classes in our task. In the standard approach, all layers of the ResNet-50 network except the last layer (classifier) are used for feature extraction. The weights of the last layer were adjusted to meet the requirements of our task. Second, a modified version of ResNet50 (ResNetF) is used to perform the training from scratch by randomly initializing the network parameters.

The training dataset was fed into our training networks during each epoch in batches form. Cross-entropy is used as the loss function. It is used when there are more than two classes in a classification problem. Adam is used as the optimizer, and the backpropagation algorithm was used to train the network. In the previous chapter, Adam and the backpropagation algorithm are described in detail.

12.5.5 Validation Stage

In this stage, a validation set is used, which is a sample of data that does not participate in the model training process. This data is used for the purpose of measuring the performance of the model after each epoch during the training phase to adjust the parameters of the model. The validation accuracy and loss compute the validation set to assess the model's performance after each epoch. This can determine whether the model suffers from bias (under-fitting) or variance (over-fitting). If the model suffers from over-fitting or under-fitting, the hyperparameters are retuned and the network is trained again. However, when the validation accuracy improves, the validation loss decreases. In this case, the training process continues until an optimal model is obtained. Then, the model with its parameters is saved as an H5 file to preserve the learned features after reaching the desired accuracy level. After that, the model is imported into the evaluation stage for final testing.

12.6 EVALUATION METRICS

Classification model performance is evaluated using unseen data (testing data) by the following metrics [19,43].

12.6.1 CONFUSION MATRIX

The confusion matrix is a two-dimensional matrix that can visualize the performance of the classification model, also known as the error matrix. By default, the confusion matrix is designed for binary-class classification. However, it can also be extended to classify multiple classes. An example of a confusion matrix for binary-class classification is shown in Table 12.2.

The row labels positive and negative refer to the model's predictions. In contrast, the column labels positive and negative refer to the dataset's ground-truth labels. As for the entries inside the confusion matrix, they represent the following:

True positive (**TP**): the number of instances correctly categorized as positive by the model.

True negative (**TN**): the number of instances correctly categorized as negative by the model.

False positive (**FP**): the number of negative instances incorrectly categorized as positive by the model.

False negative (**FN**): the number of positive instances incorrectly categorized as negative by the model.

12.6.2 ACCURACY

Model accuracy is defined as the ratio of correctly classified samples to the total number of samples. It is denoted mathematically by Equation (12.7).

$$\text{Accuracy} = \frac{TP + TN}{TP + TN + FP + FN} \ldots \tag{12.7}$$

12.6.3 RECALL

The recall is the ratio of truly positive predicted instances to all positive instances observed in the ground data. It indicates the classification performance of positively labeled instances. It is also known as sensitivity or true positive rate (TPR). It is denoted mathematically by Equation (12.8).

TABLE 12.2

Example Confusion Matrix for Binary-Class Classification

Confusion Matrix		Actual Class	
		Positive (p)	Negative (N)
Predicted class	Positive (p)	True positive (TP)	False positive (FP)
	Negative (N)	False negative (FN)	True negative (TN)

$$\text{Recall} = \frac{TP}{TP + FN} \; \cdots \tag{12.8}$$

12.6.4 PRECISION

Precision is the ratio of correctly predicted truly positive instances among all instances classified as positive. It is denoted mathematically by Equation (12.9).

$$\text{Precision} = \frac{TP}{TP + FP} \; \cdots \tag{12.9}$$

12.6.5 F1-SCORE

Precision and recall frequently have an inverse relationship, increasing one at the expense of decreasing the other. Thus, a metric that balances these two metrics is needed. This is why the F1 score was created. It is known as the harmonic mean of precision and recall. It is denoted mathematically by Equation (12.10).

$$F1 - \text{score} = 2 \; \times \frac{\textbf{Precision} \times \textbf{Recall}}{\textbf{Precision} + \textbf{Recall}} \; \cdots \tag{12.10}$$

12.7 EXPERIMENTAL RESULTS

Table 12.3 offerings the final result of the experiment ResNetF, while the accuracy of training and validation across epochs and the training loss and validation loss across epochs are shown in Figure 12.19. Table 12.4 shows the performance measures of ResNetF. Moreover, the confusion matrix of the current experiment is shown in Table 12.5.

12.8 CONCLUSION

AD is a degenerative neurological illness that worsens with age and leads to severe thinking, memory, and behavioral impairment. It is also considered the most common cause of dementia. Early diagnosis of AD is crucial because early intervention in AD slows the progression of the disease, accelerates the development of treatment options in the future, and reduces the financial burden on patients' families. Therefore, the task of early diagnosis of AD is the focus of many researchers who have built many CAD systems to diagnose AD.

TABLE 12.3
Results of ResNetF

Training Accuracy	99%
Validation accuracy	97%
Train loss	0.04
Validation loss	0.08

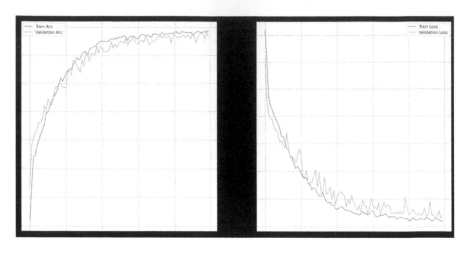

FIGURE 12.19 (a) The accuracy of training and validation across epochs and (b) the training loss and validation loss across epochs.

TABLE 12.4
Performance of ResNetF

CLASS	Accuracy	Precision	Recall	F1-score
CN	97%	0.99	0.97	0.98
MCI	97%	0.99	0.97	0.98
MD	100%	1.00	1.00	1.00
AD	99%	0.95	0.99	0.97
Avg	97%	0.98	0.98	0.98

TABLE 12.5
Confusion Matrix of ResNetF

		Actual Class			
Confusion Matrix		CN	MCI	MD	AD
Predicted class	CN	618	2	0	20
	MCI	2	173	0	4
	MD	0	0	12	0
	AD	4	0	0	444

This chapter aimed to find out whether the early diagnosis of AD can be reliably performed by using MRI of the brain together with a DL algorithm known as a CNN. Therefore, an enhanced residual neural network known as ResNetF is proposed to classify the four stages of AD by increasing the number of convolutional layers that effectively improve the network's ability to detect as many AD biomarkers as possible. Replacing the activation function (ReLU) with a leaky ReLU can also solve the problem of losing useful features that could help construct high-level discriminative features and reduce training time. To avoid over-fitting, a dropout layer is added before the fully connected layer to train all layers in our architecture from scratch without over-fitting problems.

REFERENCES

[1] J. Poirier and S. Gauthier, *Alzheimer's Disease: The Complete Introduction*. Dundurn, Canada, 2014.

[2] R. Sahyouni, A. Verma, and J. Chen, *Alzheimer's Disease Decoded: The History, Present, and Future of Alzheimer's Disease and Dementia*. 1st ed. World Scientific, Singapore, 2016.

[3] M. Prince, A. Wimo, M. Guerchet, G. Ali, Y. Wu, M. Prina, *"World Alzheimer Report 2015"*. *The Global Impact of Dementia. An Analysis of Prevalence, Incidence, Cost and Trends,* Alzheimer's Disease International, London, 2015.

[4] J. D. Kelleher, *Deep Learning*. Illustrated edition. The MIT Press, Cambridge, MA, September 10, 2019.

[5] H. Abdulkarim and M. Z. Al-Faiz, "Online multiclass EEG feature extraction and recognition using modified convolutional neural network method," *Int. J. Electr. Comput. Eng.*, vol. 11, no. 5, pp. 4016–4026, 2021, doi: 10.11591/ijece.v11i5.pp4016-4026.

[6] H. Benmeziane, "Comparison of deep learning frameworks and compilers", Thesis for the degree of Master in Computer Science, Université Polytechnique Hauts-de-France, 2020.

[7] J. Schmidhuber, "Deep learning in neural networks: An overview," *Neural Networks*, vol. 61, pp. 85–117, 2015, doi: 10.1016/j.neunet.2014.09.003.

[8] R. Wu, S. Yan, Y. Shan, Q. Dang, and G. Sun, "Deep image: Scaling up image recognition," *arXiv preprint arXiv:1501.02876*, vol. 7, no. 8, 2015.

[9] Y. Lecun, Y. Bengio, and G. Hinton, "Deep learning," *Nature*, vol. 521, no. 7553, pp. 436–444, 2015, doi: 10.1038/nature14539.

[10] M. Wu and L. Chen, "Image recognition based on deep learning," *2015 Chinese Automation Congress (CAC)*, IEEE, pp. 542–546, 2015, doi: 10.1109/CAC.2015.7382560.

[11] Q. Dou et al., "Automatic detection of cerebral microbleeds from mr images via 3D convolutional neural networks," *IEEE Trans. Med. Imaging*, vol. 35, no. 5, pp. 1182–1195, 2016, doi: 10.1109/TMI.2016.2528129.

[12] U. R. Acharya, H. Fujita, S. L. Oh, Y. Hagiwara, J. H. Tan, and M. Adam, "Application of deep convolutional neural network for automated detection of myocardial infarction using ECG signals," *Inf. Sci. (Ny).*, vol. 415–416, pp. 190–198, 2017, doi: 10.1016/j.ins.2017.06.027.

[13] M. M. Thaha, K. P. M. Kumar, B. S. Murugan, S. Dhanasekeran, P. Vijayakarthick, and A. S. Selvi, "Brain tumor segmentation using convolutional neural networks in MRI images," *J. Med. Syst.*, vol. 43, no. 9, 2019, doi: 10.1007/s10916-019-14160.

[14] M. Rahimzadeh and A. Attar, "A modified deep convolutional neural network for detecting COVID-19 and pneumonia from chest X-ray images based on the concatenation of Xception and ResNet50V2," *Informatics Med. Unlocked*, vol. 19, p. 100360, 2020, doi: 10.1016/j.imu.2020.100360.

[15] Y. Kazemi, "A deep learning pipeline for classifying different stages of Alzheimer's disease from fMRI data", Thesis for the degree of Master in Computer Science, Brock University, 2017.

[16] H. L. J. van der Maas, L. Snoek, and C. E. Stevenson, "How much intelligence is there in artificial intelligence? A 2020 update," *Intelligence*, vol. 87, no. May, p. 101548, 2021, doi: 10.1016/j.intell.2021.101548.

[17] M. Nielsen, *Neural Networks and Deep Learning*. San Francisco, CA: Determination Press, 2015.

[18] S. Sharma, S. Sharma, and A. Athaiya, "Activation functions in neural networks, " *Int. J. Eng. Appl. Sci. Technol.*, vol. 04, no. 12, pp. 310–316, 2020, doi: 10.33564/ijeast.2020. v04i12.054.

[19] T. Ateeq et al., "Ensemble-classifiers-assisted detection of cerebral microbleeds in brain MRI, " *Comput. Electr. Eng.*, vol. 69, pp. 768–781, Jul. 2018, doi: 10.1016/j. compeleceng.2018.02.021.

[20] M. Al-Smadi, M. Hammad, Q. B. Baker, and S. A. Al-Zboon, "A transfer learning with deep neural network approach for diabetic retinopathy classification, " *Int. J. Electr. Comput. Eng.*, vol. 11, no. 4, pp. 2088–8708, 2021, doi: 10.11591/ijece.v11i4. pp2088-8708.

[21] R. Poojary, R. Raina, and A. K. Mondal, "Effect of data-augmentation on fine-tuned cnn model performance, " *IAES Int. J. Artif. Intell.*, vol. 10, no. 1, pp. 84–92, 2021, doi: 10.11591/ijai.v10.i1.pp84-92.

[22] S. B. Jadhav, V. R. Udupi, and S. B. Patil, "Convolutional neural networks for leaf image-based plant disease classification, " *IAES Int. J. Artif. Intell.*, vol. 8, no. 4, pp. 328–341, 2019, doi: 10.11591/ijai.v8.i4.pp328-341.

[23] I. Goodfellow, Y. Bengio, and A. Courville, *Deep Learning*. Illustrated edition. The MIT Press, Cambridge, MA, November 18, 2016.

[24] R. Yamashita, M. Nishio, R. Do and K. Togashi, "Convolutional neural networks: An overview and application in radiology, " *Insights into Imaging*, vol. 9, no. 4, pp. 611–629, 2018, doi: 10.1007/s13244-018-0639-9.

[25] G. Currie, "Intelligent imaging: Anatomy of machine learning and deep learning, " *J. Nucl. Med. Technol.*, vol. 47, no. 4, pp. 273–281, 2019, doi: 10.2967/JNMT.119.232470.

[26] N. Aloysius and M. Geetha, "A review on deep convolutional neural networks, " *2017 International Conference on Communication and Signal Processing (ICCSP)*, IEEE, pp. 588–592, 2017, doi: 10.1109/ICCSP.2017.8286426.

[27] A. Khan, A. Sohail, U. Zahoora, and A. S. Qureshi, "A survey of the recent architectures of deep convolutional neural networks, " *Artif. Intell. Rev.*, vol. 53, no. 8, pp. 5455–5516, 2020, doi: 10.1007/s10462-020-09825-6.

[28] A. S. Lundervold and A. Lundervold, "An overview of deep learning in medical imaging focusing on MRI, " *Z. Med. Phys.*, vol. 29, no. 2, pp. 102–127, 2019, doi: 10.1016/j. zemedi.2018.11.002.

[29] P. Mianjy and R. Arora, "On convergence and generalization of dropout training, " *Adv. Neural Inf. Processing Syst.*, vol. 33, pp. 21151–21161, 2020.

[30] A. Labach, H. Salehinejad, and S. Valaee, "Survey of dropout methods for deep neural networks, " *arXiv preprint arXiv:1904.13310*, 2019.

[31] Q. Xu, M. Zhang, Z. Gu, and G. Pan, "Overfitting remedy by sparsifying regularization on fully-connected layers of CNNs, " *Neurocomputing*, vol. 328, pp. 69–74, 2019, doi: 10.1016/j.neucom.2018.03.080.

[32] M. S. AL-Huseiny and A. S. Sajit, "Transfer learning with GoogLeNet for detection of lung cancer," *Indones. J. Electr. Eng. Comput. Sci.*, vol. 22, no. 2, pp. 1078–1086, 2021, doi: 10.11591/ijeecs.v22.i2.pp1078-1086.

[33] J. Heaton, *Artificial Intelligence for Humans, Volume 3: Neural Networks and Deep Learning.* Heaton Research, Inc., CreateSpace Independent Publishing Platform, October 28, 2015.

[34] M. Nielsen, *Neural Networks and Deep Learning.* Determination Press, San Francisco, CA, 2015.

[35] R. A. Minhas, A. Javed, A. Irtaza, M. T. Mahmood, and Y. B. Joo, "Shot classification of field sports videos using AlexNet convolutional neural network," *Appl. Sci.*, vol. 9, no. 3, 2019, doi: 10.3390/app9030483.

[36] A. Ghosh, A. Sufian, F. Sultana, A. Chakrabarti and D. De, "Fundamental concepts of convolutional neural network", In *Recent trends and advances in artificial intelligence and Internet of Things 2020* (pp. 519–567). Springer, Cham.

[37] M. Mishra, T. Choudhury and T. Sarkar, "CNN based efficient image classification system for smartphone device ", 2021, doi: 10.21203/rs.3.rs-428430/v1.

[38] K. He, X. Zhang, S. Ren, and J. Sun, "Deep residual learning for image recognition", in *Proceedings of the IEEE Computer Society Conference on Computer Vision and Pattern Recognition*, pp. 770–778, 2016, doi: 10.1109/CVPR.2016.90.

[39] P. C. Nissimagoudar, A. V. Nandi, A. Patil, and H. M. Gireesha, "AlertNet: Deep convolutional-recurrent neural network model for driving alertness detection, " *Int. J. Electr. Comput. Eng.*, vol. 11, no. 4, pp. 2088–8708, 2021, doi: 10.11591/ijece.v11i4.pp2088-8708.

[40] M. A. Ihsan Aquil and W. H. Wan Ishak, "Evaluation of scratch and pre-trained convolutional neural networks for the classification of tomato plant diseases, " *IAES Int. J. Artif. Intell.*, vol. 10, no. 2, pp. 467–475, 2021, doi: 10.11591/ijai.v10.i2.pp467-475.

[41] E. M. Benyoussef, A. Elbyed, and H. El Hadiri, "Data mining approaches for Alzheimer's disease diagnosis," *International Symposium on Ubiquitous Networking*. Springer, Cham, vol. 10542 LNCS, pp. 619–631, 2017, doi: 10.1007/978-3-319-68179-5_54.

[42] M. Liu et al., "A multi-model deep convolutional neural network for automatic hippocampus segmentation and classification in Alzheimer's disease", *NeuroImage*, vol. 208, p. 116459, 2020.

[43] R. Jain, N. Jain, A. Aggarwal, and D. J. Hemanth, "Convolutional neural network based Alzheimer's disease classification from magnetic resonance brain images," *Cogn. Syst. Res.*, vol. 57, pp. 147–159, 2019, doi: 10.1016/j.cogsys.2018.12.015.

13 Plant Disease Identification Using Convolution Neural Networks

Dipra Mitra
Amity University

Shikha Gupta
Chandigarh University

Durgesh Srivastava
Chitkara University

Sudeshna Sani
Koneru Lakshmaiah University

CONTENTS

13.1 INTRODUCTION

Agriculture has a profound effect on all living organisms around the globe. In India, agriculture is considered as one of the main sources of income that has a significant impact on the gross domestic product (GDP) of the country. Agriculture accounts for roughly 17% of India's GDP and 60% of the nation's overall employment. The present world's technological advancements have enabled the world's massive population to satisfy their food requirements in an efficient manner [1]. However, climate change has adverse effects on the productivity of crops in several parts of the nation which cannot be controlled. Just like human beings, plants also are vulnerable to a variety of diseases while they progress through their phenological stages. Due to these diseases, crop production decreases, which in turn affects the net profit of the farmers.

DOI: 10.1201/9781003326182-13

Plant diseases continue to be a menace not just to the global marketplace but also to growers with smaller land holdings, whose livelihood is dependent mostly on the products they produce [2,3]. These growers generate more agricultural productivity, and also losses, which were primarily caused by crop diseases. As per studies, such types of farmers mainly contribute to individuals who are provided with a limited quantity of food. According to the Food and Agriculture Organization (FAO) of the United Nations, plant pests and diseases cause a loss of approximately 40% of agricultural harvests each year [4,5].

One way of protecting crops from diseases and preserving agricultural productivity is to use pesticides [6–9]. Since the 1950s, the utilization of pesticides has become one of the driving forces for increased agricultural productivity that satisfies the needs of its people. However, using pesticides to protect the plant from disease is not eco-friendly and is responsible for causing different acute and chronic diseases in human beings. Furthermore, the usage of these compounds has a negative impact on biodiversity, particularly bugs, birds, and fish farms, and it also degrades the quality of soil, air, and water. Despite this, there was an increase of about 78% in tones of active substances utilized between the years 1990 and 2016. Therefore, it is important to have enough knowledge about the phytosanitary conditions of the field in order to limit the use of pesticides while preserving crop productivity. It does, in fact, help farmers conduct appropriate operations in the appropriate location and at the appropriate time. Evaluating the condition of areas, on the other hand, is a difficult task that necessitates a high level of competence. Certainly, a disease can manifest itself in many ways depending on the plant species or perhaps the variety. A single ailment might be caused by a variety of issues, and these issues can coexist on the same plant [13–20]. Plants that have been affected with a disease frequently have visible markings or sores on their leaves, branches, flowers, or fruits. In essence, any illness or pest situation has its own distinct visual appearance which is utilized to identify diseases. The plant leaves are typically considered as the primary source for recognizing plant disease as the symptoms of the majority of the diseases are visible in foliage at very early stages [21–30]. Figure 13.1 depicts some of the photos of diseased plant leaves.

Therefore, due to the above-mentioned facts, farmers face challenges in producing a high-quality and disease-free crop which affects the country's economy. Therefore, it is important to detect plant disease at the earliest stages so that farmers can take essential and preventive actions to curb the disease and produce a high yield [35]. Conventionally, manual and microscopic examinations were the two most popular methods for detecting plant diseases. However, in order to recognize the disease during manual detection, one must be skillful and expert. Optical illusion, human mistakes, and excess time is taken for detecting disease are all problems that these systems face. Microscopic detection is carried out in labs by implementing immunological pathogen clustering and molecular procedures. However, such approaches necessitate a costly experimental setting as well as a legitimate lab setup, which is not a simple undertaking to bring to the whole agricultural industry [38]. Because manual and microscopic inspections are inefficient and time-consuming, automatic disease detection and recognition became the most ideal activity in agriculture. The main goal of the automatic system is to offer disease detection at a cheap cost and with a good accuracy system associated with digital signal processing techniques.

FIGURE 13.1 Example of disease-infected leaves.

The use of computer vision and ML has resulted in significant advancements in identifying diseases and diagnostics. Recently, a large variety of strategies have been presented by various researchers for detecting and recognizing crop diseases that were based on the fundamental protocols of data collection, segmentation, feature extraction, and pattern recognition [39,40].

13.2 DL-BASED PLANT DISEASE DETECTION METHODS

As discussed earlier that machine learning (ML) and deep learning (DL) approaches were mostly used by the majority of the experts in their work in order to provide optimum and more precise classification accuracy. However, due to the complex nature of ML algorithms, DL-based approaches took speed, and a number of methods were proposed. DL-based techniques are considered as one of the promising strategies for learning decisive and distinct characteristics automatically [41,42]. In a typical DL approach, a number of convolutional layers are added which reflect data-learning features. However, the biggest challenge faced by the researchers while using DL techniques was that they require mammoth-size databases for training. If the database utilized does not contain enough images for training the model, discrepancies can occur in results. In [43], the authors used the backpropagation neural network model for detecting the disease in corn and weeds at the earliest stages. Likewise, Mohanty et al. [44] utilized the two architectures of the standard convolutional neural network (CNN), i.e., AlexNet and Google Net for identifying diseases in 26 distinct plants. Ferentinos et al. [45] identified 58 distinct plant diseases using various CNN topologies with a good accuracy rate. They also put the CNN design to the test using real-time photographs. Sladojevic and his colleagues [46] proposed an enhanced DL-based plant disease detection model in which Caffe DL methodology was utilized for identifying 13 distinct plant diseases. Oyewola et al. [47] used the plain CNN and deep residual neural network (DRNN) for identifying five entirely different diseases in cassava plants. The results showcased that DRNN outperformed the PCNN by 9.25%. Selvam et al. [48] proposed a model based on the CNN for detecting the disease in the lady's finger plant. For this, the authors collected a dataset in which a total of 1,088 leaf images were present. Out of 1,088 images, 509 were healthy, 457 were unhealthy, and 122 were burned leaf images. The dataset was processed and data augmentation was applied so that more information can be added to the model. Moreover, the authors used the ReLu function for processing the layers of CNN and Softmax function was used for triggering the output layer. The results demonstrated the supremacy of the suggested approach with an accuracy rate of 96%. Hughes et al. [49] used pre-trained CNN architecture like AlexNet and GoogLeNet in their work and showcased the effectiveness of the suggested approach on various combinations. The Plant village dataset was used in which 38 crop disease pairs were categorized out of 54,306 images. In order to counteract the overfitting issue, changes were made in the ratio of training data. Around 99.34% of accuracy was achieved in the GoogLeNet-Transfer Learning-Color model with a training ratio of 80:20. Similarly, the accuracy rate was analyzed in the case of AlexNet-training from scratch with grayscale segmentation came out to be 98.21% when the training data ratio was 80:20. However, the system struggled to forecast the description and achieved an accuracy of just 31% for images taken from an external provider; nevertheless, the system can operate well on actual data once taught on massive quantities of data. Karlekar et al. [50] presented a novel mechanism for identifying the disease in soya beans. For this, the researchers of this paper used the PDDB dataset. Moreover, to eliminate the overfitting problem and to make the data more informative, data augmentation was implemented. The image analysis unit was divided into four sub-systems, where initially RGB images were converted to CIELabcolor space, and then k-mean clustering ($k=2$) was applied to partition pictures into the foreground and background. In the third unit, the bigger elements present in the image were isolated, and finally, the binary mask was mapped to RGB. The accuracy achieved by the suggested model was 98.24%. Baranwal et al. [51] employed a self-designed CNN architectural model with four layers for identifying four different diseases which include, Scab, cedar, rust, and black rot in apples. The authors of this paper also used the dataset that was collected from plant villages with four classes (three infected and one healthy). The overall accuracy rate of the current method was 98.42%. Tiwari et al. [52] presented a DL-based disease detection mode for potatoes. In this work, three pre-trained models (VGG19, VGG16, and V3) were employed. Moreover, the plant village dataset was used and testing was performed in a ratio of 70:30. the authors assessed the performance of different combinations of DNNs with traditional classifiers like KNN, SVM, NN, and LR. These results demonstrated that LR performed much better than other classifiers with an accuracy rate of 97.8%. Sulistijono et al. [53] offered a DL-based approach for categorizing four distinct types of disease that occur in potatoes. For this, they utilized various data sources like Plant village, Google images, and others for training the model. The architecture utilized was an enhanced version of VGGNet that has a 91% accuracy. Every architecture framework has the same 91% accuracy. The results demonstrated that VGG16 had a precision of 0.9131148, whereas VGG19 had a precision of 0.9096284. The VGG16 architecture model was 0.00349% more accurate than VGG19. Table 13.1 shows a comparison of different types of classifiers in DL with the accuracy level.

TABLE 13.1
Comparison of different DL Classifiers with Accuracy Level

Authors	Classifier	Database	Accuracy
[43]	Backpropagation neural network	Field data	94.28%
[44]	AlexNet and GoogLeNet	Public dataset with 54,306 images	99.35%
[45]	CNN	Open dataset of 87,848 images	99.53%
[46]	CNN	Field data	Precision equal to 96.3% average
[47]	PCNN and DRNN	NA	PCNN performed better than DRNN by over 9.25%
[48]	CNN	Public dataset with 509 images	96%
[49]	AlexNet and GoogLeNet	Plant village dataset	GoogLeNet-Transfer Learning-Color with 99.34% and GoogLeNet-Transfer Learning-Color with 98.21%
[50]	CNN with six layers	PDDB database	98.24%
[51]	CNN model with four layers	Subset of plant village database	98.42%
[52]	VGG19, VGG16 AND V3	Plant village	97.8%
[53]	Improved version of VGG16 and VGG19	Plant village, google images and others	VGG16 = 0.9131148 and VGG19 = 0.9.96284

13.3   RESULT AND DISCUSSION

This dataset was gathered from Kaggle, and it contains 4,900 photos and three kinds of disorders, all of which were diagnosed with great accuracy. This image shows a leaf that has been infected with a disease. After performing image pre-processing, the length of the dataset was calculated, with 80% of the data being used for training and 20% being used for testing. Out of the 20% of test data, 10% was examined for validation accuracy and validation loss. After image pre-processing, the dataset was fed into a CNN with all layers activated by ReLU and a maximum pooling algorithm. Figure 13.2 shows the CNN-based disease classification model in which healthy and unhealthy tomato leaves have been categorized.

In Figure 13.3, an artificial neural network has been used to minimize the image length. It also shows the total number of trainable parameters to train the model before execution. Here, the Tensor flow has been used to train the model using epochs. It has been discovered that as the number of epochs is raised, the model's accuracy improves. It has discovered 91.29 accuracy here (Figure 13.4).

The training set and the test set were created from our dataset. The training set contains 80% of our dataset's data, while the test set contains the remaining data. Some photos are derived from the test set and training set and used to create the validation set of data for validation purposes. Training loss is an error in the training

FIGURE 13.2 CNN-based disease classification.

set of data. After passing the validation batch of data through the trained network, we obtain an error. This issue is known as validation loss. With higher epochs, train and validation errors decrease. Train accuracy and validation accuracy are gradually increasing as train loss and validation loss decrease. Training loss vs. validation loss and training accuracy vs. validation accuracy is shown in Figure 13.5.

Figure 13.6 shows the predicted result after training the model with a high confidence level. If a new image dataset is fed into the model, the model will respond with accuracy.

13.4 CONCLUSION

In this research, the CNN model has been used to present a DL strategy for classifying different types of succulent tomato plants. Our network model is built using five four max-pooling layers and four convolutional layers. To reduce overfitting in the system, each completely linked layer is required to have a dropout layer. The dataset is augmented using strategies for enhancing data, such as rotation, shifting, scaling, shearing, and flipping. The model achieves 95% accuracy with the dataset after successfully completing 15 epochs. Here, three classes of succulent plants have been analyzed, and this is inadequate for model optimization or poses a challenge to additional succulent species that are unknown. As a result, our long-term goal is to

```
Model: "sequential_2"
```

Layer (type)	Output Shape	Param #
sequential (Sequential)	(32, 256, 256, 3)	0
conv2d (Conv2D)	(32, 254, 254, 32)	896
max_pooling2d (MaxPooling2D)	(32, 127, 127, 32)	0
conv2d_1 (Conv2D)	(32, 125, 125, 64)	18496
max_pooling2d_1 (MaxPooling2	(32, 62, 62, 64)	0
conv2d_2 (Conv2D)	(32, 60, 60, 64)	36928
max_pooling2d_2 (MaxPooling2	(32, 30, 30, 64)	0
conv2d_3 (Conv2D)	(32, 28, 28, 64)	36928
max_pooling2d_3 (MaxPooling2	(32, 14, 14, 64)	0
conv2d_4 (Conv2D)	(32, 12, 12, 64)	36928
max_pooling2d_4 (MaxPooling2	(32, 6, 6, 64)	0
conv2d_5 (Conv2D)	(32, 4, 4, 64)	36928
max_pooling2d_5 (MaxPooling2	(32, 2, 2, 64)	0
flatten (Flatten)	(32, 256)	0
dense (Dense)	(32, 64)	16448
dense_1 (Dense)	(32, 3)	195

```
Total params: 183,747
Trainable params: 183,747
Non-trainable params: 0
```

FIGURE 13.3 Trainable parameter findings using ANN.

Epoch 1/15
2022-05-27 09:23:15.934098: I tensorflow/core/kernels/data/shuffle_dataset_op.cc:175] Filling up shuffle buffer (this may take a while): 133 of 10000
2022-05-27 09:23:16.083187: I tensorflow/core/kernels/data/shuffle_dataset_op.cc:228] Shuffle buffer filled.
2022-05-27 09:23:16.083267: I tensorflow/core/kernels/data/shuffle_dataset_op.cc:175] Filling up shuffle buffer (this may take a while): 1 of 1000
2022-05-27 09:23:16.083709: I tensorflow/core/kernels/data/shuffle_dataset_op.cc:228] Shuffle buffer filled.
2022-05-27 09:23:17.279224: I tensorflow/stream_executor/cuda/cuda_dnn.cc:368] Loaded cuDNN version 8005
112/112 [==============================] - 52s 300ms/step - loss: 0.7569 - accuracy: 0.6604 - val_loss: 0.4151 - val_accuracy: 0.8281
Epoch 2/15
112/112 [==============================] - 28s 249ms/step - loss: 0.3514 - accuracy: 0.8555 - val_loss: 0.4329 - val_accuracy: 0.8036
Epoch 3/15
112/112 [==============================] - 27s 243ms/step - loss: 0.3632 - accuracy: 0.8497 - val_loss: 0.8477 - val_accuracy: 0.6987
Epoch 4/15
112/112 [==============================] - 28s 249ms/step - loss: 0.3637 - accuracy: 0.8550 - val_loss: 0.4819 - val_accuracy: 0.8170
Epoch 5/15
112/112 [==============================] - 28s 254ms/step - loss: 0.2842 - accuracy: 0.8869 - val_loss: 0.3325 - val_accuracy: 0.8661
Epoch 6/15
112/112 [==============================] - 27s 243ms/step - loss: 0.2897 - accuracy: 0.8782 - val_loss: 0.3158 - val_accuracy: 0.8750
Epoch 7/15
112/112 [==============================] - 27s 244ms/step - loss: 0.2699 - accuracy: 0.8970 - val_loss: 0.2745 - val_accuracy: 0.8795
Epoch 8/15
112/112 [==============================] - 27s 244ms/step - loss: 0.2500 - accuracy: 0.9015 - val_loss: 0.3700 - val_accuracy: 0.8549
Epoch 9/15
112/112 [==============================] - 28s 251ms/step - loss: 0.2427 - accuracy: 0.9031 - val_loss: 0.3597 - val_accuracy: 0.8504
Epoch 10/15
112/112 [==============================] - 28s 245ms/step - loss: 0.1953 - accuracy: 0.9244 - val_loss: 0.2608 - val_accuracy: 0.8975
Epoch 11/15
112/112 [==============================] - 28s 248ms/step - loss: 0.2377 - accuracy: 0.9079 - val_loss: 0.1977 - val_accuracy: 0.9219
Epoch 12/15
112/112 [==============================] - 29s 255ms/step - loss: 0.2005 - accuracy: 0.9197 - val_loss: 0.1955 - val_accuracy: 0.9286
Epoch 13/15
112/112 [==============================] - 30s 266ms/step - loss: 0.1971 - accuracy: 0.9208 - val_loss: 0.3555 - val_accuracy: 0.8973
Epoch 14/15
112/112 [==============================] - 33s 294ms/step - loss: 0.2117 - accuracy: 0.9155 - val_loss: 0.3020 - val_accuracy: 0.8839
Epoch 15/15
112/112 [==============================] - 29s 255ms/step - loss: 0.1825 - accuracy: 0.9289 - val_loss: 0.2253 - val_accuracy: 0.9129

FIGURE 13.4 Finding out the accuracy of the model.

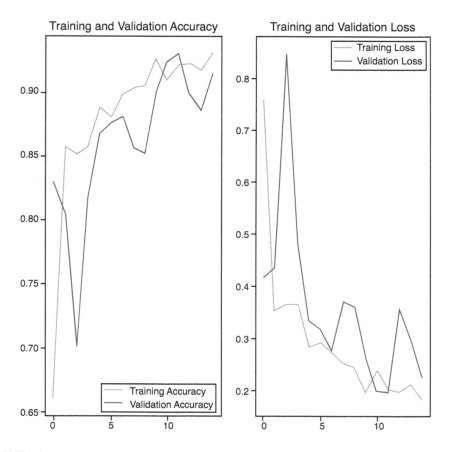

FIGURE 13.5 Training and validation accuracy, training, and validation loss.

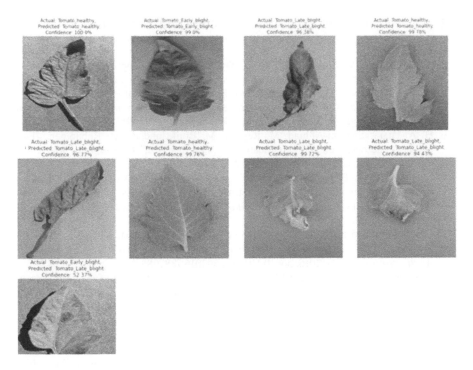

FIGURE 13.6   Predicted result after training.

increase better optimization, the number of succulent plant types, and to develop an Android app that will assist users in identifying succulent plants.

REFERENCES

1. Kamlesh Golhani, Siva K. Balasundram, Ganesan Vadamalai, and Biswajeet Pradhan, "A review of neural networks in plant disease detection using hyperspectral data," *Information Processing in Agriculture,* vol. 5, pp. 354–371, 2018.
2. Srdjan sladojevic, Marko Arsenovic, Andras Andrela, Dubravko Culibrk, and Darko Stefanovic, "Deep neural networks based recognition of plant disease by leaf image classification," *Computational Intelligence and neuroscience*, vol. 2016, pp. 201–204, 2016.
3. N. Deepa, and S.P. Chokkalingam, "Deep convolutional neural networks (CNN) for medical image analysis," *International Journal of Engineering and Advanced Technology (IJEAT)*, vol. 8, no. 3S, pp. 504–509, 2019. ISSN: 2249-8958.
4. P. Bedi, and P. Gole. "Plant disease detection using hybrid model based on convolutional autoencoder and convolutional neural network," *Artificial Intelligence in Agriculture*, vol. 5, pp. 90–101, 2021.
5. Gianni Fenu, and Francesca Maridina Malloci, "Using multioutput learning to diagnose plant disease and stress severity," *Complexity*, vol. 2021, Article ID 6663442, p. 11, 2021.
6. J. Boulent, S. Foucher, J. Théau, and P.L. St-Charles, "Convolutional neural networks for the automatic identification of plant diseases," *Frontiers in Plant Science*, vol. 2019, no. 10, p. 941, 2019. doi:10.3389/fpls.2019.00941.

7. M.A. Ebrahimi, M.H. Khoshtaghaza, S. Minaei, and B. Jamshidi, "Vision-based pest detection based on SVM classification method," *Computers and Electronics in Agriculture*, vol. 137, pp. 52–58, 2017.

8. Z. Gao, Z. Luo, W. Zhang, Z. Lv, and Y. Xu, "Deep learning application in plant stress imaging: A review," *AgriEngineering*, vol. 2, no. 3, pp. 430–446, 2020.

9. Anusha Rao, and S. B. Kulkarni. "A hybrid approach for plant leaf disease detection and classification using digital image processing methods," *The International Journal of Electrical Engineering & Education*, vol. 2, p. 0020720920953126, 2022.

10. H. Al-Hiary, S. Bani-Ahmad, M. Reyalat, M. Braik, and Z. AL Rahamneh, "Fast and accurate detection and classification of plant diseases," *International Journal of Computer Applications (0975–8887)*, vol. 17, no. 1, 2011.

11. S.H. Rasta, M.E. Partovi, H. Seyedarabi, and A. Javadzadeh, "A comparative study on preprocessing techniques in diabetic retinopathy retinal images: Illumination correction and contrast enhancement." *Journal of Medical Signals and Sensors*, vol. 5, no, 1, pp. 40–48, 2015.

12. D.S. Prabha, and J.S. Kumar, "Performance analysis of image smoothing methods for low level of distortion," *2016 IEEE International Conference on Advances in Computer Applications (ICACA)*, 2016, doi:10.1109/icaca.2016.7887983.

13. T.G. Patil, S.K. Kusekar, and M. Adasho, "Performance analysis of smoothing techniques in context with image processing," *Asian Journal for Convergence in Technology (AJCT)*, vol. 4, no. 3, ISSN 2350-1146, 2019.

14. Sheikh Tania, and Raghad Rowaida. "A comparative study of various image filtering techniques for removing various noisy pixels in aerial image," *International Journal of Signal Processing, Image Processing and Pattern Recognition*, vol. 9, no. 3, pp. 113–124, 2016.

15. Wikipedia contributors. "Median filter." Wikipedia, the free encyclopedia. Web, 2021. https://en.wikipedia.org/wiki/Median_filter

16. 2009, "Robust filters," In: *Computational Surface and Roundness Metrology*. Springer, London. doi:10.1007/978-1-84800-297-5_11.

17. K. Thangadurai, and K. Padmavathi, "Computer visionimage enhancement for plant leaves disease detection," *2014 World Congress on Computing and Communication Technologies*. Trichirappalli, India.

18. P. Raju, Daniel Ratna, and G. Neelima. "Image segmentation by using histogram thresholding," *International Journal of Computer Science Engineering and Technology,* vol. 2, no. 1, pp. 776–779, 2012.

19. K. Jeevitha, et al. "A review on various segmentation techniques in image processing," *European Journal of Molecular & Clinical Medicine,* vol. 7, no. 4, pp. 1342–1348, 2020.

20. S. Karthick, K. Sathiyasekar, and A. Puraneeswari. "A survey based on region based segmentation," *International Journal of Engineering Trends and Technology,* vol. 7, no. 3, pp. 143–147, 2014.

21. Samuel Manoharan, "Performance analysis of clustering based image segmentation techniques," *Journal of Innovative Image Processing (JIIP)*, vol. 2, no. 01, pp. 14–24, 2020.

22. Catalin Amza, "A review on neural network-based image segmentation techniques", *De Montfort University Mechanical and Manufacturing Engineering the Gateway,* vol. 4, no. 3, pp. 1–23. February 2015, ISSN: 2249-8958.

23. Dilpreet Kaur, and Yadwinder Kaur. "Various image segmentation techniques: A review," *International Journal of Computer Science and Mobile Computing,* vol. 3, no. 5, pp. 809–814, 2014.

24. B.S. Manjunath, and W.Y. Ma, "Texture features for browsing and retrieval of large image data," *IEEE PAMI*, vol. 18, no. 8, pp. 837–842, 1996.

25. S.E. Grigorescu, N. Petkov, and P. Kruizinga, "Comparison of texture features based on Gabor filters," *IEEE TIP*, vol. 11, no. 10, pp. 1160–1167, 2002.

26. Vairaprakash Gurusamy, Subbu Kannan, and G. Nalini. "Review on image segmentation techniques," *Journal of Pharmaceutical Research,* vol. 20125, pp. 4548–4553, 2013.

27. H. Wang, M. Ullah, A. Klaser, I. Laptev, and C. Schmid, *Evaluation of Local Spatio-Temporal Features for Action Recognition*, in: BMVC 2009-British Machine vision Conference, p. 124-1. BMVA Press, 2009.

28. D.S. Zhang, Md.M. Islam, and G.J. Lu, "A review on automatic image annotation techniques," *Pattern Recognition*, vol. 45, no. 1, pp. 346–362, 2012.

29. Shima Ramesh, Ramachandra Hebbar, M. Niveditha, R. Pooja, N. Prasad Bhat, N. Shashank, and P.V. Vinod, "Plant disease detection using machine learning," *2018 International Conference on Design Innovations for 3Cs Compute Communicate Control (ICDI3C)*, IEEE, 2018.

30. R. Kavya, "Feature extraction technique for robust and fast visual tracking: A typical review," *International Journal of Emerging Engineering Research and Technology,* vol. 3, no. 1, pp. 98–104, 2015.

31. Miss Meenu Sahu, Amit Saxena, and Manish Manoria, "Application of feature extraction technique: A review," *IJCSIT,* vol. 4, pp. 3014–3016, 2015.

32. S.M. Hassan, A.K. Maji, M. Jasiński, Z. Leonowicz, and E. Jasiński. "Identification of plant-leaf diseases using CNN and transfer-learning approach," *Electronics,* vol. 10, 12, p. 1388, 2021. doi:10.3390/ electronics10121388.

33. R. Zhou, S. Kaneko, F. Tanaka, M. Kayamori, and M. Shimizu, "Disease detection of cercospora leaf spot in sugar beet by robust template matching," *Computers and Electronics in Agriculture*, vol. 108, pp. 58–70, 2014.

34. D. LeitzkeBetemps, B. Vahl de Paula, S.É. Parent, S.P. Galarça, N.A. Mayer, G.A. Marodin, D.E. Rozane, W. Natale, G.W.B. Melo, L.E. Parent, et al. "Humboldtian diagnosis of peach tree (prunus persica) nutrition using machine-learning and compositional methods," *Agronomy*, vol. 10, p. 900, 2020.

35. S.K. Sarkar, J. Das, R. Ehsani, and V. Kumar, "Towards autonomous phytopathology: Outcomes and challenges of citrus greening disease detection through close-range remote sensing," *2016 IEEE International Conference on Robotics and Automation (ICRA)*, 2016, pp. 5143–5148, doi:10.1109/ICRA.2016.7487719.

36. Q. Yao, Z. Guan, Y. Zhou, J. Tang, Y. Hu, and B. Yang, "Application of support vector machine for detecting rice diseases using shape and color texture features," In: *IEEE international conference on engineering computation ICEC*, Hong Kong, pp 79–83, 2009.

37. H.X. Kan, L. Jin, and F.L. Zhou, "Classification of medicinal plant leaf image based on multi-feature extraction," *Pattern Recognition and Image Analysis*, vol. 27, no. 3, pp. 581–587, 2017.

38. Suja Radha, "Leaf disease detection using image processing," *Journal of Chemical and Pharmaceutical Sciences*, vol. 10, pp. 361–365, 2017, doi: 10.1109/ICSTCEE49637. 2020.9277379.

39. G. Saradhambal, R. Dhivya, S. Latha, and R. Rajesh, "Plant disease detection, and its solution using image classification," *International Journal of Pure and Applied Mathematics*, vol. 119, no. 14, pp. 879–884, 2018.

40. J.K. Patil, and R. Kumar, "Analysis of content based image retrieval for plant leaf diseases using color, shape and texture features," *Engineering in Agriculture, Environment and Food*, vol. 10, pp. 69–78, 2016.

41. I. Pertot, T. Kuflik, I. Gordon, S. Freeman, and Y. Elad, "Identificator: A web-based tool for visual plant disease identification, a proof of concept with a case study on strawberry," *Computers and Electronics in Agriculture*, vol. 84, pp. 144–154, 2012.

42. N. Yang, Y. Qian, H. S. EL-Mesery, R. Zhang, A. Wang, and J. Tang, "Rapid detection of rice disease using microscopy image identification based on the synergistic judgment of texture and shape features and decision tree-confusion matrix method," *Journal of the Science of Food and Agriculture*, vol. 99, no. 14, pp. 6589–6600, 2019.

43. L. Wu, Y. Wen, X. Deng, and H. Peng, "Identification of weed/corn using BP network based on wavelet features and fractal dimension," *Scientific Research and Essay*, vol. 4, pp. 1194–1200, 2009.

44. S.P. Mohanty, D.P. Hughes, and M. Salathé, "Using deep learning for image-based plant disease detection," *Frontiers in Plant Science*, vol. 7, p. 1419, 2016.

45. K.P. Ferentinos, "Deep learning models for plant disease detection and diagnosis," *Computers and Electronics in Agriculture*, vol. 145, pp. 311–318, 2018.

46. S. Sladojevic, M. Arsenovic, A. Anderla, D. Culibrk, and D. Stefanovic, "Deep neural networks based recognition of plant diseases by leaf image classification," *Computational Intelligence and Neuroscience*, vol. 2016, pp. 1–10, 2016

47. D.O. Oyewola, , E.G. Dada, S. Misra, and R. Damaševičius, "Detecting cassava mosaic disease using a deep residual convolutional neural network with distinct block processing," *PeerJ Computer Science*, vol. 7, p. e352, 2021.

48. L. Selvam, and P. Kavitha, "Classification of ladies finger plant leaf using deep learning," *Journal of Ambient Intelligence and Humanized Computing,* no. 0123456789, 2020, doi:10.1007/s12652-020-02671-y.

49. S.P. Mohanty, D.P. Hughes, and M. Salathé, "Using deep learning for image-based plant disease detection," *Frontiers in Plant Science*, vol. 7, no. September, pp. 1–10, 2016, doi:10.3389/fpls.2016.01419.

50. A. Karlekar, and A. Seal, "SoyNet: Soybean leaf diseases classification," *Computers and Electronics in Agriculture*, vol. 172, no. November 2019, 2020, doi:10.1016/j.compag.2020.105342.

51. S. Baranwal, S. Khandelwal, and A. Arora, "Deep learning convolutional neural network for apple leaves disease detection," *Proceedings of International Conference on Sustainable Computing in Science, Technology and Management (SUSCOM), Amity University Rajasthan, Jaipur - India, February 26-28, 2019*, pp. 260–267, 2019, doi: 10.2139/ssrn.3351641.

52. D. Tiwari, M. Ashish, N. Gangwar, A. Sharma, S. Patel, and S. Bhardwaj, "Potato leaf diseases detection using deep learning," *2020 4th International Conference on Intelligent Computing and Control Systems (ICICCS)*, no. Iciccs, pp. 461–466, 2020, doi:10.1109/ICICCS48265.2020.9121067.

53. R. A. Sholihati, I. A. Sulistijono, A. Risnumawan, and E. Kusumawati, "Potato leaf disease classification using deep learning approach," *2020 International Electronics Symposium (IES)*, pp. 392–397, 2020, doi:10.1109/IES50839.2020.9231784.

54. Garima Shrestha, Deepsikha, Majolica Das, Naiwrita Dey, "Plant Disease Detection Using CNN," Proceedings of *2020 IEEE Applied Signal Processing Conference (ASPCON)*, pp. 109–119, IEEE, 2020.

55. M. Brahimi, K. Boukhalfa, and A. Moussaoui, "Deep learning for tomato diseases: Classification and symptoms visualization," *Applied Artificial Intelligence*, vol. 31, no. 4, pp. 299–315, 2017, doi:10.1080/08839514.2017.1315516.

56. K.P. Ferentinos, "Deep learning models for plant disease detection and diagnosis," *Computers and Electronics in Agriculture*, vol. 145, no. January, pp. 311–318, 2018, doi:10.1016/j.compag.2018.01.009.

57. E. C. Too, L. Yujian, S. Njuki, and L. Yingchun, "A comparative study of fine-tuning deep learning models for plant disease identification," *Computers and Electronics in Agriculture*, vol. 161, no. February, pp. 272–279, 2019, doi: 10.1016/j.compag.2018.03.032.

58. R. Sujatha, J. M. Chatterjee, N. Z. Jhanjhi, and S. N. Brohi, "Performance of deep learning vs machine learning in plant leaf disease detection," *Microprocessors and Microsystems*, vol. 80, no. December 2020, p. 103615, 2021, doi:10.1016/j.micpro.2020.103615.

59. A. Cruz et al., "Detection of grapevine yellows symptoms in *Vitis vinifera L.* with artificial intelligence," *Computers and Electronics in Agriculture*, vol. 157, no. December 2018, pp. 63–76, 2019, doi:10.1016/j.compag.2018.12.028.

60. P. Jiang, Y. Chen, B. Liu, D. He, and C. Liang, "Real-time detection of apple leaf diseases using deep learning approach based on improved convolutional neural networks," *IEEE Access*, vol. 7, pp. 59069–59080, 2019, doi:10.1109/ACCESS.2019.2914929.

61. Y. Lu, S. Yi, N. Zeng, Y. Liu, and Y. Zhang, "Identification of rice diseases using deep convolutional neural networks," *Neurocomputing*, vol. 267, pp. 378–384, 2017, doi:10.1016/j.neucom.2017.06.023.

62. D. Oppenheim and G. Shani, "Potato disease classification using convolution neural networks," *Advances in Animal Biosciences*, vol. 8, no. 2, pp. 244–249, 2017, doi:10.1017/s2040470017001376.

14 Study of Health Quality Coinciding with the Handwriting Process

Atika Fatma
Integral University

Shivam Tiwari
G L Bajaj Institute of Technology & Management

CONTENTS

DOI: 10.1201/9781003326182-14

14.1 INTRODUCTION

Graphology or handwriting analysis is the science of analysing the style, features, and strokes of handwriting in order to provide valuable perception about an individual. Graphology can interpret a person's psychological state; in other words, handwriting can reveal what is going on inside an individual's brain. A skilled graphologist can reveal the confidence level, anxiety, temper, frustration, guilt, defence mechanism, fear, intensity of need for communication, suicidal tendencies, honesty, social behaviour, intellect, communication skills, emotional outlay, and present mood if happy, sad, or irritated and thus can sketch out the author's personality just by seeing a sample of handwriting. The word 'graphology' was coined by the father of graphology, Abate Jean Hippolyte Michon (1806–1881) a Frenchman, which is made up of two Greek words, 'graph' meaning 'writing' and 'logy' meaning 'study', thus meaning study of handwriting.

Graphological analysis is useful in almost all fields from criminology to medicine. Multinational companies use graphology in the recruitment process, while counsellors use it to understand their patients and it can also be used as supporting evidence in court. The authenticity of suicide notes and will statements can be checked and criminal tendencies can also be identified. Diagnosing psychological, neurodegenerative, and physical diseases is another domain where graphology is proving to be extremely helpful.

In today's time of digital evolution, men wish to use technology to do all kinds of tedious work for them. Furthermore, the accuracy of graphological analysis is comprehensively dependent upon the skills of the graphologist and thus can become a hectic and laborious work that consumes time, energy, and money as well. This point led to the advancement of graphological analysis from manual to automated graphological analysis. The steps involved in an automated handwriting analysing system (AHAS) are mentioned in Figure 14.1.

Input: Online and offline are the ways of collecting handwriting samples as input for automated handwriting analysing systems. Offline samples are images of handwriting written on A4 paper usually written with a ball pen, scanned, and converted into a .png or .jpeg format. An online handwriting sample is one taken with a digital pen or digital graphics tablet which is pressure-sensitive. These devices consider velocity and acceleration along with pressure which gives the online method an upper hand over the offline sample collection method which gives no idea of what

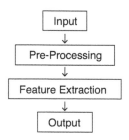

FIGURE 14.1   Block diagram for AHASs.

velocity or speed the author wrote the sample; thus, pressure and speed, two very significant characteristics of handwriting are lost.

Pre-Processing: Pre-processing is the procedure of converting a handwriting sample to a format on which further steps can be performed. Image samples are then cleaned through a threshold function, segmented, and then translated into an appropriate format for further processing.

Feature Extraction: This is the process of extracting features of handwriting such as slope, slant, connecting stroke, margin, space between words, line and letter, size, pressure, shape of letters, etc. Different systems use different algorithms to extract these features. Fuzzy technique, neural network, convolutional neural network (CNN), support vector machine (SVM), artificial neural network (ANN), and MATLAB Image processing are used to extract features from a sample of handwriting.

Output Features: Extracted features are put together by different algorithms to give traits of personality as outputs.

Due to the inefficient processing power of basic computers, there must be introduced some power computing like cloud computing. In this scenario, all data processing work will be done on a cloud platform. Cloud provides very fast processing power so that the complexity of the result acquisition is very less, which is good for the system. Thus, the accuracy matrix of the given task would be increased.

14.2   BACKGROUND

Handwriting is believed to be different for each one of us, and no two individuals are likely to have the same handwriting which gave it the name 'behavioural biometric'. It looks like handwriting is written by hand, but after carrying various experiments with people who had the misfortune to lose their hands, it has been known that even if we write with our foot or mouth, after attaining fluency, our handwriting still carries those characteristics which were present while writing with hands, so handwriting is a product of brain rather than hands. Popularly known as brainwriting, handwriting is governed by the prefrontal cortex which releases unique electric pulses for every feeling and personality trait.

The prefrontal cortex is the section of the frontal cortex that lies at the very front of the brain and is vitally involved in executive functions such as concentration, organisation, judgement, reasoning, decision-making, creativity, emotional regulation, social–relational abilities, abstract thinking, future planning, coordinating, and adjusting complex behaviour. In other words, the prefrontal cortex is implicated in a variety of complex behaviours, including planning, and greatly contributes to personality development.

Our handwriting is governed by the prefrontal cortex, the region of the brain implicated in executive functions such as planning, decision-making, short-term memory, personality expression, and social behaviour. The basic activity of this brain region is considered to be the orchestration of thoughts and actions in accordance with internal goals.

These signals from our brain can be significantly seen in our handwriting in the form of characteristics of handwriting such as strokes, slants, connecting style, size, margin, baseline, shapes of letters, space between words, letters, lines, pen pressure, etc. Handwriting can reveal the psychological state or, in other words, processes going inside our brain, and our feelings at the time of writing. Psychological diseases, namely, autism, attention deficit hyperactivity disorder (ADHD), obsessive-compulsive disorder (OCD), depression, and others can be identified through the handwriting of the patient. Alzheimer's, Parkinson's disease, and other neurodegenerative diseases can also be diagnosed through handwriting analysis.

14.3 HISTORY

Handwriting analysis has been in existence soon after man learnt to write, though the word graphology was coined much later. Ancient philosophers of China used to make deductions about the character of a person by seeing the style of writing. Okakura, a renowned Japanese scholar, Kuo Jo-Hsu, a Chinese philosopher, and the great philosopher of Greek, Aristotle, all considered that writing can identify the essence of the person writing it. Graphological analysis was used in Roman empires as well to testify if the intentions of an individual are noble or not.

The first-known article on handwriting analysis was written in the early 17th century by Alderisius Prosper followed by a book written by Camillo Baldo in 1622. Although there for centuries, graphological analysis gained its popularity near 1830 when some renowned men such as Cardinal Regnier and Abbe Louis Flandrin Sir began investigating the subject. Abate Jean Hippolyte Michon (1806–1881) studied thousands of samples and those small graphic details which he published in the book Les Mystères de l'Écriture and La Méthode Pratique de Graphologie. These formed the basis of graphology and led to further research work and Jean was titled 'the father of graphology' for the same. The next remarkable contribution towards the subject was made by other French psychologists Jules Crepieux Jamin and Alfred Binet.

14.4 LITERATURE REVIEW

Kedar et al. [1] said that handwriting is known as brain writing because it reflects all that's going inside a person's mind. Handwriting can tell a person's emotional state, i.e. happiness, fear, anxiety, anger, mental capability, and thinking capacity, and can even indicate diseases if any are present. Just like fingerprints, handwriting is also unique for everyone, and thus by analysing the handwriting of a person, a sketch of personality can be drawn and find out if the person needs physiological or psychological help or not. The author proposed a multi-stage procedure named automated emotion recognition system which takes several components such as slant, baseline, depth, size, loops, zones, margins, I-dots, T-bars, and strokes as input and identifies emotional states, mental, or physical illness. The following are the different stages of the procedure:

-Image Pre-processing
     It is a technique where a handwriting sample is converted into a specific form by which it can be processed by the system, i.e. JPEG format image.

-Feature Extraction

In this stage, the features such as baseline slants and pen pressure are extracted from the sample and are mentioned as micro or macro based on their occurrence in the sample – Classification

This is the most important stage; here, the extracted features are given as input to the classifier and then the classifier gives the mental–emotional state of the writer as the output.

Sufianita et al. [2] claim that handwriting analysis can be used to understand the human mind in a better way, it helps to know the emotional control of a person which can help a counsellor to provide better counselling, and child development, and it is also efficient in selection an employee or life partner and or business partner, as well as in criminology. It is also mentioned that the ANN popularly used to recognise features of handwriting is a good method, but its training process consumes a lot of time and data. Hence, we propose the fuzzy technique to recognise features and identify personality. This research was particularly based on determining emotional control based on the baseline or slope line of the handwriting sample. First, data is collected, and BlueJ software cleans and converts it to binary form. The height of the word is measured and divided into four components, and then the upper baseline and lower baseline are determined by calculating the number of black pixels. After that, the slope is calculated by solving centroid coordinates using the formula: $(Ya - Yb)$ $/ (Xa - Xb)$, where (Xa, Ya) are taken from the left side and (Xb, Yb) are taken from the right side. The next step is to develop fuzzy sets, using five crisp inputs: value, baseline, left slant, right slant, and emotional control. Fuzzy inference methodology uses the Mamdani technique and has been proven to be a success in determining the emotional control of a particular person.

Champa H N et al. [3] mentioned that every personality trait has a specific neurological brain pattern and each of these different brain patterns produce a unique neuromuscular movement, these movements result in stroke, baseline, size, shape, and slant of handwriting. Handwriting analysis or graphology is the branch of science that deals with identifying personality traits by analysing one's handwriting. This research paper proposes automating the process of feature extraction and predicting one's emotional state, fears, honesty, etc. by using the ANN. The author has taken only three components of handwriting as input. Polygonalisation is the technique used to check the type of baseline present in a handwriting sample while pen pressure is found by counting the number of foreground pixels in the threshold image of the handwriting sample. The height of the 't' bar is simply identified by matching the 't' present in the sample to the templates of 't' already uploaded in the system (Tables 14.1–14.3).

Esmaralda et al. [4] define graphology as the pseudo-scientific study of analysing the patterns in handwriting and signature to identify traits, attitudes, mindset, and thinking processes of a person. The basic elements of handwriting taken into account while analysing a sample are seven: pressure, shape, dimension, speed, continuity, direction, and order. This research paper discusses identifying the personality of the author by analysing handwriting based on five features and signatures based on nine features. Multi-layer perceptron (MLP) architecture is used to identify the five

TABLE 14.1
Personality Traits Based on the Baseline

S. No.	Baseline	Personality Trait
1.	Ascending	Optimistic
2.	Descending	Pessimistic
3.	Straight	Practical

TABLE 14.2
Height of T-Bar Revealing Personality Trait

S. No.	Height of t-bar	Personality Trait
1.	Crossed high on the stem	High self-esteem
2.	Crossed above the middle zone	Moderate self-esteem
3.	Crossed near the bottom of the stem	Low self-esteem
4.	Crossed above the stem	Dreamer

TABLE 14.3
Personality Traits Based upon Pen Pressure

S. No.	Pen Pressure	Personality Trait
1.	Light	Emotional intensity is low
2.	Medium	Moderate emotional intensity
3.	High	Emotions have a massive impact.

features of a signature: starting curve, shell in the middle, middle streak, ending streak, and underline. Whereas a multi-structure algorithm is used to detect four features: extreme margin, dot, separate signature, and signature streaks disconnected. Handwriting is analysed using multi-structure algorithms and ANN for recognition of margins, dominant zone, and spacing between words and lines, while the baseline patterns are recognised by hill valley extraction.

Sen Anamika et al. [5] describe handwriting as a unique pattern controlled by our brain where each stroke and curve is associated with a personality trait. Graphology is the study of identifying those traits. Handwriting can even reveal if a person has suicidal tendencies, depression, and even fatal diseases like schizophrenia, Parkinson, etc. Sen introduces a handwriting analysis system that extracts six features of handwriting using image processing and reveals the personality. Slant, margin, slope, word spacing, size, and title over 'i' are the six features. This handwriting analysis system achieved 95% accuracy in detecting features and identifying personality

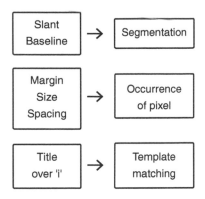

FIGURE 14.2   Features with extraction technique.

traits. Features are extracted using algorithms based on the principle mentioned in Figure 14.2.

Joshi Prachi et al. [6] state that handwriting is the most efficient way to get insight into the mind of human beings. Graphology is the science of evaluating the features of handwriting and telling what is going on inside the individual's mind and body. Analysing handwriting manually is both time-consuming and tiring; thus, Joshi proposes an automated system to analyse handwriting and save time and energy. Baseline, the imaginary line on which the writer writes reveals a lot about the author. It is determined by a method called polygonalisation. Slant is a feature that reveals the emotions and sentiments of the author, and Joshi determined the slants by template matching. The height of the 't' bar reveals traits such as the confidence and esteem of the writer and is identified by template matching. Margins are the layout of a page and determine if the author is afraid of the future or running away from the past or if everything is balanced; this can be evaluated by observing the pixels.

Khadel et al. [7] argue that handwriting is unique and no two individuals can have the same writing and refer to handwriting as behavioural biometrics. This paper has classified two different approaches to handwriting analysis namely handwriting identification or text-independent and handwriting recognition or text-dependent. The text-dependent approach is the avenue to find out if the document or signature is forged or not while the text-independent approach reveals the personality traits, behavioural patterns, abilities, fears, mental stability, and even physical health of the writer. Further, handwriting identification is also divided into two different approaches: feature extraction and feature selection. Features of handwriting were also classified into two categories: macro and micro. Khadel also highlighted some drawbacks of analysing handwriting digitally such as the fact that some features such as pen pressure and stroke order are lost while scanning the sample which is intact in the physical sample. The steps involved in analysing handwriting with text-independent approaches are shown in Figure 14.3.

Vikram et al. [8] describe graphology as the pseudoscience of decoding the signal of the neurological brain which can give us insights about personality, emotional outlay, fears, attitude towards life, and goals and can even detect diseases like

Data acquisition

↓

Feature Extraction

↓

Classification

FIGURE 14.3 Steps of handwriting analysis.

Parkinson, cancer, and Alzheimer's. This paper also mentions the ultimate need to automate handwriting analysis due to the consumption of time and energy while analysing handwriting manually. A model of an automated handwriting analysis system (AHWAS) is proposed in this paper, AHWAS uses image processing with an RGB filter and identifies eight features: size, slope, pressure, slant, spacing, margin, number of breaks, and speed. AHWAS was successfully tested with 30 samples of handwriting which gave 80% of accurate results.

Kaur et al. [9] describe graphology as a science to evaluate handwriting patterns to reveal the personality traits such as honesty, social attitude, behavioural patterns, fears, level of confidence, learning style, and dedication of the writer, in other words, handwriting analysis can draw a sketch of a person's complete personality and can give a glimpse of what going on inside author mind. Keeping in mind the amount of time and money consumed in the manual analysis of handwriting Grewal proposes a system that uses MATLAB that analyses handwriting without any human interference. The system is trained to analyse the sample based on slope, slant, pressure, and shape of letters 'f' and 'i'. The slope is the imaginary line on which the words rest and is mainly of three types: ascending, descending, and normal. The ascending baseline indicates optimism, while the descending baseline indicates a pessimist personality, and a normal slope is an indication of someone who is consistent and even-tempered. Slants are another important feature of handwriting measuring how far are the emotions in control of the author. Pen pressure determines the energy and intensity the writer invests and the polygonalisation method evaluates the slope and slant, while the grey-level thresholding technique evaluates the pressure and shape of 'f' and 'i' are selected using template matching. These extracted features are given as input to the ANN which gives personality. traits as output.

Patil et al. [10] discuss various algorithms of machine Language used by various researchers to extract features of handwriting such as the baseline, slant, the shape of letters, margin, and space between words in order to automate the process of graphological analysis or handwriting analysis. Scanned images of handwriting samples were given as input to automated handwriting analysing systems, which are further examined, and features are extracted by different techniques and algorithms, and personality traits of the author are given as the result. These AHASs are tested with several samples of handwriting in which a system using the CNN algorithm gave a 92% accuracy. The KNN classifier algorithm reached 72% of accuracy, results from the neural network classifier algorithm resulted in 90.7% accuracy, the random forest algorithm gave an 80% accuracy, while results from the support vector machine algorithm were 72% accurate.

Ravish et al. [20] conducted a study to identify stress among medical students using graphology, machine learning algorithms, and salivary cortisol. Ravish et al. mentioned that the subconscious mind sends electrical impulses which result in strokes, thus the name 'brainwriting'. They also implied that machine learning and artificial intelligence are making a significant difference in our lives and are revolutionising and automating our everyday tasks. A total of 30 features of handwriting such as boundaries, line, letter, and word spacing, text layout, size and width of letter, writing speed, rhythm. and expressing power were taken into account. Scanned handwriting samples were subjected to morphological image processing to extract individual letters. The CNN model (Inception V3) with pre-trained weights was retrained to detect negative traits such as dejection, procrastination, selective listening, gullibility, and sensitivity to criticism. A dataset of 1,000 images per class was processed with this model. The SPSS statistical program and R statistical tool were used to conduct statistical analysis. The study showed that students with low academic performance had a significantly higher number of negative traits in their handwriting.

Kowal et al. [21] consider handwriting analysis as a skillful art of personality assessment adding on to that Gupta says that handwriting is printing the brain on the paper and thus can reveal how the writer feels and thinks. The paper focuses on utilising graphology for the assessment of psychopathy which is a combination of traits such as lack of empathy, impulsivity, poor behavioural controls, egocentricity, and shallow emotional response, resulting in an inability to love, antisocial, and criminal behaviour. They not only have a destructive impact on their lives but also disrupt society. Famous criminologists Jules Crépieux-Jamin (1925), Saudek (1928), Pulver & Muhl (1949), Etienne de Greeff (1950), and Siegel (2013) have listed most commonly found signs in dishonest writers: breaks and mends, smeariness, slowness, looped arcades, and extremes in tensions either very tense or very slack. Psychiatrists can use this information combined with their own assessments to gather more detail and reassure the findings. Some ways to assess psychopathy are the Levenson Self-Report Psychopathy Scale and Psychopathy Checklist – Revised (PCL-R) developed by Hare in clinical or forensic settings. In the USA and UK, separate standings are there for psychopaths, while India is still in progress, and we can utilise automatic handwriting analysis to speed up the research for identifying antisocial personality traits. Graphological traits commonly found in criminals or psychopaths are evasiveness, covering up strokes, inhibition, defensiveness, lack of clarity, self-consciousness, deliberate calculations, impulsiveness, deceitfulness, dependency, vanity, and ostentation.

Singh et al. [22] define handwriting as the neurophysiological method that represents our feelings. Singh also mentioned that handwriting can be used as an emotional gauge as anxiety, excitement, irritability, and anger are visible in those short movements carried out by our arm. Graphology is the study and analysis of handwriting in relation to psychology to evaluate emotions and physical state. It has been established that neurological disorders such as congenital apraxia, and strephosymbolia as well as psychological illnesses such as depression, compulsive disorder, schizophrenia, and psychosis have a significant impact on handwriting. The author studies various research studies and has provided the characteristics or features of handwriting to identify anxiety, depression, ADHD, OCD, autism, Parkinson's disease, Alzheimer's, and others. Neurodegenerative Parkinson's disease is characterised by motor symptoms. Naumann et al. [23] studied handwriting movements including speed, length of strokes, and acceleration, and the results revealed a major difference in the handwriting movements of healthy ones and patients with Parkinson's disease.

Rosenblum et al. [24] conducted research among elderly people with major depressive disorder (MDD). Participants were asked to perform four handwriting tasks on digital tablets with which velocity, time on air, space, and pressure were measured. It was found that patients with depression exerted substantially less pressure, while the time taken to write was longer. An increased amount of spacing between words decreased connectivity between letters and decreased organisation was also found. ComPet – Computerised Penmanship Evaluation Tool was used to collect and analyse the data.

Singh et al. [25] state that every human develops his/her own style of penmanship based upon their personal struggles, thus giving insight into the psyche and the why behind the individual's actions. The paper elaborates on different characteristics of handwriting such as text size, word incline, spaces, margins, string, wavy line, arcades, upper zone, middle zone, pen pressure, etc. and explains what these features of handwriting reveal.

Chaubey et al. [26] explain graphology and the science behind it. The author has introduced the architecture of a CNN for handwriting analysis. The system has been trained on five personality traits: agreeableness, conscientiousness, extraversion, openness, and neuroticism. Handwriting samples of college students were taken for the experiment, and the average accuracy obtained was 42.94% (Table 14.4).

14.5 APPLICATION

14.5.1 RECRUITING

Recruiting the right candidate is as crucial as gathering funds for a company as employing one wrong person can disrupt the productivity of the whole team and can even result in some serious destruction in the company. Graphology here proves to be a great tool for recruiting the best possible candidate. Graphological analysis of the candidate can reveal the personality traits possessed, can identify tension or anxiety concealed below the surface, level of intelligence, personal harmony, i.e. positivity in the individual and can even detect if the person has signs of embezzling, fraud, or does not have the ability to maintain a healthy relationship with the boss.

14.5.2 CRIMINAL INVESTIGATION

A criminal is an individual with a mind that is psychologically disturbed and imbalanced and has no control over impulses. We know that handwriting analysis is also known as behavioural biometrics due to its ability to reveal the psychological state and draw the behavioural portrait of the author. Tendencies of being violent and cruel present in a personality can be brought to light through graphological analysis. Thus, graphological analysis can help reveal the criminal tendencies of an individual and can be used as supporting evidence in court to prove an individual guilty or innocent. Graphology can also be useful in determining if the suicide note was actually written

TABLE 14.4
Comparison of Different Handwriting Analysing Systems

Author, Year	Features Extracted	Feature Extraction Technique	Classifier
Champa H N 2010 [11]	Baseline, pen pressure, the height of the t-bar, loop of the letter 'y', and slant	Polygonalisation method, grey-level threshold, template matching, and Generalised Hough Transform (GHT)	Rule-based classifier
Vladimir Pervouchine 2006 [12]	Small letters "d", "y", "f", and grapheme "th"	MATLAB Image Processing Toolbox thinning algorithm	DistAl neural network
Sofianita Mutalib 2008 [2]	Baseline and slope	BlueJ software and an algorithm that calculates pixels	Fuzzy technique
Esmeralda Djamal 2013 [4]	Margin, spacing between lines, spacing between words, the dominance of zone, baseline, and nine features of signature	Multi-structure algorithm and multi-layer perceptron	ANN
Champa H N 2010 [3]	Pressure, baseline, height of t-bar	Polygonalisation, grey-level threshold, and template matching	ANN
Prachi Joshi 2015 [6]	Baseline, slant, height of t-bar	Polygonalisation, threshold algorithm and template matching, and margin	Mapped feature vector matrix
Parmeet Kaur Grewal 2012 [9]	Baseline, formation of small letter 'f', slant, formation of letter 'i' and pressure	Grey-level thresholding, polygonalisation, and template matching	ANN
Vishal Patil 2020 [10]	Slant, spacing between words, baseline, margin, height of t- bar	Template matching, polygonalisation, grey-level threshold, and GHT	ANN
Nikita Lemos 2018 [13]	Slant, spacing, baseline	Image pre-processing and CNN	CNN
Behnam Fallah 2016 [14]	Margin, slant, spacing between line, spacing between words, baseline, characteristics, word extension	Segmentation, pre-processing, HLAC feature, GDA	MLP neural network
Sri Hastuti Fatimah 2019 [15]	Margin, space between lines, space between words, dominant zone, slant with four letters 'a', 'g', 's', and 't'	Pre-processing, segmentation, multi-structure analysis	CNN
Anike A. Raut 2014 [16]	Pen pressure, baseline, size of the letters, slant, margins, space between letters and words, and speed of the writing	Noise removal and segmentation	Support Vector Machine (SVM)
A. Bal 2016 [17]	Baseline and writing pressure	Segmentation, normalisation, thresholding, and noise removal	Rule-based system
M. Gavrilescu 2015 [18]	Baseline, pressure, connecting strokes, slant, and formation of letter 't' and 'f'	Grey-level thresholding, normalisation, and noise removal	Neural network with 3-level architecture

(Continued)

TABLE 14.4 (*Continued*)
Comparison of Different Handwriting Analysing Systems

Author, Year	Features Extracted	Feature Extraction Technique	Classifier
Ravish H. 2021 [20]	Text layout, size, and width of letter, writing speed, etc. (30 features)	Morphological image processing	Retrained CNN (Inception V3)
Sara Rosenblum 2009 [24]	Time, space, and pressure	ComPet (Computerised penmanship evaluation tool)	ComPet and MANOVA

by the person who was suicidal or if the note is fake and the deceased was murdered. It can also help in concluding the authenticity of will statements.

14.5.3 HANDWRITING IDENTIFICATION

Handwriting analysis as explained in paper [7] by Khadel et al. has got two approaches, text-independent and text-dependent. The text-dependent approach works for finding if a document or signature is forged or not and to identify if two documents are written by the same person or not. Handwriting analysis can be of great help to the court in finding if the suicide note is authentic or the person was murdered and in finding will the statement is genuine or not.

14.5.4 DIAGNOSIS OF DISEASES

Neurodegenerative diseases cause cells to deteriorate first in the peripheral system and then in the brain, leading to the death of the patient. Graphological analysis of handwriting can diagnose Alzheimer's and Parkinson's disease at an early stage. ADHD, OCD, autism, Alzheimer's, congenital apraxia, strephosymbolia, as well as psychological illnesses such as depression, compulsive disorder, schizophrenia, and kinds of psychosis and other diseases can also be identified.

14.5.5 DEPRESSION

Depression is the most common illness across the globe starting from a usual feeling of sadness which can turn into a serious medical condition. According to the World Health Organization (WHO), 264 million people are affected with depression, causing them mental suffering and poot functioning in all aspects of life; furthermore, long-lasting major depression can lead to suicide.

14.6 MAJOR CONTRIBUTION

In this paper, our aim is to define handwriting features that indicate depression which can further be extracted by an AHAS, and identify if an individual is suffering from depression or not and can even classify its stage. It will also cover the feature of handwriting that signals suicidal tendencies so that immediate help and support can be provided to the individual.

No single feature in graphology can announce something about the author, but it is a combination of two or more features in handwriting that confirms the presence of that trait. The writing characteristics to be found in a depressed personality are listed below:

14.6.1 Margin

A margin is a layout that the writer creates when writing the text on an unruled page. The page represents the world and the margins reveal the author's approach to reaching out or interacting with the world. Extreme margins either left or right both are unhealthy; it is a balanced margin that represents a peaceful and positive approach towards life. An extreme left-tending margin reflects the author's fear of the future and wishes to stick to the past. While an extreme right margin reveals the author's will to run away from the past, this individual can be impulsive and make hasty decisions without considering the consequences.

Narrow left margin and wide right margin: A left margin represents the past, while the right margin acts as the future. Extreme left margins state that the writer is afraid of the future and is holding on to the past because it is where the security lies or due to whichever reason as shown in Figure 14.4.

FIGURE 14.4 Wide right margin.

14.6.2 BASELINE

The baseline is the imaginary line on which the word rests when the author writes on an unruled paper. Also known as the line of reality, it reveals the author's attitude towards life experiences and activities.

Descending baseline: As obvious, descending baseline manifests depression, fatigue, and pessimism.

Extremely ascending baseline: Anything extreme is hardly ever a good sign. A baseline that ascends 45 degrees or more exhibits that the person is trying too hard to be positive cause initially he is not. It can also be a sign of someone who puts a lot of energy into negative thoughts, in other words, someone who is optimistic about his pessimistic thoughts.

Drooping baseline: When a baseline is firm all over but at the end of the line a word or the last letters of the word drop. It is one of the major indicators of suicidal tendency, and this is someone who does not suicide to gain sympathy or attention and is most likely to be successful. This person will show no sign and then all of a sudden attempt suicide out of nowhere. Graphology can be very useful here to identify such people and provide immediate help to them (Figure 14.5).

14.6.3 SLANT

Slant is the measure of the angle on which an upstroke ascends, it is primarily of three types: vertical reclined and inclined which is leftward tending, rightward tending, and up straight. Slants demonstrate how willing a person is to share his true feelings, emotions, or thoughts.

Reclined slant: This is someone who represses his true emotions and is not going to reveal them to anyone easily. This person is not likely to let others know if he is feeling low or depressed. They struggle in trusting others. People with extreme reclined slants are a bit hard to understand as they seldom open up to others (Figure 14.6).

Variable slants: Variable slants are found in the handwriting of an extremely imbalanced personality which is completely withdrawn in one moment and then extremely friendly in another (Figure 14.7).

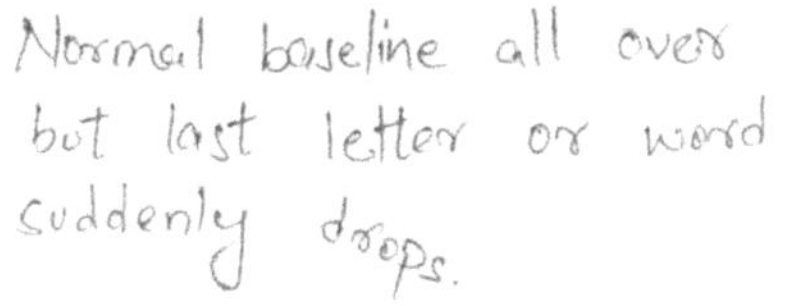

Normal baseline all over
but last letter or word
suddenly drops.

FIGURE 14.5   Suicidal baseline.

Reclined handwriting

FIGURE 14.6   Extreme left slant.

14.6.4 Pressure

The pressure exerted while writing on a piece of paper or digital tablet tells us about the emotional intensity and the physical energy the writer has available to invest in life.

Extremely light pressure: Extreme sensitivity, anxiety, nervousness, dullness, and lack of energy or interest are the major traits found in writers with extreme low pressure (Figure 14.8).

Highly inconsistent pressure: Worry, anxiety, nervousness, or even lack of involvement can be indicated by uneven pressure in handwriting (Figure 14.9).

14.6.5 Size

Size can be categorised into small, microscopic, large, normal, and huge. Size reveals how the writer is involved in an environment or in other words it tells the difference between inner and outer control of attention. It reveals the degree of introversion or extroversion.

Microscopic: Writers with too small size of writing can completely shut out the world and live with themselves. They might have no need for communication or interaction which is likely to lead to loneliness and furthermore to depression (Figure 14.10).

Huge: Extremely large writing can be a sign of a writer's inner feelings of inferiority and complex making him feel smaller than others and of no value or importance which over a long period of time may turn into major depression.

14.6.6 Spacing

Space between words, letters, and lines tell the distance the writer wishes to put between himself and others.

Variable slant

FIGURE 14.7 Variable slant.

extremely light pressure

FIGURE 14.8 Low pressure.

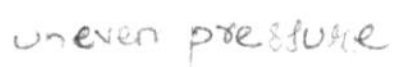

uneven pressure

FIGURE 14.9 Inconsistent pressure.

microscopic handwriting

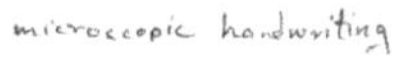

FIGURE 14.10 Microscopic writing.

FIGURE 14.11   Enormous spacing between words.

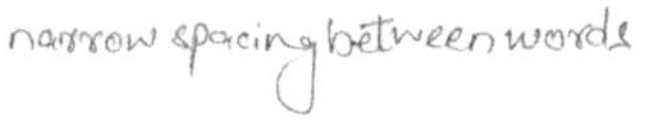

FIGURE 14.12   Narrow space between words.

FIGURE 14.13   Uneven space between words.

Enormous space between words: It is an indicator of mistrust and suspicion which ultimately result in social isolation and the writer is likely to suffer from paranoia (Figure 14.11).

Narrow spacing: Writing with narrow spacing between words reveal that the writer needs to be in constant touch with people both physically and emotionally and being lonely can drive the individual crazy (Figure 14.12).

Uneven spacing: Uneven spacing reflects inconsistency in the personality and can even be an indicator of a disturbed mind (Figure 14.13).

14.6.7 ZONES

Zones are classified into three categories: upper, lower, and middle. Each zone symbolises different parts of life. The middle zone is all about communication, relationships, and social abilities and is related to day-to-day life. The upper zone concerns imagination, ideas, and spirituality and demonstrates mental energy. It acts like the head of the body and tells what one 'should' do. The lower zone is the subconscious needs and desires that also depict the physical drive of the individual.

Poorly formed middle zone: A writing having a poorly formed middle zone expresses the inability of the writer to cope with day-to-day life, and difficulty in communication and relations all of which lead to a depressed personality (Figure 14.14).

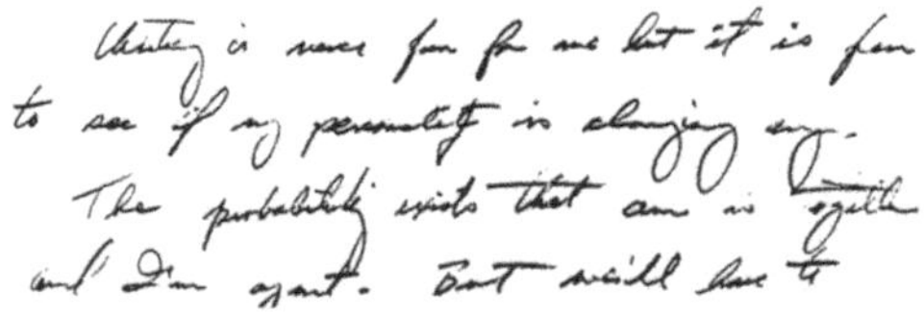

FIGURE 14.14   Poorly formed middle zone.

14.6.8 STROKES

Illegible handwriting: Illegible handwriting expresses the inability of the writer to communicate his thoughts or feelings to others.

Excessive threading: Fatigue and lack of purpose is indicated by excessive threading.

Inconsistent threading: Anxiety can be indicated by inconsistent threading (Figure 14.15).

Prominent arcade: Large arcades express the need for support the writer wants. The writer wishes to hide behind those arcades instead of dealing with the problems or situations.

Prominent angles: Anxiety, temper, and overthinking are indicated by the presence of excessive angles in handwriting (Figure 14.16).

Weak ending strokes: Unnecessary extending strokes where the pressure decreases toward the end indicate indecisiveness, passivity, and depression (Figure 14.17).

Lead-in stroke from the baseline: When lead-in stroke comes from below the baseline, it tells us that the personality is a victim of resentment consciously as well as unconsciously. Individuals are holding onto those undesirable incidents and are unable to leave any of those events behind and move on (Figure 14.18).

X-ing stroke: If an x-ing stroke is found enormously in handwriting, the writer is obsessed with the idea of death and can have self-destructing tendencies (Figure 14.19).

FIGURE 14.15   Excessive threading.

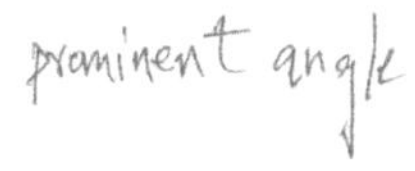

$$prominent\ angle$$

FIGURE 14.16   Prominent angles.

$$a\ e$$

FIGURE 14.17   Weak ending stroke.

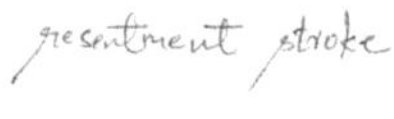

$$resentment\ stroke$$

FIGURE 14.18   Long lead-in stroke.

$$7\ 8\ 4$$

FIGURE 14.19   Unnecessary X-ing stroke.

m r n

FIGURE 14.20   Up-side down loops in m, n, and r.

broken loops

FIGURE 14.21   Broken loops in the letter 'o'.

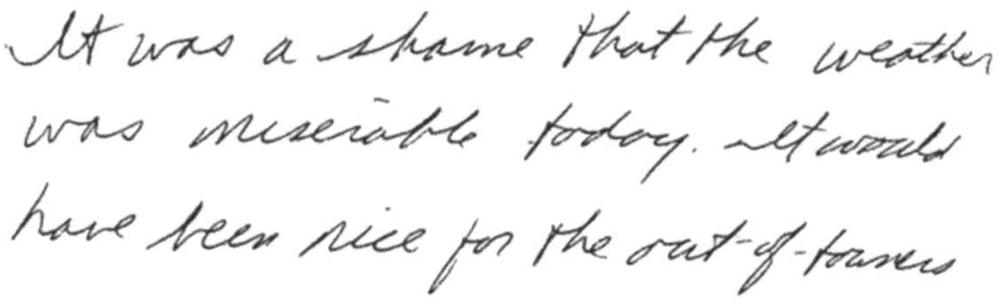

It was a shame that the weather was miserable today. It would have been nice for the out-of-towers

FIGURE 14.22   Retraced writing.

Upside-down loops: Loops that start in the air instead of starting at the baseline and even end in the air indicate the writer's tendency of worrying. Large upside-down loops indicate the individual's tendency to worry excessively over unnecessary things (Figure 14.20).

Stunted loops: Loops that are smaller in comparison to the rest of the writing indicate the writer's inability to express emotions.

Broken loops: A break while drawing a loop also indicates anxiety and worry (Figure 14.21).

Retraced writing: The presence of retraced lines in place of loops indicates a repressed personality, someone who represses the emotions not only from others but chances are that he also represses them from himself (Figure 14.22).

14.6.9   LETTERS

Inflated loop in small letter d: Excessively inflated loop in 'd' indicates a person who is extremely sensitive to criticism about self and cannot stand it.

Low t-bar: t-Bar that is near baseline indicates extremely low self-esteem, and excessive self-doubt and these writers feel unworthy or may be under an inferiority complex. The person is not a visionary and focuses on completing the nearest possible goal only (Figure 14.23).

FIGURE 14.23   Low t-bar.

FIGURE 14.24   Strikethrough signature.

14.6.10 Signature

Strikethrough signature: A signature that is cut by a long stroke indicates extreme tendencies of self-destruction. If it is struck more than once, the condition of the individual is even worse. This formation of the signature has been found in people who committed suicide with a bullet in their head (Figure 14.24).

14.7   CONCLUSION AND FUTURE RESEARCH DIRECTION

The aim of this paper is to do feature engineering for depression. Depression, a serious mental disorder, has become ubiquitous these days contributing to the number of suicides committed every year and poor functioning at both personal and professional levels. Handwriting can give insights into the human brain; this paper focuses on utilising the science of analysing handwriting to diagnose depression in individuals so that the necessary treatment and counselling can be provided to help the person recover. Key features have been identified to detect the worldwide common disease, these key features can be fed into AHASs which can save tremendous amounts of time and energy in comparison to manual handwriting analysis. AHASs should be hosted on the cloud for better processing power and thus increased efficiency of the system.

We must develop an automated handwriting analysing system to extract features mentioned in this paper in order to diagnose depression, self-destructing, and suicidal tendencies and include more features to diagnose other psychological diseases, neurodegenerative diseases, cardiovascular diseases, and other diseases as well.

REFERENCES

[1] S. V. Kedar, D. S. Bormane, A. Dhadwal, S. Alone and R. Agarwal, "Automatic emotion recognition through handwriting analysis: A review," *2015 International Conference on Computing Communication Control and Automation*, 2015, pp. 811–816, doi: 10.1109/ICCUBEA.2015.162.

[2] S. Mutalib, R. Ramli, S. A. Rahman, M. Yusoff and A. Mohamed, "Towards emotional control recognition through handwriting using fuzzy inference," *2008 International Symposium on Information Technology*, 2008, pp. 1–5, doi: 10.1109/ITSIM.2008.4631735.

[3] H. N Champa, "Artificial neural network for human behaviour prediction through handwriting analysis", *International Journal of Computer Applications (0975–8887)* 2010; 2, 2, doi: 10.5120/629-878.

[4] E. C. Djamal, R. Darmawati and S. N. Ramdlan, "Application image processing to predict personality based on structure of handwriting and signature," *2013 International Conference on Computer, Control, Informatics and Its Applications (IC3INA)*, 2013, pp. 163–168, doi: 10.1109/IC3INA.2013.6819167.

[5] A. Sen and H. Shah, "Automated handwriting analysis system using principles of graphology and image processing," *2017 International Conference on Innovations in Information, Embedded and Communication Systems (ICIIECS)*, 2017, pp. 1–6, doi: 10.1109/ICIIECS.2017.8276061.

[6] Prachi Joshi, "Handwriting analysis for detection of personality traits using machine learning approach," *International Journal of Computer Applications (0975–8887)* 2015; 130, 15, doi: 10.5120/ijca2015907189.

[7] Khaled Mohammed bin Abdl and Siti Zaiton Mohd Hashim, "Handwriting identification: A direction review," *2009 IEEE International Conference on Signal and Image Processing Applications*, 2009, pp. 459–463, doi: 10.1109/ICSIPA.2009.5478698.

[8] Vikram Kamath, Nikhil Ramaswamy, P. Navin Karanth, Vijay Desai and S. M. Kulkarni "Development of automated handwriting analysis system," *ARPN Journal of Engineering and Applied Science* 2011; 6, 9: 1819–6608.

[9] Parmeet Kaur Grewal and Deepak Prashar, "Behaviour prediction through handwriting analysis," *IJCST* 2012; 3, 2: 520–523. ISSN: 0976-8491.

[10] V. Patil and H. Mathur, "A survey: Machine learning approach for personality analysis and writer identification through handwriting," *2020 International Conference on Inventive Computation Technologies (ICICT)*, 2020, pp. 1–5, doi: 10.1109/ICICT48043.2020.9112449.

[11] H. N. Champa and K. R. AnandaKumar, "Automated human behaviour prediction through handwriting analysis," *2010 First International Conference on Integrated Intelligent Computing*, 2010, pp. 160–165, doi: 10.1109/ICIIC.2010.29.

[12] Vladimir Pervouchine and Graham Leedham, "Extraction and analysis of forensic document examiner features used for writer identification," *Pattern Recognition* 2007; 40, 3: 1004–1013, ISSN 0031-3203, doi: 10.1016/j.patcog.2006.08.008.

[13] N. Lemos, K. Shah, R. Rade and D. Shah, "Personality prediction based on handwriting using machine learning," *2018 International Conference on Computational Techniques Electronics and Mechanical Systems (CTEMS)*, 2018, pp. 110–113, doi: 10.1109/CTEMS.2018.8769221.

[14] B. Fallah and H. Khotanlou, "Identify human personality parameters based on handwriting using neural network," *2016 Artificial Intelligence and Robotics (IRANOPEN)*, 2016, pp.120–126, doi: 10.1109/RIOS.2016.7529501.

[15] S. H. Fatimah, E. C. Djamal, R. Ilyas and F. Renaldi, "Personality features identification from handwriting using convolutional neural networks," *2019 4th International Conference on Information Technology, Information Systems and Electrical Engineering (ICITISEE)*, 2019, pp. 119–124, doi: 10.1109/ICITISEE48480.2019.9003 855.

[16] Anike A. Raut and Ankur M. Bobade, "Prediction of human personality by handwriting analysis based on segmentation method using support vector machine", *International Journal of Pure and Applied Research in Engineering and Technology* 2014; 8: 24–28.

[17] A. Bal and R. Saha. "An improved method for handwritten document analysis using segmentation, baseline recognition and writing pressure detection," *Procedia Computer Science* 2016; 93: 403–415, doi: 10.1016/j.procs.2016.07.227.

[18] M. Gavrilescu, "Study on determining the Myers-Briggs personality type based on individual's handwriting," *2015 E-Health and Bioengineering Conference (EHB)*, 2015, pp. 1–6, doi: 10.1109/EHB.2015.7391603.

[19] Karen Amend and Mary S. Ruiz, *Handwriting Analysis the Complete Basic Book*, Newcastle Publishing Co Inc., Tarzana, CA, 1980.

[20] H. Ravish, S. Kumar, M.K. Sharma, B.V. Poojary and R. Raj, "Evaluation of academic stress among medical students using graphology and machine learning algorithm in correlation with salivary cortisol," *International Journal of Research and Medical Sciences* 2021; 9: 2733–2740.

[21] D.S. Kowal and P.K. Gupta, "Handwriting analysis: A psychopathic viewpoint." *International Journal of Indian Psychology* 2021; 9, 1: 1052–1058. DIP: 18.01.108/20210901, doi: 10.25215/0901.108.

[22] P. Singh and H. Yadav, Influence of neurodegenerative diseases on handwriting. *Forensic Research & Criminology International Journal* 2021; 9, 3: 110–114. doi: 10.15406/frcij.2021.09.00347.

[23] G. Naumann, G.E. Peter and P. Beth et al. "Do handwriting difficulties correlate with core symptomology, motor proficiency and attentional behaviours?" *Journal of Autism and Developmental Disorders.* 2017; 47, 4: 1006–1017.

[24] P. Werner, S. Rosenblum and B. Gady et al. "Handwriting process variables discriminating mild Alzheimer's disease and mild cognitive impairment. *The Journals of Gerontology* 2016; Series B, 61, 4: P228–P236.

[25] Singh Puja, "General characteristics of handwriting and its psychological importance," *Cognizance Journal of Multidisciplinary Studies* 2022; 2: 1–4. doi: 10.47760/cognizance.2022.v02i02.001.

[26] G. Chaubey and S. Arjaria, "Personality prediction through handwriting analysis using convolutional neural networks 2022 doi: 10.1007/978-981-16-3802-2_5.

15 E-Nose Sensor Applications and Challenges in the Health Sector

Sanad Al-Maskari, Saeid Hosseini, and Eimad Abusham
Sohar University

CONTENTS

15.1 INTRODUCTION

New smell-sensing technologies are becoming available with the emergence of new technological developments and upcoming technologies. Unfortunately, none of these techniques are comparable to humane perceptions or sensing capabilities (e.g., noise filtering, long-term tracking, evolutionary patterns, mixed decisions, similarity, differentiating, etc.). As a result, these technologies can be ineffective and can be complex. Since this technology is becoming increasingly prevalent, it is critical to develop a system capable of handling some of the common challenges faced by e-noses, such as noise, drift, imbalanced data, dynamic environments, and

DOI: 10.1201/9781003326182-15

high uncertainties. E-nose systems cannot be improved without the use of pattern-recognition methods that can infer patterns based on the data observed. Identifying valid, novel, potentially useful, and ultimately understandable patterns in data is a process that Fayyad et al. [1] define as knowledge discovery in databases. Overall, the performance of e-nose systems can be improved by making use of suitable signal processing techniques. Furthermore, e-nose systems require the development of new features and pattern-recognition techniques to improve their recognition capabilities.

Using e-nose technology to quantify, analyze, and predict odors has extensive applications. Therefore, it has been an active research area for a long time. Machine olfaction is achieved using an array of metal-oxide sensors (MOX) combined with signal processing and pattern-recognition systems. Because of this, e-nose data analysis and development have a broad appeal for both sensor and pattern-recognition communities.

15.2   E-NOSE AND GAS SENSORS

To mimic the sense of smell, Persaud and Dodd began their research in 1982 in gas sensing. They use a combination of gas sensors and a neural network to distinguish between different compounds [2]. It has since become widely recognized that an e-nose is an electronic device with an array of gas sensors built into a pattern-recognition system used to detect gases, odors, or compounds. e-Noses offered new options and low-cost alternatives to expensive methods like chromatography-mass spectroscopy for the detection and analysis of gases.

Considering their small size and low cost, e-nose technologies are becoming key enablers in many fields. There have been a number of applications of these technologies in real life, including monitoring air quality and food quality, disease detection, and security applications [3–5]. Sensor data, on the other hand, is noisy, subject to drift, and influenced by outdoor dynamic environments.

The e-nose simulates the functions of mammalian olfactory systems by using an array of sensors. With the e-nose system, each odor in a family of odors is assigned a unique pattern of response from an array of sensors. Chemical sensing systems are becoming increasingly popular. A new generation of small, fast, cheap, reproducible chemical sensors has been developed due to competitive pressure and the demand for reliable chemical processes. In the industry, there are several ways to detect chemicals, but with the invention of more reliable and cheaper chemical sensing mechanisms, the process has become more convenient.

Furthermore, it provides a vital role in addressing the emerging challenges in industries like food, agriculture, air quality, environment monitoring, medicine, water quality, and wastewater quality control. Different industries require different specifications for sensors, for instance, optimum emission control and cabin air quality require military-level specifications for the auto industry. Chemical sensors are widely used in many applications, resulting in a dramatic increase in the market for measuring chemicals. There are several lucrative markets where there is a great deal of demand, including safety (home and industrial), food freshness [6], medical applications, military applications, and many more.

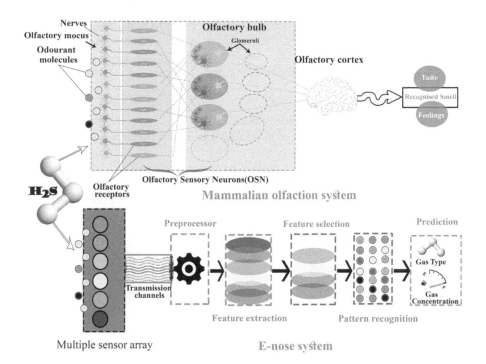

FIGURE 15.1 e-Nose concept.

Up to 650 types of receptors can detect odors in the nasal passages of humans. The functioning of the human nose remains unknown to scientists, despite decades of research. Odor information is transmitted to the brain through the receptors along with smell prints, which are then stored in the brain. A human nose works similarly to an electronic nose. The e-nose collects odor molecules by sampling through headspace sampling, diffuse methods, bubblers, and pre-concentrators [7]. A sensor array measures a reversible change in the sensing material due to contact between an odor sample and the array, which is reflected in changes to the material's electrical properties such as conductivity [8]. Pattern-recognition systems identify the changes by pre-processing and conditioning electrical signals.

Figure 15.1 shows the olfactory system in a human, and the electronic nose in a robot. Both a human nose and an electronic nose are shown in Figure 15.1. By modeling some high-level structures of biological senses, the e-nose system tries to represent biological sensors. The e-nose is different from the human nose since it has sensors that generate electrical signals in response to a specific stimulus/gas.

Figure 15.1 demonstrates the mammalian olfactory system and the e-nose system. The mammalian olfactory system is highly advanced and sophisticated equipped with very large olfactory receptors.

An electronic nose is designed to use a set of predefined sensors to distinguish stimuli and gases. A human nose, on the other hand, is one of the most complex organs in the human body, with a complex network of neurons and a large number of olfactory receptors. Humans can differentiate between 1 trillion stimuli, according to a recent study [9].

An e-nose and a human nose can be compared as follows:

Human nose
- Possesses over 100 million receptors.
- Humans are able to recognize more than 1 trillion different scents, according to a recent study [7].
- The ability to smell can be hampered by infections, which affect biological noses.
- Long-term exposure to a specific scent can lead to fatigue of the olfactory system.
- People smell based on their taste, experiences, and memories.
- In high concentrations, a human nose may be unable to detect the same gas.

e-Nose
- e-Noses can contain from 5 to 100 chemical sensors.
- For an e-nose to recognize specific scents, it has to be trained.
- The current e-nose has a short life expectancy, suffers from drift and poisoning, as well as noise.
- When trained for specific applications, an e-nose can detect gases at different concentrations than a human nose.

15.2.1 SENSOR TECHNOLOGIES

In many fields, chemical sensing technologies are key enablers. Gas and organic compounds can be detected using this technology. Sensors with varying characteristics and properties have been developed. Gas sensors come in many forms, including electrochemical sensors, chemiresistor sensors, mass sensors, and optical sensors. It is well-known and available in the market that gas chromatograph mass spectrometers (GC-MS1) are very popular, but there is a great need for portable, small, and inexpensive sensors that can be embedded in detectors and/or smart sensor arrays. Sensing devices that are cost-effective and can be used in real time can result in inexpensive, reliable, and robust measurements. MOXs are described in the next section.

One of the most common chemosensor technologies is the MOX. Certain metal oxides can perform as a semiconductor when heated. Sensors with metal-oxide elements (sintered metal-oxide with or without a catalyst) consist of a heating element and a sensor element. There is a very thin membrane that separates the two elements. Metal oxides such as ZnO and NiO, which absorb and desorb gas, were observed to change their conductivity in the early 1950s. There is no limit to the sensitivity of metal-oxide surfaces to gases since parts per billion (ppb) are possible [10,11]. Seiyama et al. published their first paper on the use of zinc oxide (ZnO) films to detect gases in 1962 [12]. Examples of a MOX gas sensor and a typical conductivity sensor are shown in Figures 15.2 and 15.3.

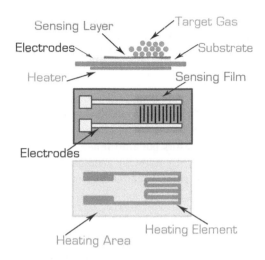

FIGURE 15.2   Typical structure of a conductivity sensor.

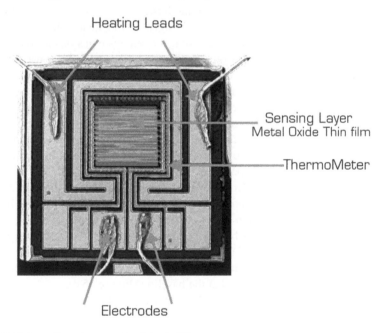

FIGURE 15.3   Microphotograph of the MOX gas sensor.

MOX sensors have a number of seemingly simple but not fully understood aspects of their sensing mechanism. A very nice description of semiconductor gas sensors was published by Yamazoe and Miura in 1992 [13]. Oxygen being absorbed on the surface of the sensing material causes a change in the surface space charge layer. The electrical resistance of polycrystalline materials can be measured as an indicator of this change. When oxygen reacts with the target gas at the surface, the equilibrium changes and the amount of oxygen absorbed changes. Material resistance can be affected by changes in the surface space charge layer. Metal-oxide powder's granularity impacts the sensor's performance. Particle sizes smaller than 6 nm produce better gas sensitivity because the average grain size is about 20 nm. On the other hand, this can lead to instability.

As with the sensitivity to different gases, the operational temperature also has an impact in a different way on different material dopants. Heating the sensing materials is usually accomplished through a coil. MOX sensors provide the user with a degree of freedom in controlling the sensors but are limited in the ability to adjust the temperature when the sensor is built. By allowing each gas sensor to operate at different temperatures, more flexibility is gained and more information can be extracted.

15.2.2 SENSOR RESPONSE

An e-nose sensor's response to a gas is generally considered a first-order response. In the case of a sensor, the response time can be calculated by using an exponential model. There are many steps involved in the analysis of odors. Initially, the sensor is flushed with a reference gas to provide the baseline. Sensors are exposed to odorants and their output signals change accordingly. In the steady-state situation, the output signal remains unchanged. As a result, the reference gas flushes out the odorant from the sensor and the sensor returns to its baseline state. Response time is the total amount of time the sensor is exposed to the odorant, while recovery time is the amount of time it takes for the sensor to return to its baseline.

Adapting sensor response to the baseline is the second step in odor analysis. It also attempts to compensate for inherently large or small signals, as well as noise and drift.

According to Pearce et al. [7], the top three most common methods for choosing a baseline manipulation include the type of sensor being employed, the application of the sensor, and the researcher's preference. The sensitivity of a sensor is the amount of change in its output resulting from a change in input. It has been shown that certain manipulation techniques are more suitable for certain sensor types. The literature review discusses the variations in such manipulation techniques.

Sensor sensitivity is defined by the change in the output parameter (y) of the e-nose sensor (S) to a change in the concentration of the odorant (O). To calculate sensitivity, however, different authors use different formulas, which are calculated with data that has been manipulated at the baseline (Figure 15.4).

At constant working temperature and concentration, this response shows that the MOX sensor can withstand 223 ppmv of ethylene and recover in pure air. In the graph, we show the response and recovery curves of the MOX sensor. The ones above are the adsorption, desorption, and steady-state stages.

15.3 APPLICATIONS

15.3.1 MACHINE OLFACTION

There are new sensing techniques available with new developments and upcoming technologies. It is unfortunate that none of the techniques can work to interpret data in

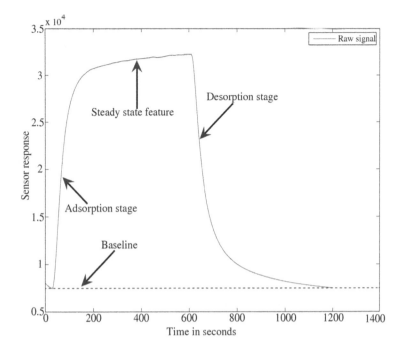

FIGURE 15.4   Raw sensor response.

the same way humans do (e.g., noise and aroma filtering, long-term recognition, sweetness, mixture recognition, and similar or different smells). In the early 1980s, Krishna et al. [14] proposed the first concept of a sensor array. The authors stated that different sensitivity curves can be used for different sensors to enable differentiation between different compounds when a neural network is applied to post-process the signals.

It has been almost a decade since the concept of an "e-nose" or "artificial nose" became widely known. The word refers to an instrument that is capable of identifying simple or even complex smells, made possible by a set of digital chemical substance devices, along with a suitable pattern-recognition system. It was only after companies started selling them that "e-nose" became more well-known. However, the phrase "e-nose" has only been used in medical publications since 1993, when its official description was published [15,16]. Several years after the e-nose term was coined, critics began to doubt its relevance [17,18]. Sensor arrays cannot perform the functions of the human nose, as Mielle et al. contend. The sensors are "obviously electronic" but not biological. E-noses and human noses are similar in their functionality.

Sensor technology, data transmission, control, and pattern recognition have all been developed in the field of gas sensing over the past two decades, with most focusing on specific applications. Nevertheless, the first attempts at research focused on replicating the mammalian biological olfactory system, leading to chemical sensing technology, which is like an engineering concept. The evolution of chemical sensing technology can be compared to the evolution of machine vision. In contrast to chemical sensing, machine vision has available stable and standard sensors (charge-coupled device), and their problems (such as camera calibration) can be clearly defined and addressed. A number of techniques are still in development, including object identification, tracking, and 3D reconstruction.

15.3.2 HEALTH AND ENVIRONMENT MONITORING

In order for information technology to be deployed effectively in environmental management systems, it must be cost-effective and capable of providing a reliable solution. Recent years have seen an explosion in the deployment of distributed sensor networks. The use of network sensors has been implemented in many applications including air pollution monitoring [19–21], habitat monitoring [22], transportation, defense, and scientific exploration. This type of sensor produces a large number of data points.

In the past 10 years, sensor networks have grown rapidly. In addition to monitoring air pollution [19–21], monitoring habitat [22], defense, transportation, and scientific exploration have also been implemented using network sensors. Data collected from these sensors produce large volumes of data that must be cleaned, pre-processed, and retrieved in order to provide information that is meaningful and useful. Management and control systems can utilize this information as a feedback loop.

Air pollution and harmful emissions continue to rise in industrial zones. In order to avoid risks and violations, environmental agencies and government organizations monitor these emissions. In order to manage an organization's environmental performance effectively, it is necessary to use systematic methods of planning, controlling, measuring, and improving it. Utilizing gas sensor networks for emission monitoring and alerts can result in significant environmental improvements (and cost savings). Many problems affecting the environment can be solved without costly pollution control devices. This is shown in the literature. This study uses inexpensive gas sensors in its experiments to address the most challenging aspects of gas sensors (drift and noise). Because of the frequent calibration required, they are not only low-cost but also perform well in the short term. The major issues of chemo gas sensors need to be addressed in order to reduce their costs, improve their reliability, and make them more efficient and reliable.

The real-time delivery of large amounts of data by gas sensor networks challenges data mining and pattern recognition. In this paper, some solutions to these challenges are proposed. Generally, data mining algorithms do not take into account the dynamics of multidimensional environmental data, for example, data generated by gas sensor networks. Scientists and researchers continue to struggle with analyzing environmental gas sensor data and identifying patterns. In addition to drift, noise, and visualization, these sensors create a complex dataset that presents many challenges in terms of data analysis and pattern recognition. It is the ultimate goal of any environmental management system (EMS) to ensure effective decision-making in order to enforce regulations, regulate behaviors, and prevent harm to the population.

15.3.3 SMART SENSING

In areas such as environmental monitoring, healthcare, smart homes, and personal lifestyles, the expansion of the Internet of things, sensor networks, and connected devices has presented new challenges and opportunities. A large-scale network of environmental sensors is used to monitor air quality and generate huge amounts of time-series data. Smartphone sensors provide information about our health, behavior, and activities. Pattern-recognition systems must be reliable, efficient, and effective for such applications to become successful. Consequently, this research study is applicable to a wide range of sensor technologies.

15.4 ISSUES AND CHALLENGES

15.4.1 LEARNING IN THE PRESENCE OF NOISE AND DRIFT

Any learning model is faced with a challenging problem due to the ways in which chemical sensor technologies work and the way they react to inputs. Chemical gas sensors' output signals are profoundly affected by drift, high levels of ambient noise, and highly variable environmental conditions. These sensors have significant performance issues due to their inability to maintain stability, selectivity, and sensitivity [23–25]. Selectivity of sensors is a measure of their specificity for one or more classes of molecules. As opposed to sensor sensitivity, it is the level of signal strength observed when a single molecule is present in a low concentration. In light of these characteristics, how can we formulate an algorithm to maximize classification performance? For any set of sensors s1..sn, maximizing the learning performance of any classifier requires minimizing noise and drift.

Drift describes the fluctuations in the signal generated by a sensor array over time, regardless of whether it is exposed to the same gas mixtures and concentrations [14,26,27]. Physico-chemical processes and unknown dynamic processes will cause a sensor array calibration curve to drift over time. Sensor poisoning, aging, and environmental change such as humidity, temperature, and pressure, along with nonspecific adsorption from system sampling, are some of the mechanisms involved in these processes. Sensor array response will be affected by all of these processes in different ways. For a systematic understanding of sensor drift, a case-by-case evaluation of chemical interactions with sensing materials must be performed for each specific e-nose. The elimination of sensor drift depends on finding such interactions to be deterministic. Therefore, concept-drift compensation seems to be the most viable approach to date [14,26,27]. Furthermore, sensor drift cannot be distinguished from noise because it is not deterministically determinable. In order to create an accurate model to compensate for drift, it is important to understand how the sensor changes physically and chemically over time while taking into consideration all factors. Therefore, simulating all parameters in a controlled environment is not feasible. Figure 15.5 demonstrates the effect of drift over time.

Two principal components are used to project ammonia in Principal Component Analysis (PCA). Drift is responsible for the variation in ammonia distribution across batches [28,29].

Drift leads to a change in sample distribution in the data space by degrading sensor selectivity and sensitivity. As a result, sensors are unable to be operated for long periods of time. Figure 15.5 shows how the distribution of ammonia samples changes over time.

To create a learning model, the initial distribution is used. The learning model is no longer able to perform as expected when the probability distribution changes, as

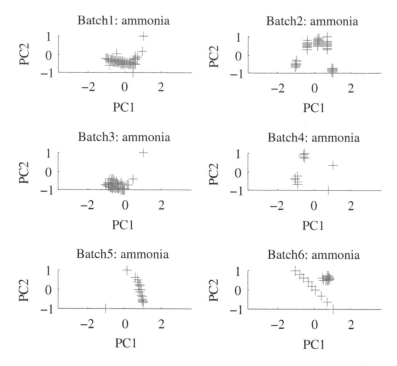

FIGURE 15.5 PCA projections over time.

shown in Figure 15.6. This requires calibrating the sensors and updating the learning model.

To train the classifiers, data from batch one is used, which is created in the calibration stage. Testing the learning model is done with batches 2–10. Although all classifiers performed well in batch two, they had difficulty exceeding 50% in the final round.

Based on data from an e-nose system created in a laboratory, Figure 15.6 illustrates the classification performance of various classifiers. Rapid degradation of an electronic nose makes it difficult for it to recognize analytes. Different classifiers, on the other hand, provide varying results. e-Nose performance can be significantly enhanced over time by learning models, as demonstrated in Figure 15.6. Accordingly, we hypothesize that an optimized feature extraction method with an appropriate learning model can enhance overall performance. It is possible to improve the stability of the system by extending the calibration period. Using data from batches 1 to 5 and testing it on the rest of the batches, providing new labeled data to the learning model could improve the learning process. It is, however, difficult to generate new labeled data.

15.4.2 Gas Quantification and Detection Using an e-Nose

Using an e-nose to detect and quantify emissions to control pollution is one of the most important aspects of air quality monitoring. Air quality monitoring and

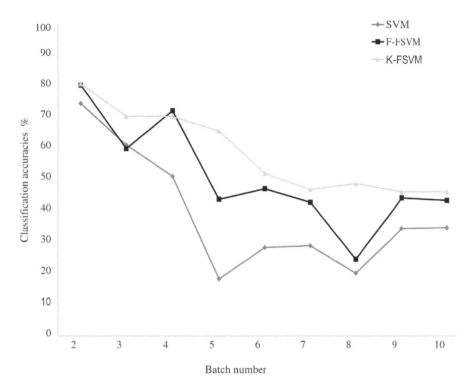

FIGURE 15.6 Learning model performance comparison.

emission control systems are typically bulky and expensive. Even though e-noses are popular, they have not been used in emission control for a variety of reasons, including sensitivity, selectivity, and stability. There has been a lot of literature written about gas detection but little about gas quantification. Quantifying emissions using an e-nose can provide environmental monitoring agencies with a very cost-effective solution. With noise, drift, and dynamic factors present in outdoor environments, using an e-nose to measure gases can be very challenging. A new research problem has been formulated in this study. In this research, the problem of gas classification with quantification is addressed with an eye on air quality limits and gas classification in a dynamic environment.

15.4.3 FEATURE EXTRACTION FOR AN e-NOSE IN A DYNAMIC ENVIRONMENT AND INFORMATION MAXIMIZATION

A critical aspect of pattern recognition is maximizing the information from gas sensors. In the literature, it is often recommended that sensors be operated after a certain stabilization period. Nevertheless, there are various ways to maximize the information extracted from the e-nose. A sensor can be switched into a different mode of operation, enabling different chemical information to be extracted from it. Different sensors respond differently at different temperatures [30,31].

Hardware manipulation is used to manipulate the sensors. Software-based techniques could be used to maximize sensor information. It would be possible to minimize the number of features applied to a pattern-recognition system so that the information gained from a single sensor would be maximized. Different feature extraction methods and ranking methods can be used to generate additional information based on their impact on specific gas types [29,32]. To maintain classification stability for a gas-sensing pattern-recognition system, an effective feature extraction, and ranking method is critical. Using too many sensors or features to classify too few samples can cause classification errors and overfitting, according to Goodner et al. [33].

15.5   CONCLUSIONS

This chapter introduces e-nose and chemical sensing technologies. It provides a brief comparison between biological and e-nose sensors. Moreover, it demonstrates an overview of the sensor's response, e-nose pattern recognition, applications, issues, and pertinent challenges. Besides discussing e-nose applications, we also elucidated the motivation for employing e-nose technology. As a final point, e-nose technologies are represented in terms of research challenges and problems.

REFERENCES

[1] U. Fayyad and R. Uthurusamy. Data mining and knowledge discovery in databases (Introduction to the special section). *Communications of the Association of Computing Machinery*, 45(8):24–26, 1996.

[2] S. Al-Maskari, X. Li, and Q. Liu. An effective approach to handling noise and drift in electronic noses. In Hua Wang and Mohamed A. Sharaf (Eds.), *Australasian Database Conference* (pp. 223–230). Springer, Cham, 2014.

[3] Satoshi Nakata, Hiroko Nakamura, and Kenichi Yoshikawa. New strategy for the development of a gas sensor based on the dynamic characteristics: Principle and preliminary experiment. *Sensors and Actuators B: Chemical*, 8(2):187–189, 1992.

[4] Sanad Al-Maskari, Wenping Guo, and Xiaoming Zhao. Biologically inspired pattern recognition for e-nose sensors. In *Advanced Data Mining and Applications: 12th International Conference, ADMA 2016, Gold Coast, QLD, Australia, December 12–15, 2016, Proceedings 12*, pp. 142–155. Springer, 2016.

[5] N. Nimsuk and T. Nakamoto. Study on the odor classification in dynamical concentration robust against humidity and temperature changes. *Sensors and Actuators B: Chemical*, 134(1):252–257, 2008.

[6] S. AL-Maskari, D.K. Saini, and Wail M. Omar. Cyber infrastructure and data quality for environmental pollution control in Oman. In *Proceedings of the 2010 DAMD International Conference on Data Analysis, Data Quality and Metada*, Mandarin Orchard Hotel, Singapore, p. 71, July 12 and 13, 2010.

[7] R. Gutierrez-Osuna. Drift reduction for metal-oxide sensor arrays using canonical correlation regression and partial least squares. In *Proceedings of the 7th International Symposium on Olfaction & Electronic Nose*, Brighton, UK, pp. 1–7, July 2000.

[8] David S Broomhead and David Lowe. Radial basis functions, multi-variable functional inter-polation and adaptive networks. Technical report, DTIC Document, 1988.

[9] C. Bushdid, M. O. Magnasco, L. B. Vosshall, and A. Keller. Humans can discriminate more than 1 trillion olfactory stimuli. *Science*, 343(6177):1370–1372, 2014.

[10] Ritaban Dutta, KR Kashwan, M Bhuyan, Evor L Hines, and JW Gardner. Electronic nose based tea quality standardization. *Neural Networks*, 16(5):847–853, 2003.

[11] Ali Gulbag and Fevzullah Temurtas. A study on quantitative classification of binary gas mixture using neural networks and adaptive neuro-fuzzy inference systems. *Sensors and ActuatorsB: Chemical*, 115(1):252–262, 2006.

[12] Sylvie Roussel, Gustaf Forsberg, Vincent Steinmetz, Pierre Grenier, and Vronique BellonMaurel. Optimisation of electronic nose measurements. Part I: Methodology of output feature selection. *Journal of Food Engineering*, 37(2):207–222, 1998.

[13] Svante Wold, Henrik Antti, Fredrik Lindgren, and Jerker hman. Orthogonal signal correction of near-infrared spectra. *Chemometrics and Intelligent Laboratory Systems*, 44(12):175–185, 1998.

[14] Sandy D Balkin and J Keith Ord. Automatic neural network modeling for Univariate time series. *International Journal of Forecasting*, 16(4):509–515, 2000.

[15] Julian W Gardner. Detection of vapours and odours from a multisensor array using pattern recognition part 1. Principal component and cluster analysis. *Sensors and Actuators B: Chemical*, 4(1):109–115, 1991.

[16] S. Marco, A. Pardo, A. Ortega, and J. Samitier. Gas identification with tin oxide sensor array and self organizing maps: Adaptive correction of sensor drifts. In *Instrumentation and Measurement Technology Conference, 1997. IMTC/97. Proceedings. Sensing, Processing, Net-working*, IEEE, vol. 2, pp. 904–907, 1997.

[17] P Mielle, B Hivert, and G Mauvais. Are gas sensors suitable for on-line monitoring and quantification of volatile compounds? Bioflavour 95, Dijon (France), Feb. 14-17, (1995), INRA, Paris 1995 (Les Colloques, n°75).

[18] L. Cheng, Q.H. Meng, A.J. Lilienthal, and P.F. Qi. Development of compact electronic noses: A review. *Measurement Science and Technology*, 32(6):062002, 2021.

[19] S. Mika, B. Schölkopf, A.J. Smola, K. Müller, M. Scholz, and G. Rätsch. Kernel PCA and de-noising in feature spaces. In *NIPS*, vol. 4, p. 7. Citeseer, 1998.

[20] Fengchun Tian, Simon X. Yang, and Kevin Dong. Circuit and noise analysis of odorant gas sensors in an e-nose. *Sensors*, 5(1):85–96, 2005.

[21] Ali Sophian, Gui Yun Tian, David Taylor, and John Rudlin. A feature extraction technique based on principal component analysis for pulsed eddy current ndt. *NDT & E International*, 36(1):37–41, 2003.

[22] S. Al-Maskari, Z. Xu, W. Guo, X. Zhao, and X. Li. Bio-inspired learning approach for electronic nose. *Computing*, 100(4):387–402, 2018.

[23] S. Al-Maskari, I.A. Ibrahim, X. Li, E. Abusham, and A. Almars. Feature extraction for smart sensing using multi-perspectives transformation. In *Australasian Database Conference* (pp. 236–248). Springer, Cham, 2018.

[24] R.K. Sharma, P.C.H. Chan, Z. Tang, G. Yan, I. Hsing, and J.K.O. Sin. Investigation of stability and reliability of tin oxide thin-film for integrated micro-machined gas sensor devices. *Sensorsand Actuators B: Chemical*, 81(1):9–16, 2001.

[25] Hang Liu and Zhenan Tang. Metal oxide gas sensor drift compensation using a dynamic classifier ensemble based on fitting. *Sensors*, 13(7): 9160–9173, 2013.

[26] Wataru Tsujita, Akihito Yoshino, Hiroshi Ishida, and Toyosaka Moriizumi. Gas sensor network for air-pollution monitoring. *Sensors and Actuators B: Chemical*, 110(2):304–311, 2005.

[27] Fengchun Tian, Simon X. Yang, and Kevin Dong. Circuit and noise analysis of odorant gas sensors in an e-nose. *Sensors*, 5(1):85–96, 2005.

[28] Tom Artursson, Tomas Eklöv, Ingemar Lundström, Per Mårtensson, Michael Sjöström, and Martin Holmberg. Drift correction for gas sensors using multivariate methods. *Journal of Chemometrics*, 14(5–6):711–723, 2000.

[29] Marzia Zuppa, Cosimo Distante, Pietro Siciliano, and Krishna C. Persaud. Drift counteraction with multiple self-organising maps for an electronic nose. *Sensors and Actuators B: Chemical*, 98(23):305–317, 2004.

[30] Alexander Vergara, Shankar Vembu, Tuba Ayhan, Margaret A. Ryan, Margie L. Homer, and Ramn Huerta. Chemical gas sensor drift compensation using classifier ensembles. *Sensors and Actuators B: Chemical*, 166–167(0):320–329, 2012.

[31] Andrew P. Lee and Brian J. Reedy. Temperature modulation in semiconductor gas sensing. *Sensors and Actuators B: Chemical*, 60(1):35–42, 1999.

[32] P.K. Clifford and D.T. Tuma. Characteristics of semiconductor gas sensors i. steady state gas response. *Sensors and Actuators*, 3:233–254, 1982.

[33] Kevin L. Goodner, J. Glen Dreher, and Russell L. Rouseff. The dangers of creating false classifications due to noise in electronic nose and similar multivariate analyses. *Sensors and Actuators B: Chemical*, 80(3):261–266, 2001

Index